Interpersonal Violence against Children and Youth

Interpersonal Violence against Children and Youth

Edited by
Hyeyoung Lim

LEXINGTON BOOKS
Lanham • Boulder • New York • London

Published by Lexington Books
An imprint of The Rowman & Littlefield Publishing Group, Inc.
4501 Forbes Boulevard, Suite 200, Lanham, Maryland 20706
www.rowman.com

86-90 Paul Street, London EC2A 4NE, United Kingdom

British Library Cataloguing in Publication Information Available

Library of Congress Cataloging-in-Publication Data

Names: Lim, Hyeyoung, 1973– editor.
Title: Interpersonal violence against children and youth / edited by Hyeyoung Lim.
Description: Lanham, Maryland : Lexington Books, [2022] | Includes bibliographical
    references and index. | Summary: "Pulling together researchers, practitioners, and
    educators from around the world, this book addresses the various practices and
    efforts different countries use to protect children and prevent interpersonal
    violence"—Provided by publisher.
Identifiers: LCCN 2021042679 (print) | LCCN 2021042680 (ebook) |
    ISBN 9781793614339 (cloth) | ISBN 9781793614353 (paper)
    ISBN 9781793614346 (epub)
Subjects: LCSH: Child abuse—Prevention. | Interpersonal conflict—Prevention. |
    Violence—Prevention.
Classification: LCC HV6626.5 .I59 2022 (print) | LCC HV6626.5 (ebook) |
    DDC 362.76—dc23
LC record available at https://lccn.loc.gov/2021042679
LC ebook record available at https://lccn.loc.gov/2021042680

Contents

Acknowledgments

This book would not have been possible without the support and contribution of the authors from various fields and countries. I am very grateful to the authors for their original contributions and persistence during the editing process, especially under the global COVID-19 pandemic circumstance. Some of the authors lost their families, friends, or colleagues due to the COVID-19, and some had to be in the frontline to control the virus, even until now. I sincerely appreciate all authors' efforts to contribute to this book under the difficult situation, personally and/or professionally, during the pandemic. I am also deeply thankful to numerous colleagues for their comments on early drafts of the papers and in the peer-review process.

Special thanks go to Becca Beurer at Lexington Books for encouraging me to publish this volume and for her support during this book project. I deeply appreciate and am thankful for the support given by Lexington's copyediting service.

Last but not least, special thanks and respects go to my parents, siblings, relatives, and friends in South Korea, who are always on my side and motivate and encourage me to do scholarly activities. Without their support, I may not be able to achieve many things or even not be able to work in the United States. I love and appreciate you all more than you think.

Hyeyoung Lim

Introduction

A Study of Global Efforts and Practices on Violence against Children and Youth

Hyeyoung Lim

Violence affects the lives of up to 1 billion children, with long-lasting and costly emotional, social, and economic consequences. (World Health Organization, 2020, p. 1)

According to the United Nations (UN), Department of Economic and Social Affairs, Population Division, the prospective world population in the age range 0–19 as of 2020 is approximately 2.6 billion (UN, 2019). The percentage of children aged 0 to 14, however, has been continuously decreasing from 38% in 1966 to 25% in 2019 (see World Bank, 2019). The worst fact is, despite the decrease in children population around the world, 40% to 45% of children in the world experience violence regardless of its type (World Health Organization (hereafter WHO), 2020). Besides, the International Labour Office (ILO) and the United Nations Children's Fund (UNICEF) (2021) report that approximately 160 million children are involved in worldwide child labor in 2020, and the number has been increasing by about 8.4 million since 2016. The report also reveals that "there were 16.8 million more children aged 5 to 11 in child labor in 2020 than in 2016" (ILO & UNICEF, 2021, p. 8). About 72% of children aged 5 to 17 in child labor worldwide are family workers, mostly working in the agricultural sector (70%) (ILO & UNICEF, 2021).

There is no doubt that protecting and caring for our children is the top priority in our society. It is not only because they are one of the vulnerable populations but also because they are our future. Nonetheless, violence against children or violation of children's fundamental human rights is very frequently observed through broadcast media and social media around the world. Child maltreatment and abuse, internet crimes against children (ICAC), bullying, youth violence, intimate partner violence or domestic

violence, sexual violence, trafficking, and emotional or psychological violence are the main forms of interpersonal violence against children under the
age of 18. These types of violence happen in all countries and any setting—
home, school, community, and online—and are committed by the hands of
the trusted people—parents, caregivers, teachers, peers, partners, relatives,
and neighbors (UNICEF, 2021). For that reason, interpersonal violence
against children and youth is often not reported and hard to be caught by the
public view, and the victims could not easily get or seek any forms of support
when they need it.

The victimization experiences during childhood have lifelong impacts
on children's well-being and health. The worst case would be any violence,
resulting in death, including but not limited to *homicide and suicide.*

Every 7 minutes, somewhere in the world, an adolescent is killed by an act of
violence. In 2015 alone, violence took the lives of around 82,000 adolescents
worldwide [. . .] nearly 2 in 3 victims died of homicide, while the rest were killed
by conflicts. (Emphasis mine) (UNICEF, 2017, p. 49)

The world homicide rate among children aged 0 to 17 in 2016 was 1.6 per
100,000 population, while the rate in the Americas (the average of 15 countries) was almost 2 times higher than that in the world (the average of 41
countries) and was 6 times higher than that in Europe (the average of 20 counties) (see UNODC, 2019). When the age range went up to 19, the homicide
rate in the Americas was about 9 times higher (5.3 per 100,000) than that in
Europe (0.6 per 100,000). In the case of the United States, Child Welfare
Information Gateway (CWIG, 2021) reports that 1,840 children died from
abuse or neglect by a parent or a primary caregiver in 2019. Although these
statistics do not include child abuse and neglect fatalities by other perpetrators and deaths by other causes, the total number of child death cases has
continuously increased since 2015 (1,660 cases) (CWIG, 2021). In terms of
homicides of children and youth (0 to 17 years old) in the United States, there
were 1,146 child victims in 2019, and the murder victim rate among Black
children aged 9 to 19 was 1.8 times higher than that among White children
(FBI, 2021). According to UNICEF (2017), the homicide victim rate among
young Black males (non-Hispanic origin) aged 10 to 19 was 19 times higher
than that among their counterpart, White adolescents, in the United States
in 2015. Although the homicide and fatality rates among children differ by
nation, region, race, gender, or age group, it is clear that many of our children
around the world experience violence and die due to maltreatment, and even
the causes of their death are classified as unknown or sudden deaths.

Another top interpersonal violence children experience is peer violence. UNICEF (2018) reported that globally 1 in 2 students aged 13 to 15

experience peer-to-peer violence in and around schools. A recent report reveals that the bullied children aged 11 to 15 are 13% less likely to graduate from school (UNICEF, 2020). Aforementioned, childhood victimization has a lifetime effect. As evidence, adults who have experienced four or more childhood violence (e.g., physical, emotional, and sexual abuse) are "7 times more likely to be involved as a victim or perpetrator [and] 30 times more likely to attempt suicide" (UNICEF, 2020, p. 9). A more surprising study finding is that the chances are 14 times higher for the male adults becoming a perpetrator of intimate partner violence and 16 times higher for female adults suffering as a victim of intimate partner violence if they were physically and sexually abused in their childhood (UNICEF, 2020).

NO VIOLENCE AGAINST CHILDREN TOLERABLE AND JUSTIFIABLE

This book is a collection of empirical studies, which provides an overview of the risk factors, different types of violence against children and youth and their victimizations (online and offline), prevention practices, strategies, and evaluation, and the international practices and challenges in child death investigation as well as the issues in policing minor. This book contains international applications across many professional fields ranging from criminology and criminal justice to forensic pathology. Researchers, practitioners, and/or educators from various countries have contributed to this book. They have addressed their respective country's practices and efforts as well as discussed what we, as a member of our global communities, need to do for protecting our children and for preventing interpersonal violence against children and youth.

The Definition of the Term *"Children"* in This Book

Prior to introducing each chapter, it is necessary to clearly describe the terms, *children* and *youth*, in terms of age range, used in this textbook, in order to prevent potential confusion. The terms *infant, child, youth, juvenile,* and *minor* are differently defined or interchangeably used for the purpose or for the scope of studies to cover certain age groups even if the legal definition of those terms indicates the same age group, 0 to 17. For example, ordinary people may define or categorize infants as anyone under 7 years old, children as 8 to 13 years old, and youth aged from 14 to 17. Or depending on the child development stages, the age groups could be more specifically categorized as the following: newborn (0 to 1 year), toddler (1 to 3 years), early childhood (3 to 8 years old), middle childhood (9 to 11 years old), and adolescence (12 to 18 years old). However, the term *children* is globally defined as persons under the age of 18. For example, in the United States, persons under the legal majority, the age of 18, are considered a minor, but individuals under the age of 21 could be considered as a minor in the context of alcohol or gambling laws. Also, the legal definition of the term *juveniles* indicates any person who is under 18, but the actual age ranges covered differ in each country.

The title of this book includes both terms, *children* and *youth*, mutually inclusively in order to avoid any confusion or misunderstanding of the subject age groups even if both terms reflect the same age ranges, *under the age of 18*. Therefore, in this book, *Interpersonal Violence against Children and Youth* is defined as any form of violence against persons under the age of 18 regardless of the perpetrator. These forms of violence include parental or caregiver initiated, actions of peers, intimate partner-related, or those among strangers and are not limited to maltreatment, bullying, emotional strife, sexual assault, or homicidal violence.

About This Book

This book is organized into three major parts. In the opening chapter of part I, Threats of Interpersonal Violence in Everyday Life, Christina M. Rodriguez addresses the multiple forms of parental physical abuse of children, starting to define the term *physical abuse*. She explores the prevalence of parental child abuse and the multiple risk factors, including epidemiological and etiological factors. And then, Rodriguez discusses the consequences of parental physical abuse and the long-term and short-term effects of interpersonal violence against children.

In chapter 2, **Kimberly A. Tyler** and **Rachel M. Schmitz** examine multiple forms of trauma as potential risk factors for sexual and physical street victimization. They analyzed how those various traumas (including street victimization) are associated with binge drinking and illicit drug use by interviewing 168 youth experiencing homelessness (YEH) in the Midwestern United States. They discuss the details of the findings that help us to understand the multiple forms of victimization YEH sustain and the problematic outcomes of victimization and inform both policy and service providers in attending to young people's multifaceted needs.

In chapter 3, **Maria José Magalhães, Cátia Pontedeira, Camila Iglesias, et al.** explore teen dating violence based on the national quantitative study conducted in Portugal. With a representative sample of 4,708 students from the seventh to twelfth grades (12 to 18 years old) in public schools, Magalhães et al. examine teen dating violence as a form of gender-based violence and the degree of the acceptance of violence by gender. They address the importance of considering teen dating violence as a form of gender-based violence, as well as the need to continue investing in its prevention from a young age.

Part II, Computer-related Interpersonal Violence, begins with the study conducted by **Adrian Scott, Chelsea J. Mainwaring, Asher Flynn, et al.** The study focuses on image-based sexual abuse (IBSA) that involves the taking or sharing (including threats to share) of intimate (i.e., nude or sexual) images (i.e., photographs and/or videos) of another person without their consent. This chapter presents survey findings relating to the IBSA and intimate image sharing experiences of 293 Australian youth, aged between 16 and 20 years. Scott et al. explore the experiences of young people from victim, perpetrator, and bystander perspectives on IBSA. They discuss the need to challenge the current victim blaming and harm minimization rhetoric associated with IBSA and intimate image sharing, particularly in the youth context.

In chapter 5, **Hyeyoung Lim** and **Hannarae Lee** examine the impact of two emotional support groups (i.e., adult and peer groups) on cyberbullying victims' social and psychological harm using data derived from the U.S. National Crime Victimization Survey (NCVS)-School Crime Supplement (SCS) data in 2011 and 2013 (N=823). This chapter reviews the trend of cyberbully studies and the definition of the term *cyberbullying* in depth, and addresses the needs for data collection and how to minimize social and psychological distress among cyberbullying victims.

Ashley Boal, Kyungshick Choi, Lisa M. Jones, et al. summarize the current state of affairs regarding ICAC and present a synthesis of research on the ICAC victimization rates, the types of victims and perpetrators, the offenses and methods used by predators, and what interventions are being used to address ICAC in chapter 6. They make in-depth discussion about what works, including the use of enhanced penalties, improved investigations and specialized task forces, and internet safety curriculum for children.

In part III, Systematic and Practical Challenges, the authors address systematic and practical issues in dealing with the incidents or crimes involved with child victims and/or offenders. **Brian Lawton** and **Hyeyoung Lim** explore controlling minors, especially when the police make a decision to use force against juveniles in chapter 7. They used the police use-of-force report data collected from the Austin Police Department in Texas, United States, and compared the use-of-force decision between minors and adult subjects and whether extra-legal factors affect the police decision to use force.

Homicidal violence is not unique to children and youth, but the investigation of pediatric deaths demands special attention to areas not immediately applicable to the general death investigation. In chapter 8, **Brandi McCleskey** and **Lily Mahler** explore medicolegal death investigation systems and address the challenges in child death investigation in the United States. They introduce medicolegal death investigation as an intersectional field of medicine, public health, and law and historical developments of the U.S. medicolegal system. McCleskey and Mahler also address the critical challenges that other countries may face similar issues in their medicolegal death investigation system.

The last chapter by **Alfredo Walker** and **Brandi McCleskey** focuses on international approaches to a pediatric medicolegal death investigation by introducing how a multidisciplinary pediatric medicolegal death investigation team is operated in other countries. Because there is no internationally standardized protocol for the medicolegal investigation of pediatric deaths, Walker and McCleskey compare multiple countries' systems to identify similarities and differences in the structures and operations. Particularly, this chapter is important to classify the causes of child deaths and to collect more accurate statistics of child mortality as well as the certification strategies and approaches to mortality-based research.

Due to its requirement of medicolegal expertise, pediatric medicolegal death investigation and children death classification introduced and discussed in the last two chapters are the areas that are not well known to and not easy to be approached by social scientists and the people in the relevant field. The two forensic medical examiners, Alfredo Walker and Brandi McCleskey, introduce the field and compare and contrast the systems in multiple countries, including but not limited to the United States and Canada, in plain language so that nonexperts can easily understand pediatric death investigation and death classification as well as the challenges in the field of forensic medical examination. Social scientists, particularly, criminologists and criminal justice practitioners, should pay more attention to these two chapters because they are more likely the end-users of the mortality statistics, children death investigation, and children death classification to establish, develop, and implement policies and laws based on those statistical outcomes.

As introduced, this book provides international applications across many professional fields ranging from criminal justice to forensic pathology. We could not provide all forms of interpersonal violence against children in this volume, but we believe big changes start with small effort. We, all contributors of this book, hope this collected edition is one of the small efforts to change our society better for our children.

REFERENCES

Child Welfare Information Gateway (2021). *Child Abuse and Neglect Fatalities 2019: Statistics and Interventions*. U.S. Department of Health and Human Services, Administration for Children and Families, Children's Bureau.

Federal Bureau of Investigation (2021). *2019 Crime in the United States: Expanded Homicide Data Table 2.* Retrieved from https://ucr.fbi.gov/crime-in-the-u.s/2019/crime-in-the-u.s.-2019/tables/expanded-homicide-data-table-2.xls

Finkelhor, D., & Ormrod, R. (2001). Homicides of Children and Youth. *Juvenile Justice Bulletin* (October 2001). Retrieved from https://www.ojp.gov/pdffiles1/ojjdp/187239.pdf

International Labour Office and United Nations Children's Fund (2021). *Child Labour: Global Estimates 2020, Trends and the Road Forward.* New York, NY: ILO and UNICEF. Retrieved from https://data.unicef.org/resources/child-labour-2020-global-estimates-trends-and-the-road-forward/

United Nations Children's Fund (2017). *A Familiar Face: Violence in the Lives of Children and Adolescents.* New York, NY: UNICEF.

United Nations Children's Fund (2018). *#ENDviolence.* Retrieved from https://www.unicef.org/end-violence?utm_source=referral&utm_medium=media&utm_campaign=evac

United Nations Children's Fund (2021). *Violence Against Children.* Retrieved from https://www.unicef.org/protection/violence-against-children

United Nations, Department of Economic and Social Affairs, Population Division (2019). *World Population Prospects 2019, Custom Data Acquired Via Website.* Received from https://population.un.org/wpp/DataQuery/

UNODC (2019). *Global Study on Homicide 2019.* Retrieved from https://www.unodc.org/documents/data-and-analysis/gsh/Booklet_6new.pdf

World Bank (2019). *World Population Prospects: 2019 Revision: Population Ages 0–14 (% Of Total Population.* Retrieved from https://data.worldbank.org/indicator/SP.POP.0014.TO.ZS?end=2019&start=1960

World Health Organization (2020a). *Global Status Report on Preventing Violence Against Children 2020: Executive Summary.* Geneva: WHO. License: CC BY-NC-SA 3.0 IGO.

World Health Organization (2020b). *Violence Against Children* (June 8, 2020). Retrieved from https://www.who.int/news-room/fact-sheets/detail/violence-against-children.

Part I

THREATS OF INTERPERSONAL
VIOLENCE IN EVERYDAY LIFE

Chapter 1

Parental Physical Abuse of Children

Characterization and Reverberations in Multiple Forms of Interpersonal Violence

Christina M. Rodriguez

Parents' physical abuse of children represents a ubiquitous public health concern with troubling adverse psychological, physical, and economic ramifications. The costs to these children's well-being are coupled with the costs from compromised productivity and from institutional responses to the consequences of maltreatment—an exorbitant price for society. Child maltreatment collectively incurs an estimated $7 trillion annually worldwide in direct and indirect economic burden (Pereznieto et al., 2014), with an estimated $428 billion annually in the United States alone for substantiated cases of maltreatment (Peterson et al., 2018). The present chapter describes some of the dilemmas involved in defining the phenomenon of physical child abuse, including issues pertaining to differences in jurisdiction and in reporting source, both of which affect prevalence estimates; overviews epidemiological and etiological risk factors in parents who perpetrate physical abuse; then turns to the consequences of physical child abuse, with particular attention to how it connects to other expressions of interpersonal violence.

PHYSICAL ABUSE DEFINITION

Defining physical abuse is far from straightforward. In the United States, physical abuse is legally recognized as "physical acts that caused or could have caused physical injury to a child" (U.S. Department of Health and Human Services [DHHS], 2020, p. 117). Although different jurisdictions diverge in their interpretation of this national guidance, most typically seek evidence that physical injury persisted for at least 48 hours after the incident.

Notably, physical abuse is seldom substantiated for incidents wherein injury only "could" have occurred, notwithstanding its inclusion in the formal definition. Critically, physical abuse is deemed an act of commission, expressly distinguished from injury ensuing from acts of omission (the latter more accurately considered neglect). The U.S. Congress mandates a surveillance report—the fourth National Incidence Study of Child Abuse and Neglect (NIS-4)—stipulating physical abuse include only cases arising from *intentional*, non-accidental incidents (Sedlak et al., 2010).

However, the role of intent in physical child abuse represents a central conundrum in its definition. Parents may not intend to physically abuse their children, but injury nonetheless arises from the intentional use of physical force principally administered as physical discipline. Parents implement physical discipline to modify children's behavior by inflicting pain. Parents thus intend to use physical force—namely, physical discipline—but inadvertent escalation may lead to physical injury. Essentially, physical discipline and physical abuse are differentiated in the United States principally by injury that is observable days after the incident. Because physical abuse typically transpires during episodes of physical discipline, robust empirical evidence documents strong links between the use of any physical discipline and the occurrence of physical abuse (Gershoff & Grogan-Kaylor, 2016). Physical discipline is conceptualized as a prerequisite for physical abuse (King et al., 2018) such that physical discipline and physical abuse lie on opposite ends of a parent-child aggression continuum (Rodriguez, 2010). As parents intensify their use of physical discipline, their aggressive behavior shifts further along this continuum, increasing their likelihood to become physically abusive (Afifi et al., 2017b).

Global definitions of physical abuse deliberately do not distinguish physical abuse from physical discipline, suggesting all forms of physical force can harm the "child's health, survival, development, or dignity" (World Health Organization (WHO), 2006, p. 10)—pointedly making no reference to injury. Accordingly, a United Nations treaty formally advocates children be protected from any form of violence, inclusive of physical discipline (U.N. Convention on the Rights of the Child, article 19, para. 1). All U.N. member nations are parties to this treaty except the United States. Consequently, over 60 nations thus far have formally banned all expressions of physical violence toward children, considering any physical discipline a form of physical abuse; in contrast, the United States adheres to the narrower definition of physical abuse that requires injury that persists after a period of days.

These definitional issues obfuscate the study of physical abuse in numerous ways. When physical abuse is narrowly defined, estimates of its scope are substantially reduced, influencing the apparent prevalence rate of physical abuse (Stoltenborg et al., 2013). Local definitions of what constitutes physical abuse also determine who is judged a potential perpetrator or victim to receive intervention services. Identifying the risk factors for abuse perpetration and the consequences for victims is also complicated by how physical abuse is defined; however, the substantial commonalities between physical discipline and physical abuse permit us to draw some conclusions in these two domains.

PREVALENCE

U.S. child protective services typically receive over 4 million reports of maltreatment annually but investigate only half of those reports and substantiate only a fraction given the narrow definition and high evidentiary standards (DHHS, 2020). Over 46% of fatalities in 2018 involved physical abuse (DHHS, 2020) with an estimated 1.6 per 1,000 children substantiated as physical abuse victims (DHHS, 2019). However, the NIS-4, which adopts a broader surveillance system, estimated 26% of all maltreatment involves physical abuse, affecting 4.4 out of every 1,000 children (Sedlak et al., 2010)—several times the rate substantiated by child protective services. Phone surveys of nationally representative samples in the United States document a rate of 84 per 1,000 children self-report lifetime experience of physical abuse, with 33 out of 1,000 reporting injury in the last year alone (Simon et al., 2018)—exponentially higher than official estimates. Furthermore, annual rates are only a snapshot in time of maltreatment, with cumulative estimates indicating one out of eight U.S. children are substantiated for maltreatment before their 18th birthday (Wildeman et al., 2014). Globally, official estimates that typically involve narrow definition report 0.3% of children are physical abused, but when those sources are combined with independent reports of abuse from children and their parents, the number rises to 22.6% (Stoltenborgh et al., 2015).

Therefore, the extent of physical abuse is not only influenced by definitional ambiguity but also by the source of the physical abuse report. Official estimates to institutional bodies are widely acknowledged to underestimate physical abuse, representing the "tip of the iceberg" (Sedlak et al., 2010; Stoltenborgh et al., 2015). Parental estimates of their abusive behavior are constrained by their reluctance to share potentially illegal activities, whereas children's reports may be affected by recall inaccuracies. Yet children's reports of abuse can be five times the rate reported to official child protective services (Euser et al., 2013). Discrepancies between parents and their children in how often they have been hit (Kremer et al., 2020) often render differences in child abuse estimates depending on the reporting source—whether parents, children, or protective services reports are used (Prevoo et al., 2017; Widom et al., 2015). Although we can conclude that physical abuse is pervasive, its exact prevalence will continue to elude us given these definitional and reporting source concerns.

PARENTAL RISK FACTORS

Physical child abuse is recognized as arising from a complex array of factors. Prevailing theoretical models suggest that the factors leading parents to abuse children derive from multiple levels of influence within an ecological model (Belsky, 1993), including characteristics of the parent; factors associated with the family; and aspects of the immediate community and wider cultural norms (Rodriguez, 2021). Risk factors can be categorized into two groups. Some risk factors are merely descriptive—namely, they do not cause a parent to physically abuse their child per se, but they characterize those at risk, consistent with epidemiological, less mutable, factors not directly addressed in interventions. Alternatively, other factors are viewed as causal risks—modifiable, etiological qualities that represent targets for child abuse prevention and intervention efforts with parents. Descriptive, epidemiological risk factors likely increase risk for physical abuse indirectly through more etiological mechanisms. This chapter reviews parental risk factors.

Epidemiological Risk Factors

Most physical abuse is perpetrated by a central attachment figure in children's lives—their caregivers. In the United States, nearly three-quarters of physical abuse is committed by parents, with an additional 19% perpetrated by non-biological caregivers (e.g., stepparents, residential partners of biological parents) (Sedlak et al., 2010). Worldwide figures on child homicide reveal that parents represent the greatest risk to their children: 56.5% of child homicides are filicides (Stöckl et al., 2017). Among biological parents, biological mothers are more likely to physically abuse than biological fathers (56%); however, among caregivers broadly, fathers and non-biological father-figures combined are somewhat more likely to physically abuse than women (54%; Sedlak et al., 2010), and male caregivers may be more likely to cause serious injury to victims (Scribano et al., 2013).

Although young parents are often considered at risk (MacMillan et al., 2013), empirical reviews summarized across studies characterize this age effect as modest (Stith et al., 2009). In terms of socioeconomic indicators, factors such as lower income (DHHS, 2019; Doidge et al., 2017a), lower educational level (Doidge et al., 2017a), and unemployment (Doidge et al., 2017a; Sedlak et al., 2010; Stith et al., 2009) are all robust predictors of physical maltreatment. Collectively, these sociodemographic epidemiological risks imply that those with more limited resources (e.g., due to age, income, or education) experience strains that likely compromise their parenting, cultivating the conditions for physical abuse to arise through more etiological risk factors.

With regard to race and ethnicity in the United States, Black, Native American, and Alaskan Native children are typically overrepresented in official surveillance reports of maltreatment (DHHS, 2020; Sedlak et al., 2010). Based on self-reports, Hispanic, Black, and Native American youth indicate they experience more physical abuse relative to White youth (Hawkins et al., 2010). However, nationally representative phone surveys of physical abuse injury do not observe racial or ethnic differences (Simon et al., 2018), which mirrors the conclusion of a global analysis of studies (Stoltenborgh et al., 2013). Therefore, the conclusions regarding racial and ethnic differences in physical child abuse victims remain inconclusive, depending again on the source of the report.

Physical abuse is more likely in neighborhoods characterized by disarray (Freisthler & Maguire-Jack, 2015) and economic disadvantage (Maguire-Jack & Font, 2017), suggesting that some community-level factors may reflect socioeconomic conditions. Cross-cultural studies have highlighted the role of societal attitudes tolerant of gender inequity as a marker for cultures where physical abuse is more prevalent (Klevens et al., 2018). However, research considering commonalities and distinctions across countries and the role of cultural norms are particularly challenged by the variability in physical abuse definition given the number of countries that now ban all forms of violence toward children. For example, countries that prohibit physical discipline of children and attain lower rates of child maltreatment fatalities have citizens who are more likely to disapprove of the use of any parental physical discipline (Gracia & Herrero, 2008).

Importantly, parents who access public supports (e.g., agencies providing financial assistance or early childhood education) or reside in communities with greater scrutiny are also more surveilled than their peers who do not interact routinely with public services. Such public interactions can thereby provide more opportunities to attract the notice of professionals who report child maltreatment. Most physical abuse occurs in the home, hidden from such surveillance. Thus, parents who are older, educated, and have higher income, and living in more affluent areas undoubtedly engage in physical abuse—despite better access to resources—through similar etiological mechanisms (cf. Rodriguez et al., 2018b), but unbeknownst to the professionals they may never encounter in highly surveilled settings.

Etiological Risk Factors

One link from socioeconomic strain to child maltreatment may be via the erosion of parental mental health (Yang, 2015). Parents are more likely to engage in physical abuse if they are experiencing mental health difficulties (Doidge et al., 2017b), including depression (Espinosa et al., 2017; Rodriguez et al., 2018b) and substance abuse (DHHS, 2020; Sedlak et al., 2010). Research also consistently identifies parents who report experiencing high levels of stress are at high risk for physical abuse (Miragoli et al., 2018; Rodriguez et al., 2017; Stith et al., 2009; Tucker et al., 2017).

Unsurprisingly, physical child abuse also often co-occurs with intimate partner violence (IPV), namely violence toward a current or former intimate partner—an overlap that has been observed globally (Chan et al., 2019; Rodriguez, 2021). Physically abusive parents can be either victims or perpetrators of IPV. A review indicates that IPV offenders are likely to use physical parent-child aggression (Chiesa et al., 2018), but IPV victims are also at increased risk to abuse their children (Ahmadabadi et al., 2018; Grasso et al., 2016). This overlap between IPV and child abuse may reflect communalities in attitudes that accept violence within the family (Gracia et al., 2020) or reflect biases in responding to conflict with aggression (Berlin et al., 2011; Martoccio et al., 2020). Additionally, both IPV victims and perpetrators are more likely to experience depression or substance use problems (Capaldi et al., 2012; Chan et al., 2019), the aforementioned mental health challenges linked to increased risk for physical child abuse perpetration that may contribute to this family violence concordance.

Mental health challenges and/or IPV likely induce *negative affect* in parents—transient emotional states such as depressive, anxious, or angry affect. Parental anger and over-reactivity are considered strong risk factors for physical child abuse (Rodriguez, 2018; Stith et al., 2009). Poor anger control epitomizes physically abusive behavior, implying that abusive parents may overreact impulsively with their children due to low frustration tolerance (Rodriguez et al., 2015, 2017). Both hostility and depressive affect are linked to increased child abuse risk (McCarthy et al., 2016), as is parental anxiety (Stith et al., 2009; Rodriguez et al., 2020b). Parents' inability to manage such negative affect—indicative of emotion dysregulation—has been implicated as the process accounting for why parents' personal history of abuse (Smith et al., 2014), rigid thinking (Lowell & Renk, 2017) and parental stress (Rodriguez et al., 2017) increase a parent's risk to abuse. Accordingly, parents confronting stress, mental health problems, and/or IPV likely experience negative affect; those unable to tolerate and manage that negative affect may react impulsively and aggressively toward their children.

When a parent encounters such strains, cognitive processes may also trigger physical abuse. One central theory organizing these cognitive processes is *Social Information Processing* (SIP) theory (Camilo et al., 2020; Milner, 2000; Rodriguez et al., 2020a). Based on SIP theory, a parent acquires cognitive beliefs about parenting and discipline during their upbringing—preexisting beliefs before they are faced with a discipline situation that contextualize how they view child behavior. Then, when their child engages in behavior prompting discipline, the parent must first accurately perceive the situation. If misperceptions occur, they may reach inaccurate conclusions about their child and interpret the child's behavior negatively. The parents may then fail to consider all relevant information, including alternatives to physical discipline, electing to implement physical aggression. Finally, failure to adequately monitor the intensity of their aggressive response is often how physical discipline escalates into physical abuse.

One preexisting belief that is central to increasing physical abuse risk pertains to parents' approval of using physical discipline in the first place. Indeed, parents who endorse physical discipline use demonstrate significantly higher physical abuse risk (McCarthy et al., 2016; Rodriguez et al., 2011). Furthermore, parents who perceive their children as troublesome also evidence higher child abuse risk (Miragoli et al. 2018; Rodriguez, 2018; Stith et al. 2009), which suggests these parents are more attuned to potentially aversive child behavior compared to positive child behavior. Parents may then conclude such child aversive behavior is intentional, displaying negative child attributions that strongly predict elevated child abuse risk (Camilo et al., 2020; Rodriguez et al., 2012, 2020a). Parents may then be unable to adequately incorporate the circumstances surrounding the child's behavior; for example, at-risk parents may neglect information that mitigates the child's responsibility (Irwin et al., 2014). Parents who cannot identify options other than physical discipline are more likely to default to such approaches, increasing their abuse risk (Rodriguez et al., 2019, 2020a); consequently, many abuse prevention programs train parents on alternatives to physical discipline (Poole et al., 2014). The final phase of SIP theory, in which parents fail to oversee the intensity of their physical discipline, is difficult to study empirically given that abusive behavior is generally unwitnessed; it seems likely, however, to be swayed by a parent's experience of negative affect and poor emotion regulation.

Together, these parental risk factors implicate a process whereby parents who are overwhelmed by personal challenges (e.g., stress, mental health, IPV) may experience compromised cognitive and affective processes that culminate in physical abuse. A parent who is overwhelmed by their own personal issues is more inclined to feel negative affect—whether depressive, anxious, or angry—when encountering a frustrating situation with their child, increasing the likelihood that the problematic social information cognitive processes are initiated (Milner, 2000). This sequence would appear most applicable to instances in which parents engage in consciously processed decisions about how to discipline their children. Yet at least some physical abuse is probably triggered via more impulsive, automatic processes (Milner,

2000; Rodriguez et al., 2020b). Consistent with other theoretical characterizations of aggressive behavior (cf. Orobio de Castro, 2004), physical abuse is likely to involve both conscious and automatic processes in which automatic processing initiates rapid perceptions of the situation, immediate affective reactions, and quick, impulsive aggression (Bluemke & Teige-Mocigemba, 2015). Research has rarely studied such automatic processes wherein parents react aggressively to their children with little forethought, representing an important future direction. Undoubtedly, overwhelming evidence portrays the etiology underlying physical child abuse as an intricate interplay of factors.

CONSEQUENCES OF PHYSICAL ABUSE

Theoretical Issues

Some consequences of physical abuse are direct and immediate, whereas others may exert delayed, indirect effects. Physical abuse can initiate short-term, immediate negative effects on children's functioning, but those short-term effects in turn spread, precipitating additional negative effects in a variety of domains—a cumulative combination of effects known as *developmental cascades* (Masten & Cicchetti, 2010). The concept of developmental cascades explains how one negative outcome proliferates into multiple negative outcomes because compromising one area of a child's functioning (e.g., health) can then interfere with other areas of their functioning (e.g., academic achievement or social skill development). Victims must contend not only with the emotional implications of abuse but also with the additional strains posed by the negative outcomes as well, compromising their ability to adaptively regulate emotion and to process information—the very risk factors that may then prompt them to later utilize physical aggression themselves.

In this regard, some short-term effects of physical abuse may operate as *mediators*, acting as the actual mechanisms for how child abuse contributes to long-term negative consequences. In other words, mediators account for and explain how physical abuse leads to later negative outcomes. Identifying such mediators is relevant for interventions because ameliorating the effect of short-term mediators provides an opportunity to avert the cascading, long-term consequences associated with child abuse. Alternatively, intervention programs are also invested in identifying factors that can serve as *moderators*. Moderators can involve qualities or experiences of child abuse victims that can either exacerbate or mitigate the adverse effects of physical abuse; recognizing moderators can detect the conditions or qualities needed for a long-term adverse consequence to emerge. In particular, intervention programs seek to minimize the effect of moderators that might exacerbate the immediate negative effects of physical abuse while promoting the moderators that could buffer negative consequences that lead to a victim's resilience.

One framework for collectively characterizing the consequences of physical abuse utilizes the *biopsychosocial model*, a comprehensive approach that integrates biological, psychological, and social elements that impact human development over time (Melchert, 2015). Physical child abuse occurs during critical periods of physical, intellectual, and psychological growth that can interfere with normative developmental processes. Such timing can thus compromise children's development across domains in terms of their physical and mental health as well as their interpersonal functioning.

Many of the psychosocial effects arising from physical child abuse materialize as expressions of interpersonal violence. Theoretically, the reason children who are physically abused proceed to engage in aggression themselves may reflect *social learning theory* (otherwise known as observational learning; Bandura, 1978). Originally proposed to explain aggression, social learning theory posits that repeated exposures to the performance of aggressive behavior (or the schema associated with those behaviors) can consolidate a script for children about aggressive responding (Allen & Anderson, 2017). Such social scripts then lead children to imitate the behaviors they observed, perpetuating aggression through cognitions aligned with SIP biases (Huesmann, 2018). For example, children with a history of physical abuse develop beliefs and biases that endorse aggression as a conflict resolution tool, which leads them to adopt similar approaches (Martoccio et al., 2020).

Nonviolent Physical Abuse Effects

For decades, physical abuse has been recognized as a core *adverse childhood experience* (ACE) (Felitti et al., 1998). ACEs are critical adversities experienced during childhood, including family violence or parental death, incarceration, or mental illness, which predict long-term negative health outcomes. Recent work affirms that any form of parent-child aggression, including physical discipline, represents an ACE (Afifi et al., 2017a; Ma et al., 2021) given the strong connection between physical discipline and child abuse (Afifi et al., 2017b). As a central ACE, physical abuse appears to incur neurobiological damage (Nemeroff, 2016; Teicher et al., 2016), initiating persistent neurochemical changes that then propagate a chain of subsequent detrimental effects (an example of the developmental cascading process). Consistent with the biopsychosocial framework, such initial neurobiological effects represent mediators to the long-term negative health outcomes associated with ACEs. Large, landmark studies document that those who retrospectively report suffering more ACEs were at increased risk for morbidity, including obesity, heart disease, liver disease, lung disease, and cancer (Felitti et al., 1998), as well as increased risk for early mortality (Brown et al., 2009). Similar effects were observed in more rigorous, prospective designs, following children into middle adulthood; blood tests and physical measurements indicated abused children were at elevated risk for lung disease, malnutrition, diabetes, as well as vision and oral health problems (Widom et al., 2012). By definition, short-term injury also occurs from physical abuse, ranging from minor cuts and bruises to the severe effects evident in head injury (Leventhal & Gaither, 2012) or bone fractures (Flaherty et al., 2014).

Mental health consequences are also apparent among the well-documented adverse outcomes of physical abuse. Indeed, 45% of all childhood-onset psychiatric disorders are attributable to child maltreatment (Green et al., 2010). Long-term, physical abuse during childhood increases the likelihood of a variety of adult psychiatric disorders, including major depression, bipolar disorder, post-traumatic stress disorder, generalized anxiety disorder, panic disorder, substance abuse, and attention-deficit disorder (Sugaya et al., 2012). A history of physical child abuse confers a greater than 2.5 increased risk of adult depression (Nelson et al., 2018) and twofold increased risk of attempted suicide (Castellví et al., 2018). Some research implicates the environmental stressors that arose from earlier physical abuse actually serve as mediators leading to adult depression (Sousa et al., 2018), consistent with the developmental cascades premise that physical abuse yields pervasive adverse effects in a variety of domains in children that ultimately erodes their adult mental and physical health.

Perhaps reflecting the impact on victims' physical and mental health, children's educational functioning is also impacted by physical abuse, likely mediating how physical abuse leads to long-term adverse achievement outcomes. Early abuse before age five can lead to poorer academic achievement (Raby et al., 2019), to grade failure and poor school performance as rated by either parents or teachers, and to fewer years of education and failure to graduate (Tanaka et al., 2015). These shorter-term educational deficits may account for victims' lower adult income and rates of employment (Currie & Widom, 2010) and their increased likelihood of being fired (Lansford et al., 2007). This pervasive impact on children's lifetime underachievement deepens the burden endured by abused children and undermines their contributions to society.

Short-Term Interpersonal Violence Effects

Peer Aggression

Consistent with social learning theory, physically abused children are significantly more likely to engage in peer aggression and bullying behavior

(Labella & Masten, 2018), with a moderately strong association between negative parenting that includes physical abuse and children's bullying behavior (Lereya et al., 2013). For both boys and girls, a history of physical abuse confers a threefold increased risk of fighting and a nearly fourfold increased risk of carrying weapons (Duke et al., 2010). Additional work identifies a reciprocal relation between these forms of aggression; harsher physical discipline of children predicted increases in later peer aggression, which was then followed by more harsh parental physical discipline (Badyar & Akcinar, 2018).

Current research suggests that the reasons physically abused children may engage in more peer aggression are attributable to a number of possible mediating mechanisms. For example, abused children appear more attuned to angry faces, an attentional bias that mediates the link between abuse history and peer aggression (Shackman & Pollak, 2014). Abused children also adopt hostile attribution biases potentially modeled by their parents; such biases mediate abuse history and peer aggression (Richey et al., 2016). Children who experience multiple forms of maltreatment also engage in aggressive antisocial behavior in part because of greater impulsivity (Thibodeau et al., 2015). Such social information processes may have been demonstrated to victims by parents who perpetrated physical abuse, consistent with social learning theory. Overall, such examples of mediators suggest physical abuse influences children's socio-cognitive development, which in turn leads to aggressive peer relations.

Although less research has considered factors that moderate the effects of physical abuse on peer aggression, some research has identified qualities that could reduce this link. Children's IQ scores were the only observed moderator of the connection between physical abuse history and aggressive antisocial behavior, wherein higher IQ reduced the likelihood of aggression; disappointingly, a stronger school connection or school retention did not reduce victims' risk of engaging in peer aggression (Klika et al., 2012). An interesting line of biopsychosocial research observed that abuse history predicted antisocial behavior based on genetic variants; peer aggression was apparent for maltreated children with specific gene profiles, suggesting some physically abused children are particularly vulnerable to become aggressive with peers, whereas those without the genetic profiles are less likely to be aggressive (Cicchetti et al., 2012; Thibodeau et al., 2015).

Family Aggression

Research on short-term intrafamilial interpersonal violence is limited, but children who have been abused are more likely to engage in violence toward their siblings (Ingram et al., 2020), with some estimates that maltreatment increases the odds of sibling aggression by 300% (Button & Gealt, 2010). Children's history of violence from either parent was also a more robust predictor of sibling aggression than children's witnessing IPV between their caregivers (Relva et al., 2013). Minimal work has examined either potential mediators or moderators of the links between physical abuse history and sibling violence, although these seem likely to align with those observed for peer aggression.

Physically abused children are also more likely to behave violently toward their parents, reflecting a broader atmosphere of family violence wherein intrafamilial physical aggression is modeled. Victims of physical abuse are nearly four times more likely to engage in physical violence toward their parents, principally toward their mothers (Lyons et al., 2015). Some have suggested that adolescent sons, relative to daughters, are particularly likely to engage in child-to-parent violence if they were abused as children (Ibabe et al., 2013). Considerably less research has explored this phenomenon, however, including a lack of work identifying potential mediators and moderators, although impaired attachment to abusive parents and social learning theory appear relevant here.

Long-Term Interpersonal Violence Effects

Intergenerational Transmission of Physical Child Abuse

If one were to ask the public at large, many would speculate that parents learn to physically abuse their children by emulating their own parents. This proposition is quintessentially the premise behind social learning theory—that children observe and model their parents' actions—in what is typically referred to as the "cycle of violence" or "intergenerational transmission of violence" hypothesis. Although the evidence for this hypothesis is substantive, the nuances in this literature are often overlooked. Systematic reviews of the literature suggest that a history of physical abuse does confer a risk of children growing up to become physically abusive parents themselves (Greene et al., 2020). Nevertheless, the estimates for the magnitude of this association across generations are considered modest (Madigan et al., 2019). In fact, the strength of the association between physical abuse history and physical abuse perpetration drops considerably when one specifically targets physical abuse (as opposed to other forms of maltreatment) and when one prioritizes estimating those effects using rigorous, methodologically sound studies (Assink et al., 2018). Indeed, a classic early review of prospective studies that followed children as they became adults estimated that only 30% of abused children become perpetrators of abuse (Kaufman & Zigler, 1987)—meaning that for decades, the science has revealed 70% do not perpetuate abuse.

The reasons for the muted effects of intergenerational transmission of physical abuse echo some of the issues noted in the earlier discussion of prevalence estimates. First among these is the source of the reports. Disparities between who identifies physical abuse (officially substantiated reports to child protective services, parent self-report, or victim retrospective report) substantially affect our estimates of abuse prevalence (Prevoo et al., 2017; Stoltenborgh et al., 2015). Thus, who reports physical abuse of the first or subsequent generation can affect the magnitude of the effects of intergenerational transmission. For instance, the estimated rate of transmission decreases when requiring that multiple reporters agree that abuse occurred; estimates using a single reporter are higher yet modest (Buisman et al., 2020). Indeed, strong research designs that follow abused children prospectively over time find limited support for intergenerational transmission given significant reporter discrepancies; those with histories of physical abuse actually appear more likely to engage in neglect rather than abuse (Widom et al., 2015).

Second, although the accuracy of parent-reports may be curtailed by legal or social desirability concerns, relying on child-reports of physical abuse are also compromised by their reluctance to share unfavorable information about their parents; retrospective reports obtained from adults about their childhood are also subject to recall errors. Although retrospective reports about child abuse are relatively stable (Fergusson et al., 2011), their accuracy is not assured. Many intergenerational effects derive from retrospective reports regarding child abuse history concurrent with their reports of perpetrating abuse, which tends to magnify those associations; true effects may be considerably weaker than assumed given that few studies conduct multiple assessments of the potential intergenerational link across time (Rodriguez et al., 2018a).

Considerable work has examined the mediating mechanisms responsible for possible transmission of physical abuse across generations. Many of these effects could be attributable to stressors impinging on the perpetrator (see Chamberlain et al., 2019 for review), some of which may be factors affecting parents' personal functioning (i.e., mental health problems, IPV, substance use, representing examples of both the consequences of abuse *and* the risk factors for abuse perpetration), whereas other risk factors are more proximate to parent-child interactions (i.e., beliefs about the child as evident in SIP theory, insecure bonding with the child). Therefore, research suggests that adults with a child abuse history are more likely to perpetrate abuse because they are experiencing depressive symptoms (Yang et al., 2018) or IPV (Greene et al., 2020). Alternatively, others have observed parents' greater delinquency or substance use did not mediate the association between abuse history and perpetration (Capaldi et al., 2019; Martoccio et al., 2020), indicating that some short-term consequences of child abuse may not be mediators in explaining the cycle of abuse.

Additional mediators may reflect affective or socio-cognitive processes. Parents' experience of negative affect and poor emotion regulation mediated the relationship between parents' abuse history and their abusive behavior (Smith et al., 2014). Further, the cycle of abuse may be mediated through beliefs and biases to respond to conflict with aggression (Berlin et al, 2011; Martoccio et al., 2020), reflecting social learning theory and the potential intergenerational transmission of SIP elements. For example, parents' greater approval of using physical discipline mediated the relation between abuse history and parental child abuse risk (Rodriguez et al., 2018a). Parents' social isolation may serve as a mediator between child abuse history and abusive behavior toward children (Berlin et al., 2011), although this mediation has not been observed consistently (Martoccio et al., 2020). Potentially the inter-generational process arises by compromising neurobiological functioning, because chronic activation of the stress response (measurable through hair cortisol) mediated the association between child abuse history and parents' own child abuse risk (Kluczniok et al., 2020). Collectively, such findings point to biopsychosocial and social information processes that may perpetu-ate the cycle of physical abuse.

Studies of moderation attempt to identify the conditions that may increase or decrease a victims' likelihood to abuse their own children. Adolescents with a history of abuse who dropped out of school and/or began living independently precociously were more likely to perpetrate abuse with their children (Augustyn et al., 2019). More proximally, parents' higher stress strengthened the intergenerational effects of harsh parenting, whereas lower parenting stress weakened it (Niu et al., 2018). In terms of additional fac-tors that may reduce intergenerational transmission of abuse, parents who describe nurturing, supportive relationships, particularly from a romantic partner, demonstrate reduced risk of abuse toward their children (Rodriguez et al., 2018a; Schofield et al., 2016). Mothers who report more engaged coping skills and fathers who report more social satisfaction and stronger emotion regulation abilities demonstrate weaker intergenerational effects (Rodriguez et al., 2018a).

Although potentially surprising to lay circles, the vast majority of children who were physically abused do not appear to perpetrate abuse with their children. Yet, we have remarkably less research inquiry into moderation. Such work is critical for intervention efforts to ascertain why the majority of physically abused children do not in fact grow up to become physically abusive parents. This research is likely to require additional inquiry on bio-psychosocial processes that could better identify those who are most vulner-able to perpetuate the cycle of violence versus those who are able to break it.

IPV and Dating Violence

Nationally representative samples of adults' retrospectively reporting a history of harsh and abusive discipline are significantly more likely to report being either a victim or perpetrator of IPV (Afifi et al., 2017b)—findings that have been affirmed by comprehensive analyses across multiple studies (Li et al., 2019). Physical abuse history confers an increased risk for both male and female perpetration of IPV (Richards et al., 2017). Similar research on increased risk for dating violence (Relva et al., 2013) has identified that a childhood history of physical abuse triples the rate of engaging in dating violence for females, with an eight-fold increase for males (Duke et al., 2010).

However, if constrained to using only official, court-documented reports of physical abuse history, the link to IPV perpetration in adulthood disappears (identifying a path only from child abuse history to becoming an IPV victim, consistent with one of the negative adult consequences of physical abuse) (Widom et al., 2014). Although relying on court records would seem to raise the threshold for physical abuse history unnecessarily high (given the low reporting previously noted through official channels), court records should have identified the most severe cases of physical abuse and thereby would have magnified the effects with IPV perpetration in adulthood (given the higher risk sample). Importantly, experiences of IPV perpetration are themselves complicated by self-report; the same social desirability concerns that reduce parents' candor in reporting the physical abuse of their children also likely render them less forthcoming about IPV perpetration.

Research that has investigated the potential mediating factors in these long-term relations has observed that psychopathology can account for the connection between physical abuse history and IPV. For example, post-traumatic stress symptoms (Lu et al., 2019) and substance abuse (Brown et al., 2015) contribute to the relation between physical child abuse and physical IPV. Alternatively, others have argued that more proximal characteristics of the couple relationship contribute to IPV (e.g., relationship dynamics) more than historical factors such as physical abuse (Kaufman-Parks et al., 2017), suggesting the need for research to consider both abuse history and more proximate conditions such as current couple functioning. Differences may also appear due to gender; men, but not women, with a history of physical abuse are more likely to be IPV victims partly attributable to their attitudes that accept family violence—a SIP characteristic (Schuster & Tomaszewska, 2020).

Apart from these gender effects, studies of moderation have identified that marital status affects this link; adults with an abuse history who are married were significantly less likely to engage in IPV than unmarried couples (Li et al., 2019). More bidirectional dating violence was also identified for White women relative to Black women with an abuse history, whereas Black men with an abuse history were more at risk of dating violence compared with White men (Kaukinen et al., 2015). Additional research should examine how sociodemographic factors may reflect differences in resources versus stressors for different subgroups to better identify the conditions whereby abuse history increases the likelihood of IPV during adulthood.

Extrafamilial Violent Criminal Behavior

Those with a history of abuse engage in antisocial behavior that manifests in higher rates of crime (Watts & McNulty, 2013). A history of physical abuse is associated with later aggressive antisocial behavior, with an 11% overall increased rate of delinquency (Braga et al., 2017). Relative to a comparison group, children who were abused were twice as likely to engage in criminally violent behavior as adults (Milaniak & Widom, 2015). Physically abused children are also twice as likely to use weapons, be arrested, and be convicted for violent offenses as adults (Topitzes et al., 2012).

In studies examining mediating mechanisms, physically abused children's unstable environments (both at home and school) and social skill deficits in part explained the link between childhood history of abuse and later antisocial violent offending for males only; for females, their adolescent problem behaviors mediated the relationship between childhood abuse and adult violent offending (Topitzes et al., 2012). Others have implicated psychopathology, such as depression (Watts & McNulty, 2013) or antisocial personality disorder (González et al., 2016), as mediators in the link between childhood victimization and adult perpetration of violence. The role of schools has also been investigated, wherein physically abused children were more likely to become violent adults in part through weak bonding and affiliation with their schools (Bartoza & Siller, 2018).

Relatively few studies have examined the factors that may moderate this long-term link. One study reported that the effect between early childhood history of physical abuse and later violent offending is stronger among women than men and among Black youth compared to White youth (Lansford et al., 2007). More recent work has delved more deeply into moderating effects, speculating that contextual factors may play a moderating role. Physically abused children were not more likely to become violent adults if residing in more disadvantaged neighborhoods; in fact, the link between childhood abuse history and later violent offending was actually reduced for those living in neighborhoods with concentrated disadvantage, and this reduction was magnified further for those living in areas with cultural norms more tolerant of family violence (Wright & Fagan, 2013). Such findings again indicate that although certain individuals may be more likely to model violence received during childhood, the long-term effects of child abuse may be strongly influenced by the proximate conditions in which the victim lives.

CONCLUSIONS

Although the definition of physical child abuse remains nebulous, research consistently documents that all forms of physical violence toward children pose a risk to children's well-being. A number of intersecting risk factors combine to amplify the risk a parent will perpetrate physical child abuse, including affective and socio-cognitive processes—echoed in the very emotional, psychological, and social effects of that abuse on their children. Evidently, physical child abuse resembles qualities of a contagion, with violence spreading from the child to other members of their family and peers, and longer-term, to their own children, partners, and members of society.

One of the greatest barriers in this field remains the division between those who construe physical abuse as qualitatively different from physical discipline and those who believe all forms of physical parent-child aggression are abusive. In modern society, parental physical discipline continues to be the only form of physical force implemented from one person toward another that is socially acceptable in some countries. This area represents a potential opportunity for public policy efforts that convey the impact of physical discipline to reframe how the public views and defines child abuse (Fortson et al., 2016). As the list of countries banning all forms of violence toward children grows, this barrier in the conceptualization of child abuse may diminish.

Without a consistent definition, identifying physical abuse victims and perpetrators is stymied. The obstacles posed by the definition of child physical abuse are compounded by reporter differences wherein parents, children, and officials may disagree. Parents may minimize their reporting, requiring researchers to develop more creative, implicit approaches to identify abuse risk (e.g., Camilo et al., 2016), and potentially requiring the confirmation of abuse by triangulating reports across multiple sources (e.g., Widom et al., 2015). However, reliance on the current child protective services system is problematic given it typically identifies the most severe cases of maltreatment, capturing only a fraction of physical abuse. Indeed, the child protection system tends to identify underserved communities more frequently because those groups experience more frequent surveillance of their family life. Alternatively, a more proactive early screening approach at multiple systems of care (e.g., through primary care settings, schools) could recognize families who might need early support before abuse occurs—consistent with a prevention approach.

The widespread public health problem of physical abuse demands more urgent attention given the substantial burden to individuals and society (Pereznieto et al., 2014). Delaying until children attract the attention of child protective services to stem its tide ignores the reality that the majority of physical child abuse is never reported nor substantiated. Intervention efforts directed at preventing the recurrence of child abuse from substantiated perpetrators are modestly effective (Vlahovicova et al., 2017). Policy makers should be reminded that preventing child abuse beforehand represents a cost-effective priority because prevention is generally acknowledged to provide an exponential return on economic investment (WHO, 2014). Yet the effectiveness of current child abuse prevention efforts remains discouraging and modest at best (van der Put et al., 2018; Rodriguez, 2021), highlighting the need to intensify research inquiry on the causal mechanisms, mediators, and moderators. With clearer insight, we can craft programs to better avert physical abuse by modifying the most salient risk factors, altering the mediators and incorporating moderators that can be used to identify how and for whom to maximize the benefits of such prevention efforts.

REFERENCES

Afifi, T.O., Ford, D., Gershoff, E.T., Merrick, M., Grogan-Kaylor, A., Ports, K.A., … Bennett, R.P. (2017a). Spanking and adult mental health impairment: The case for the designation of spanking as an adverse childhood experience. *Child Abuse & Neglect, 71*, 24–31.

Afifi, T.O., Mota, N., Sareen, J., & MacMillan, H.L. (2017b). The relationships between harsh physical punishment and child maltreatment in childhood and intimate partner violence in adulthood. *BMC Public Health, 17*, 493–593.

Ahmadabadi, Z., Najman, J.M., Williams, G.M., Clavarino, A.M., d'Abbs, P., & Abajobir, A.A. (2018). Maternal intimate partner violence victimization and child maltreatment. *Child Abuse & Neglect, 82*, 23–33.

Allen, J.J., & Anderson, C.A. (2017). General aggression model. In P. Roessler, C.A. Hoffner, & L. van Zoonen (Eds.) *International Encyclopedia of Media Effects.* Wiley-Blackwell.

Assink, M., Spruit, A., Schuts, M., Lindauer, R., van der Put, C.E., & Stams, G.J.M. (2018). The intergenerational transmission of child maltreatment: A three-level meta-analysis. *Child Abuse & Neglect, 84*, 131–145.

Augustyn, M.B., Thornberry, T.P., & Henry, K.L. (2019). The reproduction of child maltreatment: An examination of adolescent problem behavior, substance use, and precocious transitions in the link between victimization and perpetration. *Development and Psychopathology, 31*, 53–71.

Badyar, N., & Akcinar, B. (2018). Reciprocal relations between the trajectories of mothers' harsh discipline, responsiveness and aggression in early childhood. *Journal of Abnormal Child Psychology, 46*, 83–97.

Bandura, A. (1978). Social learning theory of aggression. *Journal of Communication, 28*, 12–29.

Bartoza, G.E., & Siller, L.A. (2018). Child maltreatment, school bonds, and adult violence: A serial mediation model. *Journal of Interpersonal Violence.* Online first. doi:10.1177/0886260518805763

Belsky, J. (1993). Etiology of child maltreatment: A developmental-ecological analysis. *Psychological Bulletin, 114*, 413–434.

Berlin, L.J., Appleyard, K., & Dodge, K.A. (2011). Intergenerational continuity in child maltreatment: Mediating mechanisms and implications for prevention. *Child Development, 82*, 162–176.

Bluemke, M., & Teige-Mocigemba, S. (2015). Automatic processes in aggression: Conceptual and assessment issues. *Aggressive Behavior, 41*, 44–50.

Braga, T., Gonçalves, L.C., Basto-Pereira, M., & Maia, A. (2017). Unraveling the link between maltreatment and juvenile antisocial behavior: A meta-analysis of prospective longitudinal studies. *Aggressive and Violent Behavior, 33*, 37–50.

Brown, D.W., Anda, R.F., Tiemeier, H., Felitti, V.J., Edwards V.J., & Croft, J.B., … Giles, W.H. (2009). Adverse Childhood Experiences and the risk of premature mortality. *American Journal of Preventative Medicine, 37*, 389–396.

Brown, M.J., Perera, R.A., Masho, S.W., Mezuk, B., & Cohen, S.A. (2015). Adverse Childhood Experiences and intimate partner aggression in the US: Sex differences and similarities in psychosocial mediation. *Social Science Medicine, 131*, 48–57.

Buisman, R.S.M., Pittner, K., Tollenar, M.S., Lindenberg, J., van den Berg, L.J.M., Compier-de Block, L.H.C.G., … van IJzendoorn, M.H. (2020). Intergenerational transmission of child maltreatment using a multi-informant multi-generation family design. *PLoS One, 15*, e0225839. doi:10.1371/journal.pone.0225839

Button, D.M., & Gealt, R. (2010). High risk behaviors among victims of sibling violence. *Journal of Family Violence, 25*, 131–140.

Camilo, C., Garrido, M.V., & Calheiros, M.M. (2016). Implicit measures of child abuse and neglect: A systematic review. *Aggression and Violent Behavior, 29*, 43–54.

Camilo, C., Garrido, M.V., & Calheiros, M.M. (2020). The social information processing model in child physical abuse and neglect: A meta-analytic review. *Child Abuse & Neglect, 108*, 10466.

Capaldi, D.M., Knoble, N.B., Shortt, J.W., & Kim, H.K. (2012). A systematic review of risk factors for intimate partner violence. *Partner Abuse, 3*, 231–280.

Capaldi, D.M., Tiberio, S.S., Pears, K.C., Kerr, D.C.R., & Owen, L.D. (2019). Intergenerational associations in physical maltreatment: Examination of mediation by delinquency and substance use, and moderated mediation by anger. *Development and Psychopathology, 31*, 73–82.

Castellví, P., Miranda-Mendizábal, A., Parés-Badell, O., Almenara, J., Alonso, I., Blasco, M.J., … Alonso, J. (2017). Exposure to violence, a risk for suicide in youths and young adults: A meta-analysis of longitudinal studies. *Acta Psychiatrica Scandinavica, 135*, 195–211.

Chamberlain, C., Gee, G., Harfield, S., Campbell, S., Brennan, S., Clark, Y., … Brown, S. (2019). Parenting after a history of childhood maltreatment: A scoping review and map of the evidence in the perinatal period. *PLoS ONE, 14*, e0213460. doi:10.1371/journal.pone.0213460

Chan, K.L., Chen, Q., & Chen, M. (2019). Prevalence and correlates of the co-occurrence of family violence: A meta-analysis on family polyvictimization. *Trauma, Violence, & Abuse*. Online first. doi:10.1177/1524838019841601

Chiesa, A.E., Kallechey, L., Harlaar, N., Ford, C.R., Garrido, E.F., Betts, W.R., & Maguire, S. (2018). Intimate partner violence victimization and parenting: A systematic review. *Child Abuse & Neglect, 80*, 285–300.

Cicchetti, D., Rogosch, F.A., & Thibodeau, E. (2012). The effects of child maltreatment on early signs of antisocial behavior: Genetic moderation by Tryptophan Hydrolase, Serotonin Transporter, and Monoamine Oxidase-A-Genes. *Development and Psychopathology, 24*, 907–928.

Currie, J., & Widom, C.S. (2010). Long-term consequences of child abuse and neglect on adult economic well-being. *Child Maltreatment, 15*, 111–120.

Doidge, J.C., Higgins, D.J., Delfabbro, P., Edwards, B., Vasallo, S., Toumbourou, J.W., & Segal, L. (2017a). Economic predictors of child maltreatment in an Australian population-based birth cohort. *Children and Youth Services Review, 72*, 14–25.

Doidge, J.C., Higgins, D.J., Delfabbro, P., & Segal, L. (2017b). Risk factors for child maltreatment in an Australian population-based birth cohort. *Child Abuse & Neglect, 64*, 47–60.

Duke, N.N., Pettingell, S.L., McMorris, B.J., & Borowsky, I.W. (2010) Adolescent violence perpetration: Associations with multiple types of Adverse Childhood Experiences. *Pediatrics, 125*, e778–e786.

Espinosa, A., Ruglass, L.M., Dambreville, N., Shevorykin, A., Nicholson, R., & Sykes, K.M. (2017). Correlates of child abuse potential among African American and Latina mothers: A developmental-ecological perspective. *Child Abuse & Neglect, 70*, 222–2300.

Euser, S., Alink, L.R.A., Stoltenborgh, M., Bakermans-Kranenburg, M.J., & van IJzendoorn, M.H. (2015). A gloomy picture: A meta-analysis of randomized controlled trials reveals disappointing effectiveness of programs aiming at preventing child maltreatment. *BMC Public Health, 15*. doi:10.1186/s12889-015-2387-9

Felitti, V.J., Anda, R.F., Nordenberg, D., Williamson, D.F., Spitz, A.M., Edwards, V., ... Marks, J.S. (1998). Relationship of childhood abuse and household dysfunction to many of the leading causes of death in adults: The Adverse Childhood Experiences (ACE) Study. *American Journal of Preventive Medicine, 14*, 245–258.

Fergusson, D.M., Horwood, L.J., & Boden, J.M. (2011). Structural equation modeling of repeated retrospective reports of child maltreatment. *International Journal of Methods in Psychiatric Research, 20*, 93–104.

Flaherty, E.G., Perez-Rossello, J.M., Levine, M.A., Hennrikus, W.L., & the American Academy of Pediatrics Committee on Child Abuse and Neglect. (2014). Evaluating children with fractures for child physical abuse. *Pediatrics, 133*, e477–e489.

Fortson, B.L., Klevens, J., Merrick, M.T., Gilbert, L.K., & Alexander, S.P. (2016). *Preventing child abuse and neglect: A technical package for policy, norm, and programmatic activities*. Centers for Disease Control and Prevention. www.cdc.gov/violenceprevention/pdf/CAN-Prevention-Technical-Package.pdf

Freisthler, B., & Maguire-Jack, K. (2015). Understanding the interplay between neighborhood structural factors, social processes, and alcohol outlets on child physical abuse. *Child Maltreatment, 20*, 268–277.

Gershoff, E.T., & Grogan-Kaylor, A. (2016). Spanking and child outcomes: Old controversies and new meta-analyses. *Journal of Family Psychology, 30*, 453–469.

González, R.A., Kallis, C., Ullrich, S., Barnicot, K., Keers, R., & Coid, J.W. (2016). Childhood maltreatment and violence: Mediation through psychiatric morbidity. *Child Abuse & Neglect, 52*, 70–84.

Gracia, E., & Herrero, J. (2008). Is it considered violence? The acceptability of physical punishment of children in Europe. *Journal of Marriage and Family, 70*, 210–217.

Gracia, E., Rodriguez, C.M., Martin-Fernández, M., & Lila, M. (2020). Acceptability of family violence: Underlying ties between intimate partner violence and child abuse. *Journal of Interpersonal Violence, 35*, 3217–3236.

Grasso, D.J., Henry, D., Kestler, J., Nieto, R., Wakschlag, L.S., & Briggs-Gowan, M.J. (2016). Harsh parenting as a potential mediator of the association between intimate partner violence and child disruptive behavior in families with young children. *Journal of Interpersonal Violence, 31*, 2102–2126.

Green, J.G., McLaughlin, K.A., Berglund, P.A., Gruber, M.J., Sampson, N.A., Zaslavsky, A.M., … Kessler, R.G. (2010). Childhood adversities and adult psychiatric disorders in the national comorbidity survey replication I: Associations with first onset of DSM-IV disorders. *Archives of General Psychiatry, 67*, 113–123.

Greene, C.A., Haisley, L., Wallace, C., & Ford, J.D. (2020). Intergenerational effects of childhood maltreatment: A systematic review of parenting practices of adult survivors of childhood abuse, neglect, and violence. *Clinical Psychology Review, 80*, 101891.

Hawkins, A.O., Danielson, C.K., de Arellano, M.A., Hanson, R.F., Ruggiero, K.J., Smith, D.W., … Kilpatrick, D.G. (2010). Ethnic/Racial differences in the prevalence of injurious spanking and other child physical abuse in a national survey of adolescents. *Child Maltreatment, 15*, 242–249.

Huesmann, L.R. (2018). An integrative theoretical understanding of aggression: A brief exposition. *Current Opinion in Psychology, 19*, 119–124.

Ibabe, I., Jaureguizar, J., & Bentler, P.M. (2013). Risk factors for child-to-parent violence. *Journal of Family Violence, 28*, 526–534.

Ingram, K.M., Espelage, D.L., Davis, J.P., & Merrin, G.J. (2020). Family violence, sibling, and peer aggression during adolescence: Associations with behavioral health outcomes. *Frontiers in Psychology, 11*. doi:10.3389/fpsyt.2020.00026

Irwin, L.M., Skowronski, J.J., Crouch, J.L., Milner, J.S., & Zengel, B. (2014). Reactions to children's transgressions in at-risk caregivers: Does mitigating information, type of transgression, or caregiver directive matter? *Child Abuse & Neglect, 38*, 917–927.

Kaufman, J., & Zigler, E. (1987). Do abused children become abusive parents? *American Journal of Mental Health & Social Justice, 57*, 186–192.

Kaufman-Parks, A.M., DeMaris, A., Giordano, P.C., Manning, W.D., & Longmore, M.A. (2017). Parents and partners: Moderating and mediating influences on intimate partner violence across adolescence and young adulthood. *Journal of Social and Personal Relationships, 34*, 1295–1323.

Kaukinen, C., Buchanan, L., & Gover, A.R. (2015). Child abuse and the experience of violence in college dating relationships: Examining the moderating effect of gender and race. *Journal of Family Violence, 30*, 1079–1092.

King, A.R., Ratzak, A., Ballantyne, S., Knutson, S., Russell, T.D., Pogalz, C.R., & Breen, C.M. (2018). Differentiating corporal punishment from physical abuse in the prediction of lifetime aggression. *Aggressive Behavior, 44*, 306–315.

Klevens, J., Ports, K.A., Austin, C., Ludlow, I.J., & Hurd, J. (2018). A cross-national exploration of societal-level factors associated with child physical abuse and neglect. *Global Public Health, 13*, 1495–1506.

Klika, J.B., Herrenkohl, T.I., & Lee, J.O. (2012). School factors as moderators of the relationship between physical child abuse and pathways of antisocial behavior. *Journal of Interpersonal Violence, 28*, 852–867.

Kluczniok, D., Bertsch, K., Hindi Attar, C., Neukel, C., Fuchs, A., Jaite, C., … Bermpohl, F. (2020). Early life maltreatment and depression: Mediating effect of hair cortisol concentration on child abuse potential. *Psychoneuroendocrinology, 120*, 104791.

Kremer, K.P., Kondis, J.S., & Kremer, T.R. (2020). Discordance in reporting of maternal aggression: Exploring differences by characteristics of children, mothers, and their environments. *Child Maltreatment, 25*, 339–351.

Labella, M.H., & Masten, A.S. (2018). Family influences on the development of aggression and violence. *Current Opinion in Psychology, 19*, 11–16.

Lansford, J.E., Miller-Johnson, S., Berlin, L.J., Dodge, K.A., Bates, J.E., & Pettit, G.S. (2007). Early physical abuse and later violent delinquency: A prospective longitudinal study. *Child Maltreatment, 12*, 233–245.

Lereya, S.T., Samara, M., & Wolke, D. (2013). Parenting behavior and the risk of becoming a victim and a bully/victim: A meta-analysis study. *Child Abuse & Neglect, 37*, 1091–1108.

Leventhal, J.M., & Gaither, J.R. (2012). Incidence of serious injuries due to physical abuse in the United States: 1997–2009. *Pediatrics, 130*, e847–e852.

Li, S., Zhao, F., & Yu, G. (2019). Childhood maltreatment and intimate partner violence victimization: A meta-analysis. *Child Abuse & Neglect, 88*, 212–224.

Lowell, A., & Renk, K. (2017). Predictors of child maltreatment potential in a national sample of mothers of young children. *Journal of Aggression, Maltreatment, and Trauma, 26*, 335–353.

Lu, Y., Shorey, R.C., Greeley, C.S., & Temple, J.R. (2019). Childhood physical abuse and physical dating violence in young adulthood: The mediating role of adverse mental health. *Journal of Clinical Psychology, 75*, 1916–1929.

Lyons, J., Bell, T., Fréchette, S., & Romano, E. (2015). Child-to-parent violence: Frequency and family correlates. *Journal of Family Violence, 30*, 729–742.

Ma, J., Lee, S.J., & Grogan-Kaylor, A. (2021). Adverse Childhood Experiences and spanking have similar associations with early behavior problems. *Journal of Pediatrics*. Online first. doi:10.1016/j.jpeds.2021.01.072

MacMillan, H.L., Tanaka, M., Duku, E., Vaillancourt, T., & Boyle, M.H. (2013). Child physical and sexual abuse in a community sample of young adults: Results from the Ontario Child Health Study. *Child Abuse & Neglect, 37*, 14–21.

Madigan, S., Cyr, C., Eirch, R., Fearon, R.M.P., Ly, A., Rash, C., ... Alink, L.R.A. (2019). Testing the cycle of maltreatment hypothesis: Meta-analytic evidence of the intergenerational transmission of child maltreatment. *Development and psychopathology, 31*, 23–51.

Maguire-Jack, K., & Font, S.A. (2017). Community and individual risk factors for physical abuse and child neglect: Variations by poverty status. *Child Maltreatment, 22*, 215–226.

Martoccio, T.L., Berlin, L.J., & Aparicio, E.M. (2020). Intergenerational continuity in child maltreatment: Explicating underlying mechanisms. *Journal of Interpersonal Violence*, Online First. doi:10.1177/0886260520914542

Masten, A., & Cicchetti, D. (2010). Developmental cascades. *Development and Psychopathology, 22*, 491–495.

McCarthy, R.J., Wagner, M.F., Basham, A., & Jones, C. (2016). Individual differences in parents' impressions of children and child physical abuse: A meta-analysis. *Psychology of Violence, 6*, 485–496.

Melchert, T.P. (2015). *Biopsychosocial practice: A science-based framework for behavioral health care*. American Psychological Association.

Milaniak, I., & Widom, C.S. (2015). Does child abuse and neglect increase risk for perpetration of violence inside and outside the home? *Psychology of Violence, 5*, 246–255.

Milner, J.S. (2000). Social information processing and child physical abuse: Theory and research: In D.J. Hansen (Ed.), *Nebraska symposium on motivation, Vo. 46, 1998: Motivation and child maltreatment* (pp. 39–84). Lincoln: University of Nebraska Press.

Miragoli, S., Balzarotti, S., Camisasca, E., & Di Blasio, P. (2018). Parents' perception of child behavior, parenting stress, and child abuse potential: Individual and partner influences. *Child Abuse & Neglect, 84*, 146–156.

Nelson, J., Klumparendt, A., Doebler, P., & Ehring, T. (2018). Childhood maltreatment and characteristics of adult depression: Meta-analysis. *British Journal of Psychiatry, 210*, 96–104.

Nemeroff, C.B. (2016). Paradise lost: The neurobiological and clinical consequences of child abuse and neglect. *Neuron, 89*, 892–909.

Niu, H., Liu, L., & Wang, M. (2018). Intergenerational transmission of harsh discipline: The moderating role of parenting stress and parent gender. *Child Abuse & Neglect, 79*, 1–10.

Orobio de Castro, B. (2004). The development of social information processing and aggressive behaviour: Current issues. *European Journal of Developmental Psychology, 1*, 87–102.

Pereznieto, P., Montes, A., Routier, S., & Langston, A. (2014). *The costs and economic impact of violence against children*. Overseas Development Institute. Retrieved from www.odi.org/sites/odi.org.uk/files/odi-assets/publications-opinion-files/9177.pdf.

Peterson, C., Florence, C., & Klevens, J. (2018). The economic burden of child mal-treatment in the United States, 2015. *Child Abuse & Neglect, 86*, 178–183.

Poole, M.K., Seal, D.W., & Taylor, C.A. (2014). A systematic review of universal campaigns targeting child physical abuse prevention. *Health Education Research, 29*, 388–432.

Prevoo, M.J.L., Stoltenborgh, M., Alink, L.R.A., Bakersman-Kranenburg, M.J., & van IJzendoorn, M.H. (2017). Methodological moderators in prevalence studies on child maltreatment: Review of a series of meta-analyses. *Child Abuse Review, 26*, 141–157.

Raby, K.L., Roisman, G.I., Labella, M.H., Martin, J., Fraley, R.C., & Simpson, J.A. (2019). The legacy of early abuse and neglect for social and academic competence from childhood to adulthood. *Child Development, 90*, 1684–1701.

Relva, I.C., Fernandes, O.M., & Mota, C.P. (2013). An exploration of sibling violence predictors. *Journal of Aggression, Conflict, and Peace Research, 5*, 47–61.

Richards, T.N., Tillyer, M.S., & Wright, E.M. (2017). Intimate partner violence and the overlap of perpetration and victimization: Considering the influence of physical, sexual, and emotional abuse in childhood. *Child Abuse & Neglect, 67*, 240–248.

Richey, A., Brown, S., Fite, P.J., & Bortolato, M. (2016). The role of hostile attribu-tions in the associations between child maltreatment and reactive and proactive aggression. *Journal of Aggression, Maltreatment & Trauma, 25*, 1043–1057.

Rodriguez, C.M. (2010). Parent-child aggression: Association with child abuse poten-tial and parenting styles. *Violence and Victims, 25*, 728–741.

Rodriguez, C.M. (2018). Predicting parent-child aggression risk: Cognitive factors and their interaction with anger. *Journal of Interpersonal Violence, 33*, 359–378.

Rodriguez, C.M. (2021). Mothers' non-lethal physical abuse of children. In T.K. Shackelford (Ed.), *The SAGE Handbook of Domestic Violence*. SAGE Publishing.

Rodriguez, C.M., Baker, L.R., Pu, D.F., & Tucker, M.C. (2017). Predicting parent-child aggression risk in mothers and fathers: Role of emotion regulation and frus-tration tolerance. *Journal of Child and Family Studies, 26*, 2629–2538.

Rodriguez, C.M., Bower-Russa, M., & Harmon, N. (2011). Assessing abuse risk beyond self-report: Analog task of acceptability of parent-child aggression. *Child Abuse & Neglect, 35*, 199–209.

Rodriguez, C.M., Cook, A.E., & Jedrziewski, C.T. (2012). Reading between the lines: Implicit assessment of the association of parental attributions and empathy with abuse risk. *Child Abuse & Neglect, 36*, 564–571.

Rodriguez, C.M., Russa, M.B., & Kircher, J.C. (2015). Analog assessment of frustra-tion tolerance: Association with self-reported child abuse risk and physiological reactivity. *Child Abuse & Neglect, 46*, 121–131.

Rodriguez, C.M., Silvia, P.J., Gonzalez, S., & Christl, M. (2018a). Disentangling the cycle: Potential mediators and moderators in the intergenerational transmission of parent-child aggression. *Child Maltreatment, 23*, 254–268.

Rodriguez, C.M., Silvia, P.J., Lee, S.J., & Grogan-Kaylor, A. (In press). Assessing moth-ers' automatic affective and discipline reactions to child behavior in relation to child abuse risk: A dual-processing investigation. doi.org/10.1177/10731911211020114

Rodriguez, C.M., Silvia, P.J., & Pu, D.F. (2018b). Predictors of change in mothers' and fathers' parent-child aggression risk. *Child Abuse & Neglect, 86,* 247–256.

Rodriguez, C.M., Silvia, P.J., & Gaskin, R.E. (2019). Predicting maternal and paternal parent-child aggression risk: Longitudinal multimethod investigation using Social Information Processing theory. *Psychology of Violence, 9,* 370–382.

Rodriguez, C.M., Wittig, S.M.O., & Silvia, P.J. (2020a). Refining social-information processing theory: Predicting maternal and paternal parent-child aggression risk longitudinally. *Child Abuse & Neglect, 107,* 104563.

Schofield, T.J., Conger, R.D., & Conger, K.J. (2016). Disrupting intergenerational continuity in harsh parenting: Self-control and a supportive partner. *Development and Psychopathology, 29,* 1279–1287.

Schuster, I., & Tomaszewska, P. (2020). Pathways from child sexual and physical abuse to sexual and physical intimate partner violence victimization through attitudes toward intimate partner violence. *Journal of Family Violence.* Online First. doi:10.1007/s10896-020-00180-2

Scribano, P.V., Makoroff, K.L., Feldman, K.W., & Berger, R.P. (2013). Association of perpetrator relationship to abusive head trauma clinical outcomes. *Child Abuse & Neglect, 37,* 771–777.

Sedlak, A.J., Mettenburg, J., Basena, M., Petta, I., McPherson, K., Greene, A., & Li, S. (2010). *Fourth National Incidence Study of Child Abuse and Neglect (NIS–4): Report to Congress, Executive Summary.* Retrieved from http://www.acf.hhs.gov/sites/default/files/opre/nis4_report_congress_full_pdf_jan2010.pdf

Shackman, J.E., & Pollak, S.D. (2014). Impact of physical maltreatment on the regulation of negative affect and aggression. *Development and Psychopathology, 26,* 1021–1033.

Simon, T.R., Shattuck, A., Kacha-Ochana, A., David-Ferdon, C.F., Hamby, S., Henly, M., ... Finkelhor, D. (2018). Injuries from physical abuse: National survey of children's exposure to violence I–III. *American Journal of Preventive Medicine, 54,* 129–132.

Smith, A.L., Cross, D., Winkler, J., Jovanovic, T., & Bekh, B. (2014). Emotional dysregulation and negative affect mediate the relationship between maternal history of child maltreatment and maternal child abuse potential. *Journal of Family Violence, 29,* 483–494.

Sousa, C., Mason, W.A., Herrenkohl, T.I., Prince, D., Herrenkohl, R.C., & Russo, M.J. (2018). Direct and indirect effects of child abuse and environmental stress: A lifecourse perspective on adversity and depressive symptoms. *American Journal of Orthopsychiatry, 88,* 180–188.

Stith, S.M., Liu, T., Davies, C., Boykin, E.L., Alder, M.C., Harris, J.M, ... Dees, J.E.M.E.G. (2009). Risk factors in child maltreatment: A meta-analytic review of the literature. *Aggression and Violent Behavior, 14,* 13–29.

Stöckl, H., Dekel, B., Morris-Gehring, A., Watts, C., & Abrahams, N. (2017). Child homicide perpetrators worldwide: A systematic review. *BMJ Paediatrics Open, 1.*

Stoltenborgh, M., Bakermans-Kranenburg, M.J., Alink, L.R.A., & van IJzendoorn, M.H. (2015). The Prevalence of child maltreatment across the globe: Review of a series of meta-analyses. *Child Abuse Review, 24,* 37–50.

Stoltenborgh, M., Bakermans-Kranenburg, M.J., van IJzendoorn, M.H., & Alink, L.R.A. (2013). Cultural-geographical differences in the occurrence of child physical abuse? A meta-analysis of global prevalence. *International Journal of Psychology, 48*, 81–94.

Sugaya, L., Hasin, D.S., Olfson, M., Lin, K., Grant, B.F., & Blanco, C. (2012). Child physical abuse and adult mental health: A national study. *Journal of Traumatic Stress, 25*, 384–392.

Tanaka, M., Georgiades, K., Boyle, M.H., & MacMillan, H.L. (2015). Child maltreatment and educational attainment in young adulthood: Results from the Ontario Child Health Study. *Journal of Interpersonal Violence, 30*, 195–214.

Teicher, M.H., & Samson, J.A. (2016). Annual research review: Enduring neurobiological effects of childhood abuse and neglect. *Journal of Child Psychology and Psychiatry, 57*, 241–266.

Thibodeau, E.L., Cicchetti, D., & Rogosch, F.A. (2015). Child maltreatment, impulsivity, and antisocial behavior in African-American children: Moderation effects from a cumulative dopaminergic gene index. *Development and Psychopathology, 27*, 1621–1636.

Topitzes, J., Mersky, J.P., & Reynolds, A.J. (2012). From child maltreatment to violent offending: An examination of mixed-gender and gender-specific models. *Journal of Interpersonal Violence, 27*, 2322–2347.

Tucker, M.C., Rodriguez, C.M., & Baker, L.R. (2017). Personal and couple level risk factors: Maternal and paternal parent-child aggression risk. *Child Abuse & Neglect, 69*, 213–222.

U.S. Department of Health and Human Services (2019). *Child Maltreatment, 2017.* Retrieved from https://www.acf.hhs.gov/cb/report/child-maltreatment-2017

U.S. Department of Health and Human Services (2020). *Child Maltreatment, 2018.* Retrieved from https://www.acf.hhs.gov/cb/resource/child-maltreatment-2018

van der Put, C.E., Assink, M., Gubbels, J., & Boerkhout von Solinge, N.F. (2018). Identifying effective components of child maltreatment interventions: A meta-analysis. *Clinical Child and Family Psychology Review, 21*, 171–202.

Vlahovicova, K., Melendez-Torres, G.J., Leijten, P., Knerr, W., & Gardner, F. (2017). Parenting programs for the prevention of child physical abuse recurrence: A systematic review and meta-analysis. *Clinical Child and Family Psychology Review, 20*, 351–365.

Watts, S.J., & McNulty, T.L. (2013). Childhood abuse and criminal behavior: Testing a general strain theory model. *Journal of Interpersonal Violence, 28*, 3023–3040.

Widom, C.S., Czaja, S.J., Bentley, T., & Johnson, M.S. (2012). A prospective investigation of physical health outcomes in abuse and neglected children: New findings from a 30-year follow-up. *American Journal of Public Health, 102*, 1135–1144.

Widom, C.S., Czaja, S.J., & DuMont, K.A. (2015). Intergenerational transmission of child abuse and neglect: Real or detection bias? *Science, 347*, 1480–1485.

Widom, C.S., Czaja, S., & Dutton, M.A. (2014). Child abuse and neglect and intimate partner violence victimization and perpetration: A prospective investigation. *Child Abuse & Neglect, 38*, 650–663.

Wildeman, C., Emanuel, N., Leventhal, J.M., Putnam-Hornstein, E., Waldfogel, J., & Lee, H. (2014). The prevalence of confirmed maltreatment among US children, 2004–2011. *JAMA Pediatrics, 168*, 706–713.

World Health Organization (2006). *Preventing Child Maltreatment: A guide to taking action and generating evidence.* Retrieved from http://whqlibdoc.who.int/publications/2006/9241594365_eng.pdf

World Health Organization (2014). *Global status report on violence prevention, 2014.* Retrieved from http://www.who.int/violence_injury_prevention/violence/status_report/2014/en/

Wright, E.M., & Fagan, A.A. (2013). The cycle of violence in context: Exploring the moderating roles of neighborhood disadvantage and cultural norms. *Criminology, 51*, 217–249.

Yang, M. (2015). The effect of material hardship on child protective service involvement. *Child Abuse & Neglect, 41*, 113–125.

Yang, M., Font, S.A., Ketchum, M., & Kim, Y.K. (2018). Intergenerational transmission of child abuse and neglect: Effects of maltreatment type and depressive symptoms. *Children and Youth Services Review, 91*, 364–371.

Chapter 2

Multiple Forms of Violence in the Lives of Youth Experiencing Homelessness

Risk Factors and Outcomes[1]

Kimberly A. Tyler and Rachel M. Schmitz

The National Network for Youth (2018) estimates that between 1.3 and 1.7 million youth in the United States have endured at least one night of homelessness within a specific year. Research evidence finds that many youth run away or leave home as a result of family trauma, such as experiencing child sexual and/or physical abuse (Bender, Brown, Thompson, Ferguson, & Langenderfer, 2015). Some youth are also kicked out of their family home for various reasons, in some cases, because of their sexual orientation (Cochran, Stewart, Ginzler, & Cauce, 2002). Additionally, many youth endure *further* traumatic experiences while on the street: 32% of youth reported being sexually assaulted and 94% have been physically assaulted since being on the street (Tyler & Beal, 2010). Moreover, research finds that between 9% and 20% of YEH have traded sex for money, food, drugs, or shelter (Tyler & Beal, 2010; Tyler, Gervais, & Davidson, 2013; Walls & Bell, 2011) since being on the street. Trading sex is another form of victimization that some youth experience.

Although some young people leave home to escape child abuse (Crosland, Joseph, Slattery, Hodges, & Dunlap, 2018), for at least some of these youth, violent experiences persist as they are victimized by strangers and/or acquaintances on the street (Tyler, Whitbeck, Hoyt, & Cauce, 2004; Tyler & Melander, 2010). In coping with multiple sources and experiences of victimization throughout their young lives, YEH may use substances to manage victimization stressors (Tyler & Melander, 2015). Given their multitude of victimization experiences suggests that many YEH are at significantly greater risk for abusing substances (Bender et al., 2015), experiencing mental health problems (Bender et al., 2015), and revictimization (Harris, Rice, Rhoades, Winetrobe, & Wenzel, 2017). These challenges, coupled with limited resources, suggest that YEH are extremely vulnerable to long-term negative health outcomes in the absence of intervention. As such, this chapter examines multiple forms of trauma as potential risk factors for sexual and physical street victimization, and then analyzes how these various traumas (including street victimization) are associated with binge drinking and illicit drug use among YEH. Having a better understanding of these linkages will allow for more targeted, comprehensive interventions with YEH enduring complex marginalizing life experiences.

LITERATURE REVIEW

Early Childhood Experiences of Abuse

Research finds that experiences of child abuse are a risk factor for youth running away or leaving home: over 50% of YEH have experienced child physical abuse at home prior to running away (Bender et al., 2015; Rattelade, Farrell, Aubry, & Klodawsky, 2014), and between 34% and 47% have experienced child sexual abuse (Bender et al., 2015; Tyler & Melander, 2015, respectively). Experiencing child abuse has been found to increase youth's risk of running away from home at earlier ages and running away multiple times (Tyler, Hoyt, Whitbeck, & Cauce, 2001). Additionally, some research has found that youth who have experienced child abuse are at higher risk for being revictimized while on the street (Edalati, Krausz, & Schütz, 2016; Tyler & Melander, 2015).

While general prevalence rates for child abuse are high, research finds that lesbian, gay, and bisexual (LGB) YEH have even greater rates of early childhood trauma (Rew, Whittaker, Taylor-Seehafer, & Smith, 2005; Tyler, 2008; Whitbeck, Chen, Hoyt, Tyler, & Johnson, 2004) as well as street victimization (Tyler & Beal, 2010) compared to their heterosexual counterparts. Additionally, because LGB youth are more likely to lack family support (Bouris et al., 2010) and to run away or be kicked out of their homes because of conflict surrounding their sexual orientation (Cochran et al., 2002), they may be less likely to return home and, subsequently, experience greater risk. Though child physical and sexual abuse have previously been examined as risk factors for revictimization among YEH, much of this research has not specifically examined how these experiences may differ for LGB youth compared with heterosexual youth. Moreover, there is a paucity of research that has examined other forms of trauma including being kicked out of one's family home and engaging in risky sexual behavior with strangers. Therefore, there is a critical need to learn more about these linkages and whether they vary by sexual orientation.

Victimization since Being on the Street

In addition to experiencing elevated rates of child abuse prior to leaving home, research also finds that many of these youth experience street victimization. Bender et al. (2015), for example, found that 21% of their sample of YEH had been sexually assaulted since being on the street, whereas Tyler and colleagues (2004) found a prevalence rate of 35% among their sample of YEH. Prevalence rates for physical victimization are also high: 52% of YEH in Bender et al.'s (2015) study and 94% of those young people in Tyler and Beal's study (2010) reported being physically assaulted since leaving home. Moreover, research has found that LGB youth experience higher rates of both sexual victimization (Tyler & Schmitz, 2018; Whitbeck et al., 2004) and physical assault (Gattis, 2013) compared to heterosexual youth.

Finally, trading sex is another form of victimization that some of these youth experience, which involves exchanging sexual favors for specific items youth deem necessary for survival (i.e., shelter) (Heerde & Hemphill, 2016; Whitbeck et al., 2004). Trading sex is typically viewed as an exploitative interaction because YEH usually engage in this practice when they have no other viable options to meet their basic needs (Hagan & McCarthy, 1997). Though trading sex has been linked to being sexually victimized on the street among YEH (Whitbeck et al., 2004), few studies have examined these linkages for LGB youth compared with heterosexual youth.

Substance Use

Due to the high rates of child abuse and street victimization that many YEH have endured, some researchers argue that youth often turn to substance use to cope with trauma (Kidd & Carroll, 2007; Tyler & Melander, 2015). Lifetime alcohol and drug prevalence that would likely lead to highly adverse health and legal outcomes among YEH are high: 89% report lifetime alcohol use and 48% report lifetime methamphetamine use (Bousman et al., 2005). The use of other illicit drugs including crack cocaine and hallucinogens is also common (Bailey, Camlin, & Ennett, 1998; Baron, 1999; Kral, Molnar, Booth, & Watters, 1997; Rice, Milburn, & Monro, 2011). Moreover, drug and alcohol use is 2 to 3 times more prevalent among YEH compared to youth who are not experiencing homelessness (Gomez, Thompson, & Barczyk, 2010). One proximal risk factor for substance use includes street victimization (Tyler & Schmitz, 2018): 39% and 94% of YEH have ever experienced street sexual and physical victimization, respectively (Tyler & Melander, 2015). Less is known, however, about how the associations between trauma risk factors and substance use among YEH operate for LGB youth and heterosexual youth.

THEORETICAL FRAMEWORK

We use a *life stress framework* (Lin & Ensel, 1989; Pearlin, 1989), which allows for a myriad of stressors that YEH have encountered from multiple sources and at different time points in their lives. As such, this framework provides a more comprehensive understanding of the complex life circumstances of YEH. Specifically, the life stress framework emphasizes multiple levels of influence (individual, family, and environment), as well as both distal (i.e., distant) and proximal (i.e., more recent) risk factors. These different levels or elements are fundamental to understanding the relation between early and later forms of trauma among YEH. Additionally, the life stress framework assumes that individuals exposed to one serious stressor (e.g., child sexual abuse) will be exposed to additional stressors, which can then cluster together (Pearlin, 1989). Applied to the current study, *distal stressors* (i.e., child sexual and physical abuse and ever being kicked out of one's family home) and *proximal stressors* (i.e., engaging in sexual risk behaviors with strangers, and ever having traded sex) are expected to be positively correlated with the proximal stressors of street sexual and physical victimization. Additionally, all forms of trauma, both distal and proximal, are expected to be positively associated with binge drinking and illicit drug use.

At the individual level, occupying marginalized social statuses, such as being LGB and female, are likely additional sources of stress for young people due to their socially stigmatized positions within society (Kelleher, 2009; Stanford Center on Poverty and Inequality, 2018). Individuals who identify as LGB often have to navigate chronic exposure to stigma in multiple social contexts that subordinate their sexual minority status, which in turn shapes their disproportionately elevated stress levels and resulting health disparities (Mink, Lindley, & Weinsten, 2014). Sexual minority and female YEH's exposure to stigma and adverse health outcomes may be exacerbated by the intersection between their multiple marginalized social statuses and structural vulnerability (Miller et al., 2011). Subsequently, LGB youth are more likely to experience multiple traumas as they navigate intersecting sources of stigma, prejudice, and discrimination (Meyer, 2015). The detrimental impact of experiencing homelessness on one's health, coupled with prejudice and discrimination, may lead to LGB YEH engaging in more substance use (Noell & Ochs, 2001). Perceptions and experiences of stigma may also be influenced by young people's intersecting marginalized statuses, such as biological sex, gender, and sexuality (Schmitz, Robinson, Tabler, Welch, &

Rafaqut, 2019). For example, female YEH may be more likely to exchange sex and males more likely to use substances following sexual victimization experiences (Harris et al., 2017).

METHODS

Data are from the Social Network and Homeless Youth Project, a study designed to examine the effect of social network characteristics on YEH's HIV-risk behaviors. The original sample included 249 YEH, ages 14 to 21 years who were interviewed in shelters and on the streets from January 2008 to March 2009 in three Midwestern cities in the United States. To participate in the study, youth had to be within the age range and meet the definition of being homeless or a runaway on the night prior to screening. *Homeless* includes those who lack *permanent* housing such as spending the previous night in a shelter, public place, on the street, staying with friends or in a transitional facility, or other places not intended as a domicile (National Center for Homeless Education, 2017). *Runaway* refers to youth under age 18 who have spent the previous night away from home without parental permission (Ennett, Bailey, & Federman, 1999). The current analysis uses a subsample ($n = 168$) given the current study focuses on youth (i.e., those 19 years of age or younger).

Experienced interviewers who have worked on past YEH projects, who have served for several years in agencies and shelters that support at-risk youth, and who were very familiar with local street cultures, such as knowing where to locate youth and where they congregate, conducted the interviews. All interviewers had completed the Collaborative Institutional Review Board (IRB) Training Initiative course for the protection of human subjects. Interviewers approached shelter residents and located other eligible respondents in areas of the cities where YEH congregate. They varied the times of the day on both weekdays and weekends that they visited these locations. This sampling protocol was conducted repeatedly over the course of 15 months. All participants gave informed consent. While some respondents were not at the age of majority but were mature minors, a request for waiver of parental consent was approved by the supervising IRB. All respondents were told that their responses would remain confidential and that their participation was voluntary. The interviews were typically conducted in shelter conference rooms or quiet corners of fast-food restaurants if taking the youth back to the shelter was not feasible because of distance or safety concerns. The interview lasted approximately 45 minutes, and all participants received $25 for their involvement and $5 for a meal. Referrals for shelter, counseling services, and food services were also offered to youth at the time of the interview. All youth present were screened for eligibility and invited to participate. The response rate was 97% based on the number of initial contacts. The IRB at the University of Nebraska-Lincoln approved this study.

Measures

Demographic Variables

Sex was coded 0 = male and 1 = female.

Sexual orientation was measured by asking youth to describe their sexual orientation; coded 0 = lesbian, gay, or bisexual; 1 = straight or heterosexual.

Distal Risk Factors

Child physical abuse was a single item indicator which asked youth if they have ever been physically abused as a child (under the age of 18) (0 = no; 1 = yes).

Child sexual abuse was a single item indicator which asked youth if they have ever been sexually abused as a child (under the age of 18) (0 = no; 1 = yes).

Ever kicked out was a single item indicator that asked youth if their parents/caretaker ever kicked them out (0 = no; 1 = yes).

Proximal Risk Factors

Sexual risk behavior with strangers included seven items which asked youth, for example, if they ever had sex with an intravenous drug user or had sex with a person after the youth had used drugs or had too much to drink (0 = no; 1 = yes). The items were summed such that a higher score indicated a greater number of sexual risk behaviors ($\alpha = .82$). This scale has been used in prior research with YEH (Ennett et al., 1999).

Ever traded sex was measured by asking participants if they have ever traded sex for food, shelter, money, or drugs (0 = no; 1 = yes) used in prior research with this population (Tyler et al., 2013; Walls & Bell, 2011).

Physical street victimization included six items such as "how often were you beaten up" since leaving home (0 = never to 3 = many times). A mean scale was created; higher scores indicated more street physical victimization ($\alpha = .76$). These items have been used in previous studies of YEH (Tyler, Olson, & Ray, 2018; $\alpha = .85$).

Sexual street victimization included four items such as how often were you "touched sexually when you didn't want to be" since leaving home (0 = never to 3 = many times) ($\alpha = .85$). Due to skewness, the individual items were dichotomized and then a count variable was created; a higher score indicated more sexual victimization. This scale has been used in prior research with YEH (Tyler & Beal, 2010; α = .83).

Dependent Variables

Binge drinking was a single item indicator that asked youth if they had more than five drinks at one time in the past month (0 = no; 1 = yes).

Illicit drug use asked youth how often they have used a series of eight illicit drugs such as cocaine, hallucinogens and amphetamines during the past six months. Due to skewness, the final variable was dichotomized into 0 = never used any of these drugs in the past six months and 1 = used one or more of these drugs at least once in the past six months.

Data Analytic Plan

Chi-square tests were used to assess bivariate associations between heterosexual youth and LGB youth and between males and females on dichotomous variables. Student's *t*-tests were used to assess bivariate associations between heterosexual youth and LGB youth and between males and females on continuous variables. Second, we added a correlation matrix to show bivariate associations between all study variables. Third, due to the continuous nature of two of our proximal risk factors, street sexual victimization and street physical victimization, ordinary least squares (OLS) regression was used to examine these risk factors' associations with distal variables and two additional proximal variables (i.e., sexual risk behavior with strangers and trading sex). Finally, logistic regression models were used to examine associations between all trauma variables, including street sexual and physical victimization, with illicit drug use and binge drinking due to the dichotomous nature of these two substance use outcome variables. A p-value of ≤ .05 was considered significant. Stata version 15.1 was used.

Sample Characteristics

The subsample included 168 youth, 59% female (n = 99). Ages ranged from 14 to 19 years of age (mean = 17.58). Approximately 17% of youth (n = 28) identified as LGB. In terms of abuse, 54% of youth (n = 91) reported that they had experienced child physical abuse, while 30% of youth (n = 50) indicated that they had experienced child sexual abuse. Forty-seven percent of youth (n = 79) reported that they had been kicked out of their parents/caretakers' home.

RESULTS

Bivariate Results

Table 2.1 results revealed that LGB youth were significantly more likely to have experienced child sexual abuse (χ^2 = 8.96; p < .01) and to have ever traded sex (χ^2 = 5.53; p < .05) compared to heterosexual youth. LGB youth also were more likely to have ever used illicit drugs (χ^2 = 6.65; p < .01) and to have binge drank in the past month (χ^2 = 10.92; p < .01) compared to their heterosexual counterparts. On the right side of table 2.1, results are presented for male and female youth and revealed two significant differences: females were more likely to have experienced child sexual abuse (χ^2 = 15.26; p < .01) compared to males, whereas males reported ever using illicit drugs more than females (χ^2 = 6.42; p < .01). As the cell sizes for trading sex are small, caution is recommended in interpreting these findings.

The lower portion of table 2.1, which shows the results from t-tests, revealed that sexual risk behaviors with strangers (t = 4.73; p < .01) and street sexual victimization (t = 4.32; p < .01) were both significantly higher among LGB youth than heterosexual youth. On the bottom right side of table 2.1, results comparing male and female youth revealed that experiencing more street *sexual* victimization (t = −6.07; p < .01) was significantly higher for females than males, whereas experiencing more street *physical* victimization (t = 2.21; p < .05) was significantly higher for males than females (see table 2.2 for bivariate correlations).

Multivariate Analysis

OLS regression models are shown in table 2.3. In Model 1 for sexual victimization, results revealed that females were significantly more likely to have experienced more street sexual victimization compared to males (β = .32; CI = .56–1.32). Additionally, youth who had ever been sexually abused as a child (β = .37; CI = .72–1.59) and those who had engaged in sexual risk behavior with strangers (β = .16; CI = .02–.20) reported more experiences of street sexual victimization. Model 1 explained 43% of the variance in street sexual victimization. In Model 2, the variable ever traded sex was added and was significantly associated with street sexual victimization (β = .29; CI = .78–2.05). Prior significant variables in Model 1 remained significant in Model 2 with two exceptions: heterosexual youth were less likely to have experienced street sexual victimization compared to LGB youth (β = −.11; CI = −.89 to .05) and sexual risk behavior with strangers was no longer significant in Model 2. Model 2 explained 49% of the variance in street sexual victimization, which is a significant improvement in model fit with the addition of the trading sex variable.

Table 2.1 Bivariate Results

Chi-Square Test and Descriptive Statistics for Dichotomous Variables by Sexual Orientation and Sex

	Heterosexual		LGB		χ^2	Male		Female		χ^2
	N	%	N	%		N	%	N	%	
Child physical abuse	74	52.9	17	60.7	.58	41	59.4	50	50.5	1.30
Child sexual abuse	35	25.2	15	53.6	8.96**	9	13.2	41	41.4	15.26**
Ever kicked out	64	46.0	15	53.6	.53	37	54.4	42	42.4	2.32
Ever traded sex	10	7.1	6	21.4	5.53*	3	4.3	13	13.1	3.64
Illicit drug use	21	15.0	10	35.7	6.65**	19	27.5	12	12.1	6.42**
Binge drinking	32	22.9	15	53.6	10.92**	24	34.8	23	23.2	2.69

Student's t-test and Mean for Continuous Variables by Sexual Orientation and Sex

	Mean (SD)		t-test	Mean (SD)		t-test
	n = 140	n = 28		n = 69	n = 99	
Correlate	Heterosexual	LGB	t	Male	Female	t
Sexual risk behavior with strangers	1.68 (1.88)	3.61 (2.39)	4.73**	2.06 (2.05)	1.96 (2.13)	.30
Street sexual victimization	.88 (1.35)	2.11 (1.47)	4.32**	.35 (.72)	1.60 (1.57)	−6.07**
Street physical victimization	3.49 (3.16)	4.25 (3.04)	1.18	4.25 (3.79)	3.17 (2.54)	2.21*

Note: $**p < .01$; $*p < .05$. LGB = lesbian, gay, bisexual. SD = standard deviation.
Source: Data created by author study

48   *Kimberly A. Tyler and Rachel M. Schmitz*

Table 2.2 Correlation Matrix for All Study Variables

	1	2	3	4	5	6	7	8	9	10	11
1 Female	–										
2 Heterosexual	−.24**	–									
3 Physical abuse	−.08	−.06	–								
4 Sexual abuse	.30**	−.23**	.40**	–							
5 Kicked out	−.11	−.06	.32**	.17*	–						
6 Sexual risk beh.	−.03	−.35**	.19*	.22**	.14	–					
7 Traded sex	.14	−.18*	.18*	.32**	.06	.48**	–				
8 Sexual vict.	.44**	−.32**	.24**	.56**	.16*	.29**	.48**	–			
9 Physical vict.	−.17*	−.09	.25**	.24**	.11	.40**	.32**	.30**	–		
10 Illicit drug use	−.20**	−.20*	.17*	.12	.11	.61**	.37**	.14	.39**	–	
11 Binge drinking	−.14	−.25**	.18*	.08	.13	.49**	.11	.11	.26**	.49**	–
Mean	.60	.83	.54	.30	.47	2.01	.10	1.08	3.61	.19	.28
SD	.49	.38	.50	.46	.50	2.09	.29	1.44	3.15	.39	.45

Note: **p < .01, *p < .05. SD = standard deviation. Beh = behavior. Vict = victimization.
Source: Data created by author study

Table 2.3 OLS Regression Models for Correlates of Street Sexual and Physical Victimization

	Model 1		Model 2		Model 3		Model 4	
	β	95% CI	β	95% CI	β	95% CI	β	95% CI
	Sexual Victimization				Physical Victimization			
Female	.32**	.56–1.32	.29**	.49–1.21	−.21**	−2.29 to −.34	−.22**	−2.40 to −.46
Heterosexual	−.10	−.87 to .13	−.11+	−.89 to .05	.03	−1.05 to 1.50	.02	−1.10 to 1.43
Child physical abuse	.05	−.25 to .53	.04	−.27 to .47	.10	−.39 to 1.61	.09	−.43 to 1.56
Child sexual abuse	.37**	.72–1.59	.32**	.57–1.41	.19*	.19–2.43	.16*	−.02 to 2.24
Ever kicked out	.09	−.11 to .61	.10	−.06 to .62	−.02	−1.05 to .79	−.02	−1.00 to .82
Sexual risk behavior with strangers	.16**	.02–.20	.03	−.07 to .11	.34**	.29–.74	.27**	.16–.66
Ever traded sex			.29**	.78–2.05			.16*	−.02 to 3.39
Adjusted R²	.43		.49		.21		.22	

Note: CI = confidence interval. **p ≤ .01; *p ≤ .05; +p < .10.
Source: Data created by author study.

On the right side of table 2.3 for street physical victimization, Model 3 revealed that females were significantly less likely to have experienced more street physical victimization compared to males ($\beta = -.21$; CI = −2.29 to −.34). Additionally, youth who had ever been sexually abused as a child ($\beta = .19$; CI = .19–2.43) and those who engaged in more sexual risk behavior with strangers ($\beta = .34$; CI = .29–.74) reported more experiences of street physical victimization. Model 3 explained 21% of the variance in street physical victimization. In Model 4, the variable ever traded sex was added and was significantly associated with street physical victimization ($\beta = .16$;

CI = −.02 to 3.39). All prior significant variables in Model 3 remained significant in Model 4. Model 4 explained 22% of the variance in street physical victimization.

Results for illicit drug use and binge drinking are shown in table 2.4, respectively. On the left side of table 2.4, results for illicit drug use revealed that females had 85% lower odds of having used illicit drugs in the past six months compared to males (OR = .15; CI = .05–.44), whereas heterosexual youth had 82% lower odds of using illicit drugs in the past six months compared to LGB youth (OR = .18; CI = .06–.56). The addition of the proximal variables in model 2 significantly improved the fit of the model. Results showed that youth who engaged in sexual risk behavior with strangers were more than twice as likely to have reported illicit drug use in the prior six months (OR = 2.30; CI = 1.59–3.32) compared to those who did not have these experiences with strangers.

The right side of table 2.4 (model 3) showed similar results for binge drinking: females had 65% lower odds (OR = .35; CI = .15–.82) and heterosexuals had 82% lower odds (OR = .18; CI = .07–.48) of binge drinking in the prior month compared to males and LGB youth, respectively. Model 4 revealed that youth who engaged in sexual risk behavior with strangers were over one- and one-half times more likely to have reported binge drinking in the past month (OR = 1.79; CI = 1.40–2.29) compared to youth without these experiences. Additionally, youth who ever traded sex had 82% lower odds of binge

Table 2.4 Logistic Regression Models for Correlates of Illicit Drug Use and Binge Drinking

	Model 1		Model 2		Model 3		Model 4	
	Illicit Drug Use				*Binge Drinking*			
	OR	95% CI	OR	95% CI	OR	95% CI	OR	95% CI
Female	.15**	.05–.44	.06**	.01–.43	.35*	.15–.82	.41	.13–1.22
Heterosexual	.18**	.06–.56	.53	.12–2.40	.18**	.07–.48	.40	.13–1.19
Child physical abuse	1.69	.63–4.52	1.21	.35–4.23	1.92	.83–4.44	1.81	.70–4.65
Child sexual abuse	2.35	.79–6.97	1.13	.20–6.55	1.13	.45–2.83	.69	.21–2.25
Ever kicked out	1.11	.46–2.69	.77	.23–2.55	1.29	.60–2.76	1.07	.45–2.55
Sexual risk behavior with strangers			2.30**	1.59–3.32			1.79**	1.40–2.29
Ever traded sex			2.30	.28–18.96			.18*	.03–.99
Street physical victimization			1.11	.93–1.33			1.05	.91–1.21
Street sexual victimization			1.36	.67–2.79			1.21	.79–1.86
LRχ²	24.21		77.41		22.05		52.95	
d.f.	5		9		5		9	
Pseudo R²	.15		.48		.11		.27	

Note: OR = odds ratio; CI = confidence interval. **p ≤ .01; *p ≤ .05; †p < .10.
Source: Data created by author study

drinking in the past month compared to those who had not traded sex (OR = .18; CI = .03–.99). The addition of the proximal variables in Model 4 resulted in the variables sex and sexual orientation no longer being significant.

DISCUSSION

The purpose of this chapter was to examine different forms of trauma as risk factors for sexual and physical street victimization, as well as delineate how these various traumas are associated with binge drinking and illicit drug use among YEH. Overall, results indicate that at the bivariate level, LGB youth experience more trauma compared to their heterosexual counterparts as indicated by their greater experiences of child sexual abuse, ever having traded sex, sexual risk behavior with strangers, and street sexual victimization. Moreover, LGB youth report illicit drug use and binge drinking more than heterosexual youth. In terms of biological sex, results show that females experience child sexual abuse and street sexual victimization more than males, whereas males report more street physical victimization than females. Males also report illicit drug use more than females. The sex pattern observed for sexual and physical street victimization and substance use at the bivariate level generally holds when controlling for other variables at the multivariate level. For LGB youth, the pattern of illicit drug use and binge drinking holds when controlling for other variables, whereas the pattern for street victimization is not significantly different for LGB youth compared to heterosexual youth.

Some of the current findings are consistent with previous research (Edalati et al., 2016; Tyler & Melander, 2015), such as child sexual abuse experiences continue to impact youth as indicated by its positive association with both sexual and physical victimization on the street. It is noteworthy, however, that there are no significant differences between LGB and heterosexual youth for street victimization. One possible explanation for this lack of a significant difference may be because females also experience high prevalence rates of child sexual abuse and street sexual victimization, and many of them identify as heterosexual. Another potential explanation is that because LGB YEH may strategically conceal their sexual identity to avoid prejudice and discrimination (Schmitz & Tyler, 2018), this could serve as a buffer for potential anti-LGB victimization if their sexual orientation is not publicly known.

Additionally, results show that being kicked out of one's family home was not associated with the dependent variables, nor were there any significant differences for being kicked out across sexual orientation or respondent's biological sex. One possible explanation is that even though LGB youth report prevalence rates of child sexual abuse that are more than double that of heterosexual youth, rates of physical abuse are more similar between the groups.

Thus, it is possible youth are leaving home not only to escape sexual abuse but also to avoid further physical abuse. Subsequently, some youth may be leaving home to escape physical abuse, and others are running to avoid sexual abuse, while still some youth are fleeing from both types of abuse. Therefore, some young people may have already planned to run away or leave home to escape further abuse before their parent/caretaker could kick them out. This might explain why being kicked out is not associated with street victimization. Relatedly, research has found that some youth leave home multiple times (Tyler & Whitbeck, 2004), sometimes initiated by the youth themselves, to escape abuse, regardless of whether a parent/caretaker kicks them out. Thus, the impact of experiencing sexual abuse as a precursor to leaving home may be more influential for youth's outcomes than being kicked out by one's parent/caregiver.

Engaging in more sexual risk behavior with strangers and trading sex are both significant correlates of sexual and physical street victimization, which is consistent with some prior research (Whitbeck et al., 2004). Youth who trade sex for specific items of necessity are likely to be in vulnerable positions (i.e., they are unable to meet their basic needs) making it more difficult for them to say no. Additionally, it is possible that the individuals the youth are trading sex with victimize them at some future date as they already know the youths' precarious situation and may exploit the situation, taking further advantage of these youth. Moreover, youth who have been victimized as children while at home suffer from numerous mental health issues including depression and anxiety (Tyler & Ray, 2021), which also makes them more vulnerable to future victimization on the street. Specifically, results show that females and LGB youth are especially vulnerable to sexual revictimization, which may be attributed to their social status. This finding highlights the importance of a life stress framework in holistically understanding the numerous stressors young people experience relating to their intersecting stigmatized statuses across housing instability and processes of gender and sexual marginalization (Meyer, 2015; Pearlin, 1989).

Results show that males and LGB youth are more likely to report using illicit drugs and binge drinking compared to females and heterosexual youth, respectively, when controlling for distal factors, which is consistent with prior work (Cochran et al., 2002; Harris et al., 2017). Contrary to what was expected, however, neither sexual or physical abuse nor sexual or physical street victimization was associated with either type of substance use. One possible explanation is that youth were asked about illicit drug use for the past six months, which is a short time period given the youths' ages. Moreover, because of the limited time frame, illicit drug use had to be dichotomized due to a smaller number of youths who reported multiple uses. As such, the lack of variance in both substance use variables (i.e., yes/no responses) may explain why the abuse and victimization variables were not significantly associated with either substance. At the bivariate level, results show that LGB youth are using illicit drugs and binge drinking more than their heterosexual counterparts. It is possible that because of the elevated stressors that some LGB youth endure stemming from their socially marginalized status, they may turn to substance use as a means of coping with the layered stress of managing both stigma and homelessness (Goldbach, Tanner-Smith, Bagwell, & Dunlap, 2014). Males' elevated rates of substance use, on the other hand, could possibly be related to their conforming to ideals of stereotypical masculinity (Iwamoto & Smiler, 2013), especially when they are faced with stressful life events and in need of coping outlets.

Finally, the addition of the proximal variables significantly improved model fit for both the illicit drug use and binge drinking models. Though sexual and physical street victimization is not significantly associated with either substance use variable, sexual risk behavior with strangers is a significant correlate in both models, whereas trading sex is linked with binge drinking only. Consistent with expectations and our theoretical model of a life stress framework (Lin & Ensel, 1989; Pearlin, 1989), youth exposed to multiple stressors and trauma may be using illicit drugs as a method of coping with their current situation. Specifically, some youth who engage in sexual risk behavior with strangers may use illicit drugs and alcohol as a result of these encounters or more broadly to cope with the numerous stressors associated with experiencing homelessness. Though trading sex was associated with binge drinking, it was in the opposite direction of what was expected. One possible explanation for this finding is that we measured sexual risk behavior with strangers (e.g., having sex with a stranger after using too much alcohol and/or drugs) in the same model, but because sexual risk behavior with strangers is a continuous variable, it has more variance and is better able to explain binge drinking compared to the dichotomous trading sex variable.

Overall, this study contributes to the existing literature by examining how experiences of trauma may differ for LGB youth and heterosexual youth, which has previously been understudied in research. Because individuals who identify as LGB often have to navigate exposure to stigma in various social contexts, this can lead to higher levels of stress and result in poorer health outcomes and disparities (Mink et al., 2014). Additionally, there is a paucity of research that has examined specific forms of trauma including being kicked out of one's family home and engaging in risky sexual behavior with strangers. Understanding more about the multiple forms of complex trauma (in addition to child abuse) that many of these young people have experienced provides a more comprehensive understanding of potential linkages with alcohol and drug use. Subsequently, this study's findings can inform more targeted interventions with this population with the goal of mitigating the long-term negative health outcomes to which many YEH are vulnerable.

LIMITATIONS

There are some limitations to this study that should be noted. First, these data are cross-sectional and though some of the variables are time ordered, such as child abuse occurs prior to being on the street, whereas street victimization occurs after leaving home, the timing for substance use and trading sex, for example, is less certain. That is, though it was expected that trading sex would result in binge drinking and/or illicit drug use, it is also possible that youth who are binge drinking are at greater risk for trading sex. Notwithstanding the order of these variables, results do show important, significant linkages among key variables. Another limitation is small cell sizes with the trading sex variable once it is broken down into subgroups (e.g., by sexual orientation and then biological sex). Additionally, these data were collected in the Midwest, and it is possible that YEH in other areas of the country may have different experiences or different prevalence rates than those found in the current study. Thus, these results cannot be generalized to all YEH. Finally, the measures of child sexual and physical abuse were dichotomous so it is possible that their association with the outcome variables may have been different with the use of continuous variables. That is, some research has found a positive link between child abuse and substance use (Tyler & Melander, 2015), but these early distal variables were not associated with either illicit drug use or binge drinking in the current study.

CONCLUSION

These findings demonstrate that many YEH have undergone multiple forms of trauma both at home as well as on the street. Ironically, many young people run from home to escape abusive situations only to find themselves in similar precarious circumstances in the street environment where the likelihood for revictimization is exceedingly high. Such risks are especially prevalent for specific subgroups of YEH including females and LGB youth. The sexual exploitation that these young people have experienced in their family of origin continues on the street as seen through participation in sexual risk behavior with strangers and trading sex for specific items of necessity. The negative outcomes suffered by many YEH include the use of illicit drugs and/ or binge drinking, both of which are higher for LGB youth and males.

Overall, the multiple forms of trauma YEH sustain along with numerous negative outcomes underscore the need for multifaceted, formalized services for youth. Specifically, our findings show that early exposure to child sexual abuse is associated with both sexual and physical victimization on the street. Moreover, we observed biological sex differences in the forms of street victimization that young women and men experience as well as differences in the likelihood of using illicit drugs and binge drinking by sexual orientation. Service providers may be able to provide more comprehensive services by knowing about the diverse forms of trauma experienced by YEH and that the level of exposure may vary. Additionally, service providers should know that the origins of trauma may be unique and outcomes of these early forms of trauma may also be distinct by group membership. Services that attend to the multiple stressors that YEH have experienced as well as programs that focus on developing healthy methods of coping are vital.

Additionally, we find that LGB youth and males are at higher risk for using illicit drugs and binge drinking compared to heterosexual youth and females, respectively. It is possible that some of these young people are unaware of services or perhaps feel they do not need them. Moreover, it is possible that some LGB youth may be hesitant to use services for fear of prejudice or discrimination (Hunter, 2008). Thus, it may benefit providers to advertise services specifically tailored to the needs of LGB youth. LGB youth who are also managing additional stressors related to sexual identity may require distinctive supports that are specifically targeted to their needs in navigating stigma. Informing LGB youth that they have a safe place to go with available services may reduce the risk of further trauma. Additionally, LGB staff members who are open about their non-normative sexual orientation may also increase the likelihood that LGB youth will seek services (Choi, Wilson, Shelton, & Gates, 2015). Finally, providing all young people with supportive and positive role models can increase their social support and subsequently lower their risk for poor mental health outcomes (Tyler, Schmitz, & Ray, 2018), which may lead to reduced substance use and other street risk behaviors.

NOTE

1. This book chapter is based on research funded by a grant from the National Institute on Drug Abuse (DA021079). Dr. Kimberly A. Tyler, PI.

REFERENCES

Bailey, S. L., Camlin, C. S., & Ennett, S. T. (1998). Substance use and risky sexual behavior among homeless and runaway youth. *Journal of Adolescent Health, 23*, 378–388.

Baron, S. W. (1999). Street youths and substance use: The role of background, street lifestyle, and economic factors. *Youth and Society, 31*, 3–26.

Bender, K., Brown, S. M., Thompson, S. J., Ferguson, K. M., & Langenderfer, L. (2015). Multiple victimizations before and after leaving home associated with

PTSD, depression, and substance use disorder among homeless youth. *Child Maltreatment, 20*, 115–124.

Bousman, C. A., Blumberg, E. J., Shillington, A. M., Hovell, M. F., Ji, M., Lehman, S., & Clapp, J. (2005). Predictors of substance use among homeless youth in San Diego. *Addictive Behaviors, 30*, 1100–1110.

Bouris, A., Guilamo-Ramos, V., Pickard, A., Shiu, C., Loosier, P. S., Dittus, P., Gloppen, K., & Waldmiller, J. M. (2010). A systematic review of parental influences on the health and well-being of lesbian, gay, and bisexual youth: Time for a new public health research and practice agenda. *The Journal of Primary Prevention, 31*, 273–309.

Choi, S. K., Wilson, B. D. M., Shelton, J., & Gates, G. J. (2015). Serving our youth 2015: The needs and experiences of lesbian, gay, bisexual, transgender, and questioning youth experiencing homelessness. The Williams Institute. Retrieved February 3, 2016 (http://eprints.cdlib.org/uc/item/1pd9886n#page-1).

Cochran, B. N., Stewart, A. J., Ginzler, J. A., & Cauce, A. M. (2002). Challenges faced by homeless sexual minorities: Comparison of gay, lesbian, bisexual, and transgender homeless adolescents with their heterosexual counterparts. *American Journal of Public Health, 92*, 773–777.

Crosland, K., Joseph, R., Slattery, L., Hodges, S., & Dunlap, G. (2018). Why youth run: Assessing run function to stabilize foster care placement. *Children and Youth Services Review, 85*, 35–42.

Edalati, H., Krausz, M., & Schütz, C. G. (2016). Childhood maltreatment and revictimization in a homeless population. *Journal of Interpersonal Violence, 31*, 2492–2512.

Ennett, S. T., Bailey, S. L., & Federman, E. B. (1999). Social network characteristics associated with risky behaviors among runaway and homeless youth. *Journal of Health and Social Behavior, 40*, 63–78.

Gattis, M. N. (2013). An ecological systems comparison between homeless sexual minority youths and homeless heterosexual youths. *Journal of Social Service Research, 39*, 38–49.

Goldbach, J. T., Tanner-Smith, E. E., Bagwell, M., & Dunlap, S. (2014). Minority stress and substance use in sexual minority adolescents: A meta-analysis. *Prevention Science, 15*, 350–363.

Gomez, R., Thompson, S. J. & Barczyk, A. N. (2010). Factors associated with substance use among homeless young adults. *Substance Abuse, 31*, 24–34.

Hagan, J., & McCarthy, B. (1997). *Mean streets: Youth crime and homelessness.* Cambridge: Cambridge University Press.

Harris, T., Rice, E., Rhoades, H., Winetrobe, H., & Wenzel, S. (2017). Gender differences in the path from sexual victimization to HIV risk behavior among homeless youth. *Journal of Child Sexual Abuse, 26*, 334–351.

Heerde, J. & Hemphill, S. (2016). Sexual risk behaviors, sexual offenses, and sexual victimization among homeless youth: A systematic review of associations with substance use. *Trauma, Violence & Abuse, 17*, 468–489.

Hunter, E. (2008). What's good for the gays is good for the gander: Making homeless youth housing safer for lesbian, gay, bisexual, and transgender youth. *Family Court Review, 46*, 543–557.

Iwamoto, D. K., & Smiler, A. P. (2013). Alcohol makes you macho and helps you make friends: The role of masculine norms and peer pressure in adolescent boys' and girls' alcohol use. *Substance Use & Misuse, 48*, 371–378.

Kelleher, C. (2009). Minority stress and health: Implications for lesbian, gay, bisexual, transgender, and questioning (LGBTQ) young people. *Counselling Psychology Quarterly, 22*, 373–379.

Kidd, S. A., & Carroll, M. R. (2007). Coping and suicidality among homeless youth. *Journal of Adolescence, 30*, 283–296.

Kral, A. H., Molnar, B. E., Booth, R. E., & Watters, J. K. (1997). Prevalence of sexual risk behavior and substance use among runaway and homeless adolescents in San Francisco, Denver and New York City. *International Journal of STD and AIDS, 8*, 109–117.

Lin, N., & Ensel, W. M. (1989). Life stress and health: Stressors and resources. *American Sociological Review, 54*, 382–399.

Meyer, I. H. (2015). Resilience in the study of minority stress and health of sexual and gender minorities. *Psychology of Sexual Orientation and Gender Diversity, 2*, 209–213.

Miller, C. L., Fielden, S. J., Tyndall, M. W., Zhang, R., Gibson, K., & Shannon, K. (2011). Individual and structural vulnerability among female youth who exchange sex for survival. *Journal of Adolescent Health, 49*, 36–41.

Mink, M. D., Lindley, L. L., & Weinstein, A. A. (2014). Stress, stigma, and sexual minority status: The intersectional ecology model of LGBTQ health. *Journal of Gay & Lesbian Social Services, 26*, 502–521.

National Center for Homeless Education & The (NCHE) and the National Association for the Education of Homeless Children and Youth (NAEHCY). (updated 2017). Definitions of homelessness for federal programs serving children, youth, and families. Retrieved 24 of February 2018. https://nche.ed.gov/downloads/briefs/introduction.pdf

National Network for Youth. (2018). How many homeless youth are in America? Retrieved May 4, 2018 (https://www.nn4youth.org/learn/how-many-homeless/).

Noell, J. W., & Ochs, L. M. (2001). Relationship of sexual orientation to substance use, suicidal ideation, suicide attempts, and other factors in a population of homeless adolescents. *Journal of Adolescent Health, 29*, 31–36.

Pearlin, L. I. (1989). The sociological study of stress. *Journal of Health and Social Behavior, 30*, 241–256.

Rattelade, S., Farrell, S., Aubry, T., & Klodawsky, F. (2014). The relationship between victimization and mental health functioning in homeless youth and adults. *Journal of Interpersonal Violence, 29*, 1606–1622.

Rew, L., Whittaker, T. A., Taylor-Seehafer, M. A., & Smith, L. R. (2005). Sexual health risks and protective resources in gay, lesbian, and bisexual, and heterosexual homeless youth. *Journal for Specialists in Pediatric Nursing, 10*, 11–19.

Rice, E., Milburn, N. G., Monro, W. (2011). Social networking technology, social network composition, and reductions in substance use among homeless adolescents. *Prevention Science, 12*, 80–88.

Schmitz, R. M., Robinson, B. A., Tabler, J., Welch, B., & Rafaqut, S. (2019). LGBTQ+ Latino/a young people's interpretations of stigma and mental health: An intersectional minority stress perspective. *Society and Mental Health*. doi:10.1177/2156869319847248

Schmitz, R. M., & Tyler, K. A. (2018). Contextual constraints and choices: Strategic identity management among LGBTQ youth. *Journal of LGBT Youth*, *15*, 212–226.

Stanford Center on Poverty and Inequality. (2018). State of the union: The poverty and inequality report. Special issue, *Pathways Magazine*. https://inequality.stanford.edu/sites/default/files/Pathways_SOTU_2018.pdf

Tyler, K. A. (2008). A comparison of risk factors for sexual victimization among gay, lesbian, bisexual, and heterosexual homeless young adults. *Violence & Victims, 23*, 586–602.

Tyler, K. A., & Beal, M. R. (2010). The high-risk environment of homeless young adults: Consequences for physical and sexual victimization. *Violence & Victims, 25*, 101–115.

Tyler, K. A., Gervais, S. J., & Davidson, M. M. (2013). The relationship between victimization and substance use among homeless and runaway female adolescents. *Journal of Interpersonal Violence, 28*, 474–493.

Tyler, K. A., Hoyt, D. R., Whitbeck, L. B., & Cauce, A. M. (2001). The impact of childhood sexual abuse on later sexual victimization among runaway youth. *The Journal of Research on Adolescence, 11*, 151–176.

Tyler, K. A., & Melander, L. A. (2010). The effect of drug and sexual risk behaviors with social network and non-network members on homeless youth's STI and HIV testing. *Sexual Health, 7*, 434–440.

Tyler, K. A., & Melander, L. A. (2015). Child abuse, street victimization, and substance use among homeless young adults. *Youth & Society, 47*, 502–519.

Tyler, K. A., Olson, K. & Ray, C. M. (2018). Understanding the link between victimization and alcohol use among homeless youth using an ecological momentary assessment. *Socius: Sociological Research for a Dynamic World, 4*, 1–7. Published Online June 6, 2018. journals.sagepub.com/doi/full/10.1177/2378023118779832.

Tyler, K. A., & Ray, C. M. (2019). A latent class analysis of lifetime victimization among homeless youth. *Journal of Interpersonal Violence, 36*, 7202–7222. Published Online March 7, 2019. https://doi.org/10.1177/0886260519834090

Tyler, K. A., & Schmitz, R. M. (2018). A comparison of risk factors for various forms of trauma in the lives of lesbian, gay, bisexual and heterosexual homeless youth. *Journal of Trauma & Dissociation, 19*, 431–443.

Tyler, K. A., Schmitz, R. M. & Ray, C. M. (2018). Role of social environmental protective factors on anxiety and depressive symptoms among midwestern homeless youth. *Journal of Research on Adolescence, 28*, 199–210.

Tyler, K. A., & Whitbeck, L. B. (2004). Lost childhoods: Risk and resiliency among runaway and homeless adolescents. In P. Allen-Meares & M. W. Fraser (Eds.) *Intervention with children & adolescents: An interdisciplinary perspective* (pp. 378–397). Boston, MA: Pearson Education.

Tyler, K. A., Whitbeck, L. B., Hoyt, D. R., & Cauce, A. M. (2004). Risk factors for sexual victimization among male and female homeless and runaway youth. *Journal of Interpersonal Violence, 19*, 503–520.

Walls, N. E., & Bell, S. (2011). Correlates of engaging in survival sex among homeless youth and young adults. *Journal of Sex Research, 48*, 423–436.

Whitbeck, L. B., Chen, X., Hoyt, D. R., Tyler, K. A., & Johnson, K. D. (2004). Mental disorder, subsistence strategies, and victimization among gay, lesbian, and bisexual homeless and runaway adolescents. *The Journal of Sex Research, 41*, 329–342.

Chapter 3

Teen Dating Violence

Results from a National Study in Portugal[1]

Maria José Magalhães, Cátia Pontedeira,
Camila Iglesias, Ana Guerreiro,
Margarida Teixeira, and Ana Beires

Dating violence among young people is an increasing social and political concern, drawing the attention of a variety of stakeholders, from governments to schools and academics. Recently, a considerable amount of literature has focused on teen dating violence, namely on its high prevalence and consequences for young people who experience it (Bergman, 1992; Exner-Corterns, 2014; Foshee & Reyes, 2011; Gómez, Delgado, & Gómez, 2014; Hellevik & Øverlien, 2016; Smith, White, & Holland, 2003; Wincentak, Connolly, & Card, 2017).

In the last decade, some Portuguese studies have provided relevant information about the topic (Guerreiro et al., 2015; Oliveira, 2009). In order to better understand this rising problem, as of 2017, a Portuguese non-governmental organization named UMAR—Alternative and Response Women's Association—has carried out a national quantitative study about teen dating violence. This study is conducted on an annual basis, with a representative sample of young people.

This chapter provides an analysis of the results of the 2019 national study on teen dating violence and is structured in three parts: (1) theoretical overview of the main concepts behind dating violence; (2) empirical study—description of the methodological approach, analysis, and results; and (3) discussion of the results in line with previous research findings. The study's main limitations and recommendations for future research are included at the end of the chapter.

THEORETICAL OVERVIEW

Gender-based Violence as a Social Problem

Gender-based violence is set on a power imbalance between genders, and its most prominent forms (e.g., IPV, rape, etc.) affect women disproportionally (Council of Europe, 2011). This form of violence is linked to the idea of "hegemonic masculinity," which was first introduced in the 1980s and further developed to address a form of masculinity or a configuration of gender that contrasts against and dominates other subordinated forms of masculinity (Connell & Messerschmidt, 2005; Hearn, 2004). The term hegemonic masculinity recognizes that society tends to validate only one of a multitude of expressions of masculinity and prioritize it above all others. Consequently, other forms of masculinity and all expressions of femininity are denied, invisible, persecuted, and subjected to violence. Men and women are socialized according to hegemonic gender roles (Hearn, 2004) in which the models of masculine behavior include controlling the other person and engaging in violent behaviors (Connell, 2002; Johnson, 2008; Connell & Pearse, 2015).

IPV perpetrated against women is considered a clear expression of hegemonic masculinity. According to the World Health Organization (2012, 2013), IPV is also one of the most recognized forms of gender-based violence. For Dobash & Dobash (1997), there are four main explanations for it: (1) men's possessiveness and jealousy (also mentioned in Wilson & Daly, 1998); (2) men's expectations concerning women's domestic work; (3) men's sense of the right to punish women for perceived wrongdoings; and (4) the importance for men to maintain and exercise their position of authority. Gender stereotypes influence what is expected of each gender in terms of roles, prerogatives, and access to power (or lack thereof).

With the emergence of knowledge about domestic violence and the first shelters, feminist academics evidenced that this form of violence has specific patterns. Domestic violence can be characterized by cycles of violence (Walker, 1984) and is part of a *continuum of violence* (Kelly, 1987) accounting for the ways the patriarchal structure is actualized in everyday interactions, in public and private spheres. Researchers, professionals, and activists working with the narratives of IPV victims noticed that the cycle of violence often begins in the relationship's early stages (Hagemann-White, & Grafe, 2016; Kelly, 1988). The nature of this type of violence makes it difficult for the victim to acknowledge it while still experiencing feelings of entrapment when the acts of violence are severe and happening with increased frequency (LaViolette & Barnett, 2000).

Teen Dating Violence

As stated by the World Health Organization (2010, p. 14), dating violence "refers to physical or sexual violence occurring in the context of a 'dating relationship' [. . .]. These range from casual first encounters to longer-term sexual partnerships." This organization's report further adds that "dating" can be considered as all stages of a relationship that occur during adolescence into young adulthood and that is neither marriage nor a long-term cohabiting relationship (WHO, 2010).

Although the above definition is a crucial step toward clarifying the concept of teen dating violence, it remains insufficient to encompass all forms and manifestations of this phenomenon. From a broader and more actual perspective, teen dating violence can be defined as any form of "physical, sexual, or psychological/emotional violence within a romantic or dating relationship, including stalking" (Debnam & Mauer, 2019, p. 1).

Adolescence is a social category covering an age range between childhood and adulthood (10–19 years old) that has been studied as a particular phase in the lifespan and is characterized by different and complex biological, social, economic, personal, intimate, and sexual transitions (WHO, 2018). It is also a transitional phase, classified as a contradictory period, in which adolescents are the future of society but are also commonly perceived as being disrupting (Minayo, 2011). During adolescence, sexuality and identity become important issues for young people (Erickson, 1968; Furman & Shaffer, 2003).

In the Western world, romantic love and dating relationships made their way through the twentieth century, expanding the model of romance between men of the noblesse and young women of middle and working classes to all social classes (Ariès, 1981; Bloch, 1991). This romanticized model was popular in literature, advertising, and, more recently, the mass media, which undoubtedly contributed to its rapid turning into a hegemonic model for intimate relationships, especially among young people. Karandashev (2015) mentions that even though love is a universal emotion, its expression might vary across cultures, as some of them place emphasis on "explicit and direct ways of love expression to a romantic partner, while others on implicit and indirect ways" (p.15). Love as a romantic feeling and passion prevails in the hegemonic discourse around intimate relationships. Similarly, dating relationships are perceived as a phase of experiences within intimacy and sexual interactions. As dating is considered a time of promise and ideal love, it came as a surprise when researchers and professionals found the first signs of IPV at a very early stage in dating relationships (Exner-Cortens, 2014).

When debating about love and romance, especially at a young age, there is an essential link with jealousy (Baroncelli, 2011). Jealousy is an attempt to control and exercise power over someone and is often normalized through common sense discourses and even judicial discourses. As young people tend to take on gender differences in their roles within the romantic relationship, they can become accepting of jealousy and control of partners as a normal expression of affection. Control can actually be perceived by young people as a problem within the relationship but not as a form of violence (Baker & Helm, 2010). As Foucault (1984) mentioned, in terms of emotions, men and women are seen differently by society. This different and sexist conception about feelings legitimates young males' expression of jealousy through controlling behaviors. Jealousy in dating relationships is the fear of losing or not possessing someone, more frequently manifested by males, who feel a sense of ownership over their partners (Almeida, Rodrigues, & Silva, 2008). Sesar & colleagues (2012) found that the expression of jealousy by a male partner had a significant correlation with the perpetration of sexual abuse, while the same behavior was not a predictor of any form of dating violence if manifested by a female partner. A Spanish study with 567 adolescents also found a strong link between jealousy and perpetration of verbal-emotional and physical violence (Fernández-Fuertes & Fuertes, 2010). Moreover, other researchers further discussed that violence could be used intentionally to increase jealousy (Sanhueza & Lessard, 2018).

Results of a qualitative study conducted with Australian secondary school students (15–19 years old) showed that their conceptions about what is acceptable or unacceptable in dating relationships reinforce the patriarchal notion of abuse by underestimating violence as well as its consequences (Chung, 2005).

Towns & Scott (2013) suggested that there is a sense of "ownership" in young people's intimate heterosexual relationships that could lead to domestic violence through adulthood. This concept can be related to "sexual proprietariness," developed by Wilson and Daly (1998). As such, Miller & White (2003, p. 1244) argue that these practices are "embedded within the fabric of gendered power and inequality within our society more broadly."

Prevalence and Acceptance of Teen Dating Violence

One of the first studies on dating violence was published by James Makepeace (1981), who used a sample of college students to point out a lack of scientific literature related to this subject. Since then, and over the past three decades, scholars have been developing scientific research about dating violence, particularly in terms of its prevalence among young people (Foshee & Reyes, 2011; Rubio-Garay, López-González, Carrasco, & Amor, 2017; Ulloa, Kissee, Castaneda, & Hokoda, 2013). Despite their inconsistent results, the emergence of studies shows increased concern and awareness regarding the prevalence of dating violence (Gómez et al., 2014). Such variation is a consequence of adopting different methodologies, inclusion and exclusion criteria, instruments, and strategies of analysis. Notwithstanding, White (2009) mentioned that dating violence statistics are very similar to adult domestic violence rates, and Martsolf & colleagues (2012) estimated that between 20% and 50% of young people have experienced some type of violence during a relationship.

Results from a systematic review about the prevalence of dating violence among adolescents and young adults (12–35 years old) pointed out that men perpetrated more than 90% of physical, psychological, and sexual violence against women. Regarding age, this study found a higher prevalence of violent behaviors in adolescents than in young adults (Rubio-Garay et al., 2017). A meta-analytical review of 101 studies published between 1980 and 2013 on teen dating violence among young people (aged 13 to 18) indicated a prevalence range of physical violence from 1% to 61%. When considering comparable samples, results demonstrated that one in five young people reported having experienced physical violence in dating relationships (Wincentak et al., 2017). Furthermore, when it comes to physical aggression, in a sample of 193 high school students, Avery-Leaf and her colleagues (1997) found that 21% of males and 53% of females were victims of aggression during an intimate relationship. Watson & colleagues (2001) found that physical dating violence affects around 45.5% of high school students in New York. Regarding sexual violence, Rhynard & colleagues (1997) conducted a study with a sample of 192 students in Canada (aged between 13 and 18) and found that 26.1% of the participants reported having suffered sexual abuse, and almost half of those (40%) experienced it more than once. Similarly, Coker & collaborators (2000) stated that 16.2% of female South Carolina high school students from ninth to twelfth grade were forced to engage in sexual activity.

Due to the emergence and advancement of new technologies, young people have been exposed to new forms of violence, named by some authors as digital violence (see, for example, Hellevik & Øverlien, 2016). Digital violence has been discussed as one of the most common forms of violence among young people. On account of the increasing use of digital media among young people, this form of communication is also used to send and receive unwanted sexual messages (Dake, Price, Maziarz, & Ward 2012). Moreover, some authors found a positive association between sending sexual messages and sexual victimization (Dake et al., 2012; Hellevik & Øverlien, 2016).

Several authors have been studying the acceptance of these forms of violence by young people (Fernández-González, Calvete, & Orue, 2017; Guerreiro et al., 2015; Karlsson, Calvert, Rodriguez, Weston, & Temple, 2018). According to a Spanish study conducted with high school students, when comparing both genders, males displayed a higher acceptance of dating violence

(Fernández-González et al., 2017). In addition, students who had had a dating relationship in the previous year manifested higher acceptance rates of violence compared to those who had not (Fernández-González et al., 2017). This result is not a recent pattern, given that, in 1999, Price and Byers tested the *Attitudes towards Dating Violence Scale* with 823 students (from grades 7, 9, and 11), and found that males accepted more dating violence than females.

Further studies should continue to be developed since the tolerance or acceptance of violence might be predictive of violent behavior in the relational context and of the actual perpetration of violence (Oliveira, 2015).

Teen Dating Violence in Portugal

In Portugal, there has been a surge of political and social attention toward dating violence among young people. Initially, studies on the subject were more focused on university populations rather than on younger people (see, for example, Alexandra & Figueiredo, 2006; Oliveira & Sani, 2005; Paiva & Figueiredo, 2004). However, in 2009, Oliveira highlighted that this form of violence is also a reality in the lives of younger students, namely those who attend secondary schools (aged between 15 and 19). According to Oliveira (2009), 42.9% of participants who were in an existing dating relationship reported having been victims of abusive behavior perpetrated by their current partner, and 37.6% admitted to having committed some of these forms of violence. These numbers are even higher when considering previous intimate relationships, where 57% of participants reported some form of victimization, and 45.1% admitted to having committed some of the referred violent behaviors against their intimate partner.

Since 2017, UMAR has been annually conducting the National Dating Violence Study in Portugal. Over the years, the results have been pointing toward a slightly increasing trend in victimization indicators. These results might represent either an actual increase in the prevalence of these forms of violence and/or a greater awareness of young people regarding their occurrence (see the annual reports: UMAR, 2017, 2018, 2019 and 2020). Similar to previously cited studies, these annual reports displayed males as having a higher acceptance rate of dating violence when compared to females.

It is essential, however, to keep in consideration that the real figures of teen dating violence are hidden, just as not all cases of domestic violence, and even fewer of dating violence, are reported. Two main reasons for dating violence having low reporting rates can be traced to, first, young people who don't always recognize their relationship as a violent one (Gómez et al., 2014); and second, the society that has only recently started to pay attention to this form of violence happening at such a young age, by acknowledging the overwhelming presence of violence in a patriarchal society (Hagemann-White 1998), the continuum of violence (Kelly, 1987) in the lives of girls and women, and the cumulative effect of the female experiences since an early age (see also Hunter, 2006, Magalhães et al., 2016b; Magalhães et al., 2007; Sousa, 1999).

The study of IPV at an early age allows for a better understanding of how the culture of violence against women is still present in young people's relationships (Hagemann-White, 1998; Kelly, 1988; Neves et al., 2019; UMAR, 2020; Wood, 2001). It is essential to keep researching how these values and norms are reinforced, challenged, and reproduced in societies (Neves & Correia, 2018; White, 2009). Moreover, young people that have been physically injured are more likely to be victims of violence in their freshman year at universities (Smith et al., 2003), which increases the importance of focusing on early interventions to prevent potential victimization later in life.

Current Study

The current study aimed to approach teen dating violence in Portugal and address mainly three research questions: first, to understand which are the most common forms of violence suffered and accepted by young people; secondly, to consider which are the most prevalent and accepted forms of violence reported by males and females; and finally, to understand if having suffered some form of dating violence can be associated with higher acceptance in its different forms.

METHOD

This quantitative study on teen dating violence was conducted in Portuguese schools with students from basic to secondary schools. For this purpose, any person between the ages of 10 and 18 years old is considered a teenager, and dating violence is defined as any form of violence (psychological, physical, verbal, and sexual) happening in the past or present, long-term or casual intimate relationship. Data collection took place between November 2018 and January 2019.

Instrument

A self-report questionnaire was used for data collection. The idea for the questionnaire first emerged during an intervention in a holistic gender-based violence prevention program of UMAR, in which the NGO facilitators became aware that young people did not recognize dating violence behaviors. The instrument was created based on the insights provided by the literature review, the experience of these facilitators, and the students' feedback while discussing the topic of dating violence during the program implementation. The approach of having an author-designed questionnaire is not a novel one (see, for example, Bergman, 1992, or more recently, Kaukinen, Gover, & Hartman, 2012). Prior to its wider application, a pilot study was conducted with about 500 students (selected for the pilot only), and the questionnaire was modified and adapted according to the pilot's findings and the students' feedback.

The final version of the instrument consisted of 15 simple and fast-to-complete questions, written in a comprehensive and straightforward language that takes into consideration the cognitive and socio-emotional development of the participants at a young age. The questions are grouped into six forms of violence: psychological violence, physical violence, sexual violence, controlling behaviors, stalking, and violence through social media. This self-report questionnaire is separated into two sections: (1) victimization indicators and (2) acceptance of teen dating violence. All 15 questions are related to both victimization indicators (if students have ever experienced the behavior) and acceptance of violence (if they perceive that behavior as teen dating violence). The average response time is 15 minutes. All questions are of a "Yes" or "No" response type. Participants are also asked about their gender, age, and if they are or have ever been in a long-term or casual dating relationship. In Portugal, it is not recommended to ask minors about their sexual orientation, other gender identities (apart from masculine and feminine identities), social class, or ethnicity. Therefore, those items were not included in the current study.

The research team purposely chose the expression *victimization indicators* when referring to data and results retrieved from the questionnaire, but the word "victim" is never mentioned in the instrument. As such, participants are not asked to identify themselves as victims—they only have to indicate whether a particular (violent) behavior has ever happened to them. The words "victim" and "violence," or similar, were deliberately taken out of the questionnaire, given that (young) people might not self-identify as victims of violence and might not recognize a specific (violent) behavior as violence. With this approach, the results of this study must be interpreted as being indicators of victimization. In this chapter, participants who reported having suffered any form of violence from a dating partner are identified as the "V" group, and those who reported not having been subjected to any of the forms of violence in the questionnaire are identified as "NV" group.

Before its application in schools, the questionnaire was submitted and authorized for ethical approval to the Directorate-General for Education and to the Portuguese National Data Protection Commission.

Participants

The questionnaire was administered in the academic year of 2018/2019, from November 2018 until January 2019, in Portuguese public schools. Portugal is the westernmost European country, geographically divided into 18 districts and 2 archipelagos (Madeira and Azores), with an estimated population of 10 million people. National representativity was ensured through schools from different contexts (rural areas, coastline, North and South of the country, and the Islands). Schools were chosen randomly from a list, and once school boards agreed to participate, classes (from seventh to twelfth grades) were chosen according to their availability for data collection, assuring a randomized selection of students. Prior to application, an explanation of the study was handed out to all students and their parents.

Given that most students were minors, authorizations from parents or legal guardians were obtained. Only authorized and motivated students participated in the study, but the research team also ensured that students were free to stop participation at any moment if they so wished.

A total of 81 schools participated in the study, which resulted in 4938 respondents. Data from participants who reported being more than 18 years of age were excluded from this analysis. The final sample was comprised of 4,708 participants, all students, aged between 12 and 18 years (M: 15.17, SD=1.68). A sample of 54% (n=2,524) of students identified themselves as female, and 45% (n=2,133) identified themselves as male. About 70% (n=3,277) of the students mentioned that they were or had been in a previous intimate relationship.

Data Collection Procedure

Data were collected by previously designated researchers, who were trained in dating violence and survey techniques. All team members have previous experience in quantitative research and primary prevention of violence in schools. The aims of the questionnaire and study were explained to the students, and doubts and questions were addressed before its distribution. During the questionnaire implementation, anonymity, confidentiality, and respect for the children's rights were ensured. For that purpose, two researchers were present during data collection so that participants felt supported. Neither teachers nor the school board had access to the students' results. Confidentiality was also ensured by not disclosing information that could lead to the location and identification of schools, classes, or participating students.

Data Analysis

Data analysis was performed using Microsoft Excel and the Statistical Package for the Social Sciences, version 26.0 for Windows, focusing on descriptive and inferential statistical analysis (chi-square tests).

For the rates of victimization indicators, only the responses from those 70% (n=3277) of participants who mentioned having had a relationship (current or past) were considered. For the indicators of acceptance of violence, all responses were included (n=4708). In the association test between gender and dating violence, responses from both males and females were considered (participants who had not replied to the "sex" question were excluded). This study had three main research questions. The first relates to the prevalence and acceptance of dating violence, the second focuses on the comparability between male and female participants, and the third concerns the influence of having suffered any form of dating violence in acceptance rates. For the latter research question, acceptance rates of the students who claimed they had not suffered any form of violence were compared with those who identified themselves as having been subjected to any form of violence. Only students who had previously dated were considered in this research question. Two groups for data analysis were created: (1) "V" group—Students who answered having suffered from at least one of the questioned behaviors; (2) "NV" group—Students who had dated but reported never having experienced any form of violence.

RESULTS

The results are described by forms of violence (as per the first research question), by gender (second research question) and by the influence that the victimization indicators have on the acceptance of violence (third research question).

Prevalence and Acceptance of Teen Dating Violence in Portugal

Results from table 3.1 suggest that the most prevalent forms of violence are psychological violence and controlling behaviors. Of all participants, 30.3% (n=987) identified themselves as having been targets of a partner's insults during an argument. Controlling and restrictive behaviors, such as forbidding the partner from speaking to or going out with friends or colleagues, are also prevalent (reported by 21.0%, n=686). The unauthorized use of the partner's phone or social media accounts was signalized by 20.1% (n=658) of students, and stalking behaviors were reported by 17.6% of participants (n=576). Sexual violence was also reported, with 9.3% (n=300) of participants mentioning that their partners had subjected them to forced intimacy and unwanted public displays of affection (e.g., kissing) and 4.8% (n=156) reported having been

Table 3.1 Descriptive Results of Victimization Indicators and Acceptance of Dating Violence

Question	Have any of your partners of a romantic, dating or casual intimate relationship ever...?[1]				Do you consider the following behaviors as dating violence: your partner of a romantic, dating or casual intimate relationship to...			
	n= 3,277				N= 4,708			
	Yes		No		Yes		No	
	n	%	n	%	n	%	n	%
Control								
...forbidden you to go out without him/her?	173	5.3	3,096	94.7	3,244	70.6	1,354	29.4
...make you do something you didn't want, and you felt bad about it?	296	9.1	2,965	90.9	3,949	85.8	655	14.2
...pick up your phone, or sign in to your Facebook (or other social networks) without asking you for permission?	658	20.1	2,611	79.9	2,848	61.9	1,751	38.1
...forbidden you to be with or talk to a friend or colleague?	686	21.0	2,579	79.0	3,285	71.5	1,311	28.5
...forbidden you to wear certain clothing?	255	7.8	3,012	92.2	2,900	63.2	1,692	36.8
Psychological violence								
...insult you during an argument?	987	30.3	2,271	69.7	3,330	72.6	1,259	27.4
...threaten you by saying, for example, that he/she would leave or injure you?	362	11.1	2,903	88.9	4,186	90.9	418	9.1
...humiliate you by saying things that put you down?	540	16.5	2,727	83.5	4,007	87.0	597	13.0
Physical violence								
...physically hurt you, leaving a wound or bruise?	134	4.1	3,129	95.9	4,370	94.7	245	5.3
...pushed you or slapped you, even without leaving any bruise?	245	7.5	3,017	92.5	4,242	92.2	360	7.8
Sexual violence								
...pressured you to kiss him/her in front of friends?	300	9.2	2,967	90.8	2,956	64.4	1,634	35.6
...pressured you to have sex with him/her?	156	4.8	3,109	95.2	4,008	87.1	595	12.9
Violence through social networks								
...shared intimate photos, videos, and/or messages over the internet without your permission?	95	2.9	3,170	97.1	3,934	85.5	669	14.5
...insulted you, or said bad things about you, via social / internet networks (Facebook, Instagram, Twitter...)?	388	11.9	2,879	88.1	3,754	81.6	845	18.4
Stalking								
...stalk you, bothered you, looking for you insistently (walked behind you, waited for you at the door of your home and/or school, called you all the time...)?	576	17.6	2,689	82.4	3439	74.7	1,165	25.3

[1] Considered participants who have dated before.
Source: Data created by author study.

pressured to have sexual intercourse. The least prevalent identified forms of violence are the sharing of unauthorized personal content online (2.9%, n= 95) and physical violence with visible bruises (4.1%, n= 134).

Regarding the acceptance of dating violence, controlling behaviors were the most commonly accepted. The unauthorized use of the partner's phone or social media accounts (38.1%, n=1,751) and restrictions on the partners' clothing choice (36.8%, n=1692) were the behaviors least considered as dating violence and, therefore, the most accepted by young people. Similarly, sexual violence, specifically pressuring to kiss in front of other people, was not recognized as violence by 35.6% of the sample (n=1,634). Physical violence showed the lowest acceptance rates: violence resulting in visible bruising and without visible bruising was accepted by 5.3% (n=245) and 7.8% (n=360) of participants, respectively.

Victimization Indicators and Acceptance of Teen Dating Violence by Gender

Regarding the second research question, the results of female participants were statistically compared with the male's results in two aspects: victimization indicators and acceptance of dating violence. As shown in table 3.2, almost all forms of violence victimization were reported as more prevalent among females than among male students. Results were statistically different for several forms of controlling behavior, psychological, physical, and sexual violence, and stalking. The most significant difference between males and females was found in restricting behaviors toward the partner's choice of clothing (3.2% vs. 11.7%, χ^2=81.599, p=.000); humiliating one's partner (11.4% vs. 21.0%, χ^2=53.375, p=.000); forcing a partner into something they do not want to do (6.9% vs. 11.0%, χ^2=16.070, p=.000); threatening their significant other (8.7% vs. 13.2%, χ^2=15.951, p=.000); and pressuring them to have sex (3.4% vs. 6.0%, χ^2=11.740, p=.001). The victimization indicators regarding physical violence with visible bruises (4.2% vs. 4.0%, no statistical difference), physical violence without visible bruises (8.9% vs. 6.4%, χ^2=7.543, p=.006), and sharing unauthorized intimate content online (2.9% vs. 2.8%, no statistical difference) were higher in males than in females.

When considering the recognition of those behaviors as violence, gender differences were even more significant (see table 3.3). Male participants showed a lower recognition level for all dating violence behaviors in the questionnaire, and all results were statistically significant. While the most accepted forms of violence by males were restricting a partner's clothing choices (48.5%, n=1004) and pressuring a partner to kiss in public (48.3%, n= 999), the most accepted forms of violence by females were the unauthorized use of the partner's phone or social media (32.9%, n=812) and restricting

Table 3.2 Association between Gender and Indicators of Teen Dating Violence

Have any of your partners of a romantic, dating, or casual intimate relationship ever...?	Male				Female				χ^2
	Yes		No		Yes		No		statistic[a]
	n	%	n	%	n	%	n	%	
Control									
...forbidden you to go out without him/her?	60	4.1	1,419	95.9	112	6.3	1,654	93.7	8.374**
...make you do something you didn't want, and you felt bad about it?	102	6.9	1,376	93.1	193	11.0	1,566	89.0	16.070***
...pick up your phone, or sign in to your Facebook (or other social networks) without asking you for permission?	295	19.9	1,185	80.1	361	20.5	1,404	79.5	.135
...forbidden you to be with or talk to a friend or colleague?	286	19.3	1,193	80.7	396	22.5	1,366	77.5	4.763*
...forbidden you to wear certain clothing?	47	3.2	1,432	96.8	207	11.7	1,557	88.3	81.599***
Psychological violence									
...insult you during an argument?	437	29.6	1,039	70.4	542	30.8	1,216	69.2	.569
...threaten you by saying, for example, that he/she would leave or injure you?	129	8.7	1,349	91.3	232	13.2	1,531	86.8	15.951***
...humiliate you by saying things that put you down?	169	11.4	1,312	88.6	370	21.0	1,392	79.0	53.375***
Physical violence									
...physically hurt you, leaving a wound or bruise?	62	4.2	1,416	95.8	70	4.0	1,691	96.0	.099
...pushed you or slapped you, even without leaving any bruise?	132	8.9	1347	91.1	112	6.4	1,647	93.6	7.543**
Sexual violence									
...pressured you to kiss him/her in front of friends?	135	9.1	1345	90.9	164	9.3	1,599	90.7	.031
...pressured you to have sex with him/her?	50	3.4	1429	96.6	105	6.0	1,657	94.0	11.740***
Violence through social networks									
...shared intimate photos, videos and/or messages over the internet without your permission?	43	2.9	1435	97.1	50	2.8	1,713	97.2	.015
...insulted you, or said bad things about you, via social / internet networks (Facebook, Instagram, Twitter...)?	175	11.8	1305	88.2	209	11.9	1,554	88.1	.001
Stalking									
...stalk you, bothered you, looking for you insistently (walked behind you, waited for you at the door of your home and/or school, called you all the time...)?	236	16.0	1241	84.0	337	19.1	1,427	80.9	5.397*

[a] Chi-square test for independence; *p < .05. **p < .01. ***p < .001.
Source: Data created by author study.

a significant other's clothing choices (26.8%, n=664). In another set of questioned behaviors, the acceptance was three times higher among males than females: forcing the partner to do something they do not want to do (22.3% vs. 7.2%, χ^2=213.692, p=.000) and physical violence without visible bruises (12.4% vs. 3.9%, χ^2=115.285, p=.000). These results are significantly

Maria José Magalhães et al.

Table 3.3 Association between Gender and Acceptance of Teen Dating Violence

Do you consider the following behaviors as dating violence: your partner of a romantic, dating, or casual intimate relationship to...	Male				Female				χ^2
	Yes		No		Yes		No		
	n	%	n	%	n	%	n	%	statistic[a]
Control									
...forbidden you to go out without him/her?	1,257	60.5	821	39.5	1,953	79.0	518	21.0	186.917***
...make you do something you didn't want, and you felt bad about it?	1,614	77.7	464	22.3	2,297	92.8	178	7.2	213.692***
...pick up your phone, or sign in to your Facebook (or other social networks) without asking you for permission?	1,155	55.6	923	44.4	1,659	67.1	812	32.9	63.895***
...forbidden you to be with or talk to a friend or colleague?	1,309	63.1	766	36.9	1,942	78.6	530	21.4	132.575***
...forbidden you to wear certain clothing?	1,066	51.5	1,004	48.5	1,809	73.2	664	26.8	227.361***
Psychological violence									
...insult you during an argument?	1,346	64.8	730	35.2	1,954	79.3	509	20.7	119.310***
...threaten you by saying, for example, that he/she would leave or injure you?	1,790	86.1	290	13.9	2,359	95.3	117	4.7	118.041***
...humiliate you by saying things that put you down?	1,699	81.6	383	18.4	2,267	91.7	206	8.3	101.724***
Physical violence									
...physically hurt you, leaving a wound or bruise?	1,914	92.0	166	8.0	2,415	97.2	70	2.8	61.586***
...pushed you or slapped you, even without leaving any bruise?	1,818	87.6	258	12.4	2,382	96.1	96	3.9	115.285***
Sexual Violence									
...pressured you to kiss him/her in front of friends?	1,070	51.7	999	48.3	1,853	75.0	618	25.0	266.008***
...pressured you to have sex with him/her?	1,609	77.5	467	22.5	2,364	95.4	114	4.6	324.994***
Violence through social networks									
...shared intimate photos, videos and/or messages over the internet without your permission?	1,630	78.4	448	21.6	2,266	91.5	210	8.5	156.319***
...insulted you, or said bad things about you, via social / internet networks (Facebook, Instagram, Twitter...)?	1,571	75.7	504	24.3	2147	86.7	328	13.3	92.012***
Stalking									
...stalk you, bothered you, looking for you insistently (walked behind you, waited for you at the door of your home and/or school, called you all the time...)?	1,345	64.9	729	35.1	2059	83.0	421	17.0	197.629***

[a] Chi-square test for independence; *p < .05. **p < .01. ***p < .001.
Source: Data created by author study.

Table 3.4 Association between Acceptance of Teen Dating Violence and Victimization

Do you consider as dating violence the following behaviors: your partner of a romantic, dating or casual intimate relationship to...	V Group [1]				NV Group [2]				χ^2
	Yes		No		Yes		No		statistic[a]
	n	%	n	%	n	%	n	%	
Control									
...forbidden you to go out without him/her?	1,196	65.1	641	34.9	974	72.5	370	27.5	19.413***
...make you do something you didn't want, and you felt bad about it?	1,522	82.9	315	17.1	1175	87.2	172	12.8	11.499***
...pick up your phone, or sign into your Facebook (or other social network) without asking you for permission?	1,035	56.3	805	43.8	869	64.7	474	35.3	23.095***
...forbidden you to be with or talk to a friend or colleague?	1,216	66.1	625	33.9	997	74.2	346	25.8	24.548***
...forbidden you to wear a certain clothing?	1,085	59.1	750	40.9	902	67.2	441	32.8	21.366***
Psychological violence									
...insult you during an argument?	1,257	69.0	565	31.0	1,082	80.2	267	19.8	50.395***
...threaten you by saying, for example, that he/she would leave or injure you?	1,626	88.5	211	11.5	1,257	93.3	90	6.7	20.958***
...humiliate you by saying things that put you down?	1,567	85.3	271	14.7	1,206	89.5	141	10.5	12.623***
Physical violence									
...physically hurt you, leaving a wound or bruise?	1,732	93.9	113	6.1	1,285	95.3	64	4.7	2.837
...pushed you or slapped you, even without leaving any bruise?	1,664	90.5	174	9.5	1,273	94.4	75	5.6	16.443***
Sexual violence									
...pressured you to kiss him/her in front of friends?	1,027	55.9	810	44.1	928	69.3	411	30.7	58.757***
...pressured you to have sex with him/her?	1,544	84.0	294	16.0	1,203	89.2	145	10.8	17.966***
Violence through social networks									
...shared intimate photos, videos and/or messages over the internet without your permission?	1,526	83.0	313	17.0	1,164	86.4	183	13.6	6.977**
...insulted you, or said bad things about you, via social / internet networks (Facebook, Instagram, Twitter...)?	1,454	79.0	386	21.0	1,139	84.8	204	15.2	17.226***
Stalking									
...stalk you, bothered you, looking for you insistently (walked behind you, waited for you at the door of your home and/or school, called you all the time...)?	1,295	70.5	541	29.5	1,053	78.1	295	21.9	23.078***

[a] Chi-square test for independence; *p < .05. **p < .01. ***p < .001.
[1] Considered participants who have dated before and had reported suffered at least one form of violence.
[2] Considered participants who have dated before and had not identified to have suffered any form of violence.
Source: Data created by author study.

different. Moreover, regarding sexual violence, the gender difference is outstanding: while 4.6% (n=114) of the females do not recognize the pressure to have sex as a form of dating violence, for males, the rate was 22.5% (n= 467), four times higher (χ^2=324.994, p=.000). Physical violence was the least accepted form of violence by both female and male participants.

Acceptance of Dating Violence by "V" and "NV" Groups: Does It Make a Difference?

The third research question means to understand if the acceptance of violence by those who reported having suffered at least one of the violent behaviors (V) was statistically different from that of those who had previously dated but did not report any of those behaviors (NV). Results demonstrate that all forms of violence were less recognized by participants who had suffered dating violence. As per table 3.4, in all forms of violence included in this study, the V group had higher percentages of acceptance of dating violence when compared with the NV group, and almost all were significantly different.

The most considerable difference between the groups is in pressuring to kiss one's partner in front of other people, in which the acceptance rate of the V group was 44.1% versus 30.7% (χ^2=58.757, p=.000) in the NV group. Insults during arguments are also more accepted by those who referred to having suffered some form of violence (31.0% vs. 19.8%, χ^2= 50.395, p=.000). The only behavior that is not significantly different between the two groups is physical violence resulting in visible bruises (6.1%V vs. 4.7%NV, not significant).

DISCUSSION

Most findings fall in line with previous research, both regarding victimization indicators and acceptance of violence. According to this study, 57% of the participants who had been in a relationship reported having suffered at least one of the forms of violence referenced in the questionnaire, which confirms the need to continue developing studies in this field and investing in gender-based violence prevention programs.

The results indicate that the most prevalent forms of violence are those related to psychological violence, including insults and controlling behaviors. This finding is consistent with previous studies, such as those developed by James & colleagues (2000), Hellevik & Øverlien (2016), and Magalhães & colleagues (2016a). Johnson (2008) highlighted that controlling an intimate partner is a consistent element of violence, especially when the perpetrator is male. In accordance, in this study, controlling behaviors were most commonly perpetrated by males against female partners. In line with this result, Beserra et al. (2016) also found that male adolescents were the greatest perpetrators of psychological violence, mainly with controlling behaviors. Moreover, likewise agreeing with previous research (Guerreiro et al., 2015; Hellevik & Øverlien, 2016; Magalhães et al., 2016b), physical violence was the least reported form of violence suffered by young people in this study.

Considering the average age of participants, the prevalence of sexual violence is especially concerning. Similar to previous research, the current study demonstrates that the prevalence of sexual violence victimization is higher among females (see, e.g., Bergman, 1992 or Wincentak et al., 2017). The only form of violence in which male participants reported higher victimization indicators than females was physical violence. Although it is not possible to establish the context for the precedent behaviors, a possible explanation is that females are becoming more physically aggressive in response to abusive behavior and, as such, are physically reacting in self-defense (Watson et al., 2001).

Similar to what Baker & Helm (2010) discussed, digital violence and the unauthorized use of a partner's phone are the most prevalent behaviors, while, simultaneously, the participants who reported having suffered from these forms of violence do not always recognize it as such (43% of students). As Hellevik & Øverlien (2016) suggested, more research is needed on the role of digital media in dating violence. The fact that this set of behaviors is the least recognized as violence might raise important considerations for future prevention practices in terms of resource allocation and attention.

Both Jaycox & collaborators (2006) and Fernández-Gonzáles & colleagues (2017) found that all forms of violence were less accepted by females than by males, meaning that the latter group accepts violence in relationships the most. This result also emerged from the current study and can be related to hegemonic masculinity and gender bias in society, which attribute more power to males while maintaining the stereotypes about women and men, especially in their roles in intimate relationships.

As discussed in some studies, higher levels of acceptance of violence increase the probability of young people experiencing dating violence, be it as a victim or perpetrator (Oliveira, 2015; UMAR, 2017). It is, then, fundamental to contradict this trend and empower young people to have healthy relationships that are based on mutual respect and trust. This study contributes to an adequate knowledge of the prevalence and attitudes of young people concerning teen dating violence, namely gender differences and victimization effects. The main conclusion that can be drawn from these results, and a potential policy recommendation, is that there is an urgent and essential need for preventive actions that focus on the deconstruction of these toxic relationships and gender-based stereotypes.

Limitations and Further Research

Firstly, where methodological limitations are concerned, students whose legal tutors did not authorize their participation were not included in this study. Moreover, the questionnaire includes 15 questions, whereas the scope of violence is not limited to this chosen set, which means that the prevalence of violence might be higher than the one reported for this study. As it is a self-report questionnaire, participants might, on the one hand, still not report all forms of violence that they have suffered, and on the other, fill out the questionnaire considering social desirability.

Secondly, the research team has classified as acceptable the violent behaviors that were not classified as violence by participants. However, when participants respond that they do not regard a certain behavior like violence, it might not mean that they accept those behaviors in their relationships. Furthermore, this study does not explore the context in which violence happens nor the perpetration of violence, meaning that it is not possible to distinguish self-defense behaviors from bilateral forms of dating violence. Additional research is needed to combine these quantitative results with qualitative methodologies so that the context in which these forms of violence are happening can be further understood.

Finally, this study focuses on the dichotomous results between male and female participants, not taking into consideration different gender identities nor identifying the participants' sexual orientation (despite each question being phrased to include other orientations beyond heterosexual), which limits the scope of the results. Regarding the analysis, this study focused on univariate and bivariate tests, leaving multivariate analysis for future research. It would be important, for example, to study how age influences the participants' responses.

Notwithstanding its limitations, the current study is a significant contribution to the understanding of dating violence among young people in Portugal and provides important background for upcoming gender-based violence research and relevant policies, especially considering the limited number of existing national scientific papers on these subject matters.

CONCLUSION

Teen dating violence has proved to be a current and important topic of research. The current study addressed the Portuguese data about teen dating violence and confirmed that this is a social problem affecting both genders. The findings are consistent with other studies: victimization indicators are higher in females when compared to males; acceptance of violence is more common in males; and, in general, participants who had previously experienced one of the behaviors presented in the questionnaire were more likely to accept dating violence.

Results demonstrate that it is essential to conduct additional studies by combining methodologies in order to deepen the understanding of this complex phenomenon experienced by young people. Additional knowledge about dating violence will prove key in setting and framing it as a gendered issue which, in turn, will further support the development of guidelines that promote appropriate primary prevention programs for children and young people. This study also highlights the gendered differences in attitudes toward dating violence; therefore, it is crucial that prevention programs address boys and girls differently and explore their beliefs. Only by focusing on the gendered issue of dating violence, it will be possible to prevent it. Moreover, it is recommended that countries develop specific educational policies based on human rights and gender equality to effectively combat gender-based violence and its acceptance.

NOTE

1. This study was funded by national funds through Fundação para a Ciência e Tecnologia (FCT), I.P., under project UIDP/04304/2020.

REFERENCES

Alexandra, C., & Figueiredo, B. (2006). Versão portuguesa das "Escalas de Táticas de Conflito Revisadas": estudo de validação. *Psicologia: Teoria e Prática, 8*(2), 14–39. Retrieved from http://editorarevistas.mackenzie.br/index.php/ptp/article/view/1045/

Almeida, T., Rodrigues, K., & Silva, A. (2008). O ciúme romântico e os relacionamentos amorosos heterossexuais contemporâneos. *Estudos de Psicologia, 13*(1), 83–90. doi: 10.1590/S1413-294X2008000100010

Ariès, P. (1981). *História social da criança e da família.* Rio de Janeiro: LCT- Livros Técnicos e Científicos Editora S.A.

Avery-Leaf, S., Cascardi, M., O'Leary, K. D., & Cano, A. (1997). Efficacy of a dating violence prevention program on attitudes justifying aggression. *Journal of Adolescent Health, 21*, 11–17. doi: 10.1016/S1054-139X(96)00309-6

Baker, C. K., & Helm, S. (2010). Pacific youth and shifting thresholds: Understanding teen dating violence in Hawaii. *Journal of School Violence, 9*(2), 154–173. doi: 10.1080/15388220903585879

Baroncelli, L. (2011). Love, and jealousy in the contemporary world: Psychological reflections. *Psicologia & Sociedade, 23*(1), 163–170. doi: S0102-71822011000100018

Bergman, L. (1992). Dating violence among high school students. *Social Work, 37*(1), 21–27. doi: 10.1093/sw/37.1.21

Beserra, M., Leitão, M., Fabião, J., Dixe, M., Veríssimo, C., & Ferriani, M. (2016). Prevalence and characteristics of dating violence among school-aged adolescents in Portugal. *Escola Anna Nery, 20*(1), 183–191. doi: 10.5935/1414-8145.20160024

Bloch, H. (1991). *Medieval misogyny and the invention of western romantic love.* Chicago: The University Chicago Press.

Chung, D. (2005). Violence, control, romance and gender equality: Young women and heterosexual relationships. *Women's Studies International Forum, 28*(6), 445–455. doi: 10.1016/j.wsif.2005.09.005

Coker, A., McKeown, R., Sanderson, M., Davis, K., Valois, R., & Huebner, E. S. (2000). Severe dating violence and quality of life among South Carolina high school students. *American Journal of Preventive Medicine, 19,* 220–227. doi: 10.1016/S0749-3797(00)00227-0

Connel, R. W. (2002). On hegemonic masculinity and violence: Response to Jefferson and Hall. *Theoretical Criminology, 6*(1), 89–99. doi: 10.1177/136248060200600104

Connel, R. W., & Messerschmidt, J. (2005). Hegemonic masculinity rethinking the concept. *Gender & Society, 19*(6), 829–859. doi: 10.1177/0891243205278639

Connell, R. W., & Pearse, R. (2015). *Gender: In world perspective.* Cambridge: Polity Press.

Council of Europe (2011). *Convention on preventing and combating violence against women and domestic violence (Istanbul convention).* Retrieved from: https://rm.coe.int/168008482e

Dake, J., Price, J., Maziarz, L., & Ward, B. (2012). Prevalence and correlates of sexting behavior in adolescents. *American Journal of Sexuality Education, 7*(1), 1–15. doi: 10.1080/15546128.2012.650959

Debnam, K., & Mauer, V. (2019). Who, when, how, and why bystanders intervene in physical and psychological teen dating violence. *Trauma, Violence, & Abuse.* doi: 10.1177/1524838018806505

Dobash, R., & Dobash, R. (1997). Violence against women. In L. O'Toole & J. Schiffman (Eds.) *Gender violence: Interdisciplinary perspectives* (pp. 266–278). New York University Press.

Erickson, E. H. (1968). *Identity: Youth in crisis.* New York: Norton.

Exner-Coterns, D. (2014). Theory and teen dating violence victimization: Considering adolescent development. *Developmental Review, 34*(2), 168–188. doi: 10.1016/j.dr.2014.03.001

Exner-Cortens, D., Eckenrode, J., & Rothman, E. (2013). Longitudinal associations between teen dating violence victimization and adverse health outcomes. *Pediatrics, 131*(1), 71–78. doi: 10.1542/peds.2012-1029

Fernández-Fuertes, A. A., & Fuertes, A. (2010). Physical and psychological aggression in dating relationships of Spanish adolescents: Motives and consequences. *Child Abuse & Neglect, 34*(3), 183–191. https://doi.org/10.1016/j.chiabu.2010.01.002

Fernández-González, L., Calvete, E., & Orue, I. (2017). The acceptance of dating violence scale (ADV): Psychometric properties of the Spanish version. *Psicothema, 29*(2), 241–246. https://doi.org/10.7334/psicothema2016.229

Foshee, V., & Reyes, H. (2011). Dating abuse: Prevalence, consequences, and predictors. In R. J. R. Levesque (Ed.) *Encyclopedia of adolescence,* Springer Science + Business Media (pp. 602–615). New York: Springer.

Foucault, M. (1984). *Histoire de la Sexualité 3: Le souci de soi*. Paris: Edition Gallimard.

Furman, W., & Shaffer, L. (2003). The role of romantic relationships in adolescent development. In P. Florsheim (Ed.) A*dolescent romantic relations and sexual behaviors: Theory, research, and practical implications* (pp. 3–22). doi: 10.4324/9781410607782.

Garcia-Moreno, C., & Watts, C. (2011). Violence against women: An urgent public health priority. *Bulletin of the World Health Organization, 89*, 2. doi: 10.2471/BLT.10.085217

Gómez, M., Delgado, A., & Gómez, A. (2014). Violencia en relaciones de pareja de jóvenes y adolescentes. *Revista Latinoamericana de Psicología, 46*(3), 148–159. doi: 10.1016/S0120-0534(14)70018-4

Guerreiro, A., Pontedeira, C., Sousa, R., Magalhães, M. J., Oliveira, E., & Ribeiro, P. (2015). Intimidade e violência no namoro: refletir a problemática nos/as jovens. *Atas do colóquio internacional "@s jovens e o crime: transgressões e justiça tutelar"*. Retrieved from https://repositorio-aberto.up.pt/bitstream/10216/78885/2/101832.pdf

Hagemann-White, C. (1998). Violence without end? Some reflections on achievements, contradictions, and perspectives of the feminist movement in Germany. In R. Klein (Ed.) *Multidisciplinary perspectives on family violence* (pp. 176–191). London: Routledge.

Hagemann-White, C., & Grafe, B. (2016). *Experiences of intervention against violence: An anthology of stories*. Germany: Barbara Budrich Publishers.

Hearn, J. (2004). From hegemonic masculinity to the hegemony of men. *Feminist Theory, 5*(1), 49–72. doi: 10.1177/1464700104040813

Hellevik, P., & Øverlien, C. (2016). Teenage intimate partner violence: Factors associated with victimization among Norwegian youths. *Scandinavian Journal of Public Health, 44*(7), 702–708. doi: 10.1177/1403494816657264

Hunter, R. (2006). Narratives of domestic violence. *Sydney Law Review, 28*, 734–776.

James, W. H., West, C., Deters, K. E., & Armijo, E. (2000). Youth dating violence. *Adolescence, 35*(139), 455–465. Retrieved from http://search.proquest.com/openview/e95beb0184bfcac4be7208f2950ec0fc/1?pq-origsite=gscholar&cbl=41539

Jaycox, L., McCaffrey, D., Eiseman, B., Aronoff, J., Shelley, G., Collins, R., Marshall, G. (2006). Impact of a school-based dating violence prevention program among Latino teens: Randomized controlled effectiveness trial. *Journal of Adolescent Health, 39*(5), 694–704. doi: 10.1177/1403494816657264

Johnson, M (2008). *A typology of domestic violence: Intimate terrorism, violent resistance, and situational couple violence*. Boston: Northeastern University Press.

Karandashev, V. (2015). A cultural perspective on romantic love. *Online Readings in Psychology and Culture, 5*(4), 3–21. doi:10.9707/2307-0919.1135

Karlsson, M., Calvert, M., Rodriguez, J., Weston, R., & Temple, J. (2018). Changes in acceptance of dating violence and physical dating violence victimization in a longitudinal study with teens. *Child Abuse & Neglect, 86*, 123–135. doi:10.1016/j.chiabu.2018.09.010

Kaukinen, C., Gover, A. R., & Hartman, J. L. (2012). College women's experiences of dating violence in casual and exclusive relationships. *American Journal of Criminal Justice, 37*, 146–162. doi: 10.1007/s12103-011-9113-7

Kelly, L. (1987). *Surviving sexual violence.* Cambridge: Polity Press.

Kelly, L. (1988). How women define their experiences of violence. In K. Yllö & M. Bograd (Eds.) *Feminist perspectives on wife abuse* (pp. 114–132). Newbury Park, Calif: SAGE Focused Editions.

LaViolette, A., & Barnett, O. (2000). *It could happen to anyone - Why women stay.* Thousand Oaks, CA: Sage Publications.

Magalhães, M. J., Canotilho, A. P., & Brasil, E. (2007). *Gostar de mim, gostar de ti: Aprender a prevenir a violência de géne*ro. Maia: UMAR.

Magalhães, M. J., Pontedeira, C., Guerreiro, A., & Ribeiro, P. (2016a). *CENAS. IGUALDADE: Programa de prevenção da violência e delinquência juvenil.* Porto: UMAR.

Magalhães, M. J., Teixeira, A. M., Dias, A. T., Cordeiro, J., Silva, M., & Mendes, T. (2016b). *Prevenir a violência: construir a igualdade.* Porto: UMAR.

Makepeace, J. M. (1981). Courtship violence among college students. *Family Relations, 1*(30), 97–102. doi: 10.2307/584242

Martsolf, D. S., Colbert, C., & Drauker, C. B. (2012). Adolescent dating violence prevention and intervention in a community setting: Perspectives of young adults and professionals. *The Qualitative Report, 17*(50), 1–23. Retrieved from https://nsuworks.nova.edu/tqr/vol17/iss50/1

Miller, J., & White, N. (2003). Gender and adolescent relationship violence: A contextual examination. *Criminology, 41*(4), 1207–1248. doi:10.1111/j.1745-9125.2003.tb01018.x

Minayo, M. C. (2011). A condição juvenil no século XXI. In M. C. Minayo, S. G. Assis, & K. Njaine (Eds.) *Amor e violência: um paradoxo das relações de namoro e do 'ficar' entre jovens brasileiros* (pp. 17–43). Rio de Janeiro: Editora Fiocruz.

Neves, S., & Correia, A. (2018). *Violências no namoro.* Maia: Edições ISMAI.

Neves, S., Ferreira, M., Abreu, A., & Borges, J. (2019). *Estudo Nacional sobre a Violência no Namoro em Contexto Universitário: Crenças e Práticas.* Porto: Associação Plano I. Retrieved from: https://drive.google.com/file/d/1RNTCbW 9DJ1X5D9aqRKnM64zVacwmczJz/view

Oliveira, M. S. (2009). *A intergeracionalidade da violência nas relações de namoro.* (Master's thesis, University of Porto). Retrieved from https://repositorio-aberto.up .pt/bitstream/10216/22140/3/Dissertao%20de%20Mestrado.pdf

Oliveira, M. S. (2015). *Transmissão intergeracional da violência.* Lisboa: Chiado Editora.

Oliveira, M., & Sani, A. (2005). Comportamentos dos jovens universitários face à violência nas relações amorosas. In *Bento Silva e Leandro Almeida (Coords), Atas do VIII Congresso Galaico-Português de Psicopedagogia* (pp. 1061–1074). Braga: Centro de Investigação em Educação.

Paiva, C., & Figueiredo, B. (2004). Abuso no relacionamento íntimo: Estudo de prevalência em jovens adultos portugueses. *Psychologica, 36*, 75–107. Retrieved from https://repositorium.sdum.uminho.pt/handle/1822/4211~

Price, E. L., & Byers, E. S. (1999). The attitudes towards dating violence scales: Development and initial validation. *Journal of Family Violence, 14*(4), 351–375. https://doi.org/10.1023/A:1022830114772

Rhynard, J., Krebs, M., & Glover, J. (1997). Sexual assault in dating relationships. *Journal of School Health, 67*(3), 89–93. doi: 10.1111/j.1746-1561.1997.tb03419.x

Rubio-Garay, F., López-González, M. A., Carrasco, M. A., & Amor, P. J. (2017). The prevalence of dating violence: A systematic review. *Psychologist Papers, 38*(2), 135–147. doi: 10.23923/pap.psicol2017.2831

Sanhueza, T., & Lessard, G. (2018). Representations of dating violence in Chilean adolescents: A qualitative study. *Children and Youth Services Review, 87*(C), 41–55. doi: 10.1111/j.1746-1561.1997.tb03419.x

Sesar, K., Pavela, I., Simic, N., Barisic, M., & Banai, B. (2012). The relation of jealousy and various forms of violent behavior in the relationships of adolescents. *Paediatrics Today, 8*(2), 133–146. doi: 10.5457/p2005-114.48

Smith, P. H., White, J. W., & Holland, L. J. (2003). A longitudinal perspective on dating violence among adolescent and college-age women. *Journal of American Public Health Association, 93*(7), 1104–1109. doi: 10.2105/AJPH.93.7.1104

Sousa, C. A. (1999). Teen dating violence: The hidden epidemic. *Family & Conciliation Courts Review, 37*(3), 356–374. doi: 10.1111/j.174-1617.1999. tb01310.x

Towns, A., & Scott, H. (2013). 'I couldn't even dress the way I wanted.' Young women talk of 'ownership' by boyfriends: An opportunity for the prevention of domestic violence?. *Feminism & Psychology, 23*(4), 536–555. doi: 10.1177/0959353513481955

Ulloa, E. C., Kissee, J., Castaneda, D., & Hokoda, A. (2013). A global examination of teen relationship violence. In J. A. Sigal & F. L. Denmark (Eds.) *Violence against girls and women: International perspectives* (pp. 211–238). Westport: Praeger.

UMAR (2017). *Relatório de Imprensa 2017: Resultados Nacionais apontam a gravidade do problema.* Porto: UMAR.

UMAR (2018). *Violência no Namoro: resultados nacionais.* Porto: UMAR.

UMAR (2019). *Estudo Nacional sobre a Violência no Namoro.* Porto: UMAR.

UMAR (2020). *Estudo Nacional sobre a Violência no Namoro.* Porto: UMAR.

Walker, L. (1984). *The battered woman syndrome.* New York: Springer Publishing Company.

Watson, J. M., Cascardi, M., Avery-Leaf, S., & O'Leary, K. D. (2001). High school students' responses to dating aggression. *Violence and Victims, 16*, 339–348. doi: 10.1891/0886-6708.16.3.339

White, J. W. (2009). A gendered approach to adolescent dating violence: Conceptual and methodological issues. *Psychology of Women Quarterly, 33*(1), 1–15. doi: 10.1111/j.1471-6402.2008.01467.x

WHO (2010). *Preventing intimate partner and sexual violence against women- taking action and generating evidence.* Retrieved from https://www.who.int/violence _injury_prevention/publications/violence/9789241564007_eng.pdf

WHO (2012). *Understanding and addressing violence against women: Intimate partner violence.*

WHO (2013). *Global and regional estimates of violence against women: Prevalence and health effects of intimate partner violence and non-partner sexual violence.* Department of Reproductive Health and Research, London School of Hygiene and Tropical Medicine, South African Medical Research Council. Retrieved from https://apps.who.int/iris/bitstream/handle/10665/77432/WHO_RHR_12.36_eng .pdf;jsessionid=17E4C50C35D368CAE0395CE531AAC1A8?sequence=1

WHO (2018). *Recognizing adolescence.* Retrieved from http://apps.who.int/adolescent/second-decade/section2/page1/recognizing-adolescence.html.

Wilson, M., & Daly, M. (1998). Lethal and nonlethal violence against wives and the evolutionary psychology of male sexual proprietariness. In R. E. Dobash & R. P. Dobash (Eds.) *Rethinking violence against women* (pp. 199–230). Sage: Thousand Oaks, CA.

Wincentak, K., Connolly, J., & Card, N. (2017). Teen dating violence: A meta-analytic review of prevalence rates. *Psychology of Violence, 7*(2), 224. doi: 10.1037/ a0040194

Wood, J. T. (2001). The normalization of violence in heterosexual romantic relationships: Women's narratives of love and violence. *Journal of Social and Personal Relationships, 18*(2), 239–261.

Part II

COMPUTER-RELATED INTERPERSONAL VIOLENCE

Chapter 4

Image-Based Sexual Abuse among Australian Youths

The Experiences and Perspectives of Victims, Perpetrators, and Bystanders

Adrian J. Scott, Chelsea Mainwaring, Asher Flynn,
Anastasia Powell, and Nicola Henry

Image-based sexual abuse (IBSA) involves the taking or sharing (including threats to share) of intimate (i.e., nude or sexual) images (i.e., photographs and/or videos) of another person without their consent. Although a growing body of research has examined the consensual sexting behaviors (i.e., the sending of intimate images) of youth, little research has specifically examined the extent and nature of IBSA (or the "non-consensual sexting" behaviors) of young people. This chapter presents survey findings relating to the IBSA and intimate image sharing experiences of 293 Australian youth, aged between 16 and 20 years. The study is the first of its kind to examine the experiences of young people from victim, perpetrator, and bystander perspectives, although it is important to acknowledge that these perspectives are not mutually exclusive (i.e., the same respondents may have been victims, perpetrators, and/or bystanders). In the context of this chapter, victims comprise respondents who reported having intimate images of themselves taken, shared, and/or threatened to be shared without their consent. Perpetrators comprise respondents who reported having taken, shared, and/or threatened to share intimate images of another person without their consent. Bystanders comprise respondents who reported having been shown and/or sent intimate images of another person.

This chapter briefly reviews the relevant literature relating to interpersonal violence, technology-mediated sexual interaction (TMSI), and IBSA. It then examines the extent and nature of IBSA and intimate image sharing among Australian youth, before exploring the impacts and fears of victims, the motivations of perpetrators, and the reactions of bystanders. Finally, it discusses the findings with respect to the need to challenge the current victim blaming and harm minimization rhetoric associated with IBSA and intimate image sharing, particularly in the youth context.

LITERATURE REVIEW

Interpersonal Violence

Interpersonal violence among young people is a pervasive problem that is well documented in the existing research literature. For example, Ybarra, Espelage, Langhinrichsen-Rohling, Korchmaros, & Boyd (2016) examined youth (aged between 14 and 17 years) experiences of psychological, physical, and sexual abuse in the United States. They found that between 10% and 26% of females, and between 7% and 26% of males, had experienced physical dating abuse; and that between 11% and 15% of females, and between 3% and 12% of males, had experienced sexual dating abuse. Similarly, Barter et al. (2017) examined young people's (aged between 14 and 17 years) experiences of interpersonal violence and abuse across five European countries. They found that between 9% and 22% of females, and between 8% and 15% of males, had experienced physical violence; and that between 31% and 59% of females, and between 19% and 41% of males, had experienced face-to-face emotional violence. With regard to online emotional violence, approximately 40% of males and females had experienced this form of victimization.

A recent meta-analysis of 96 studies examined adolescent (aged between 13 and 18 years) dating violence and found that the prevalence of physical dating violence ranged from 1% to 61%, with an average of 20% (Wincentak, Connolly, & Card, 2017). Overall, females were more likely to report being perpetrators of physical dating violence, but there were no gender differences in victimization. Using a subsample of 31 studies, they found that the prevalence of sexual dating violence ranged from less than 1% to 54%, with an average of 9%. Overall, males were more likely to report being perpetrators of sexual dating violence, and females were more likely to report being victims of sexual dating violence (Wincentak et al., 2017).

Given the prevalence of online emotional violence and the increasing capacity (and therefore potential) for digital technology to be used to perpetrate violence, it is important to consider young people's use of technology. Sudan, Olsen, Sigsgaard, & Kheifets (2016) examined trends in mobile phone use in Denmark and found that 37% of children aged 7 years used mobile phones, compared with 94% of children aged 11 years. Furthermore, research by the International Telecommunications Union (2017) found that young people (aged between 15 and 24 years) from developed countries were more likely to use the internet than the population as a whole (94% vs. 81%). Research also suggests that technology is increasingly becoming a "ubiquitous element" of young people's lives (Anderson & Jiang, 2018). For example, the Pew Research Center found that the percentage of adolescents (aged between 13 and 17 years) with access to a smartphone increased from 73% in 2014/2015 to 95% in 2018 (Anderson & Jiang, 2018; Lenhart, 2015). Furthermore, the number of adolescents who described themselves as being online "almost constantly" increased from 24% to 45% over the same time period.

Technology-Mediated Sexual Interaction

TMSI refers to any form of interpersonal interaction where self-created, sexually explicit content (messages and/or images) is exchanged using digital technology (Courtice & Shaughnessy, 2017). "Sexting" represents a highly prevalent form of TMSI and refers to the taking and sharing of intimate messages and/or images via mobile phones or social media (Powell & Henry, 2014).

According to Symons, Ponnet, Walrave, & Heirman (2018), sexting plays an increasing role in young people's sexual development. A recent systematic review of 29 studies examined the experiences of adolescents and young adults (aged between 10 and 30 years) who engaged in TMSI across Australia, Europe, South Korea, and the United States (Courtice & Shaughnessy, 2017). The review found that between 1% and 31% of adolescents and young adults reported sending sexually explicit images of themselves to another person and that between 17% and 49% reported receiving sexually explicit images from another person. A more recent survey of adolescents (aged between 14 and 17 years) across five European countries found that between 6% and 44% of females, and between 15% and 32% of males, reported sending a sexual message or image to a partner (Stanley et al., 2018). Stanley et al. also found that between 9% and 49% of females, and between 20% and 47% of males, reported receiving a sexual message or image from a partner. A similar pattern was found by Reed, Boyer, Meskunas, Tolman, & Ward (2020) in their study of adolescents' (aged between 13 and 19 years) sexting experiences in dating relationships. They found that females were more likely to report having sent intimate images, but that males were more likely to report having received intimate images.

Research has highlighted the normative nature of TMSI and sexting, with many young people describing their experiences as a common, normal, and safe way to relieve sexual tensions, to flirt, and/or to provide sexual stimulation (Crofts, Lee, McGovern, & Milivojevic, 2016; Stanley et al., 2018; Yeung, Horyniak, Vella, Hellard, & Lim, 2014). Motivations for sexting are generally positive, and research suggests that the sharing of sexually explicit content can be beneficial for young people. For example, sexting is often motivated by the desire to have fun or to flirt with another person (Reed et al., 2020). Furthermore, Drouin, Coupe, & Temple (2017) found that 57% of students (average age of 20 years) believed that sexting had a positive impact on their sexual and emotional relationships.

It is important to acknowledge, however, that a number of studies suggest females experience fewer positive, and more negative, emotional responses to the sending and receiving of sexts than males (Del Rey, Ojeda, Casas, Mora-Merchán, & Elipe, 2019; Gassó, Klettke, Agustina, & Montiel, 2019; Reed et al., 2020). Individual characteristics, and the wider social context, have also been shown to influence young people's emotional responses to, and engagement with, TMSI and sexting. For example, Reed et al. (2020) found that young people's emotional responses to sexting differed according to age, religiosity, self-sexualization, attachment avoidance and anxiety, and peer norms. Furthermore, research has shown that young people's pornography use, and perceptions of peer norms regarding sexting, influences their engagement with sexting (Maheux et al., 2020; Symons et al., 2018). Finally, several studies have reported associations between sexting and anxiety and depression, although these associations appear to weaken with age (Gassó et al., 2019; Mori, Temple, Browne, & Madigan, 2019).

Image-Based Sexual Abuse

The taking and sharing of sexual images is not a new phenomenon, but the increasing capacity of technology and opportunity for TMSI are associated with concerns regarding the safety of young people (McGlynn & Rackley, 2017; Powell & Henry, 2014), specifically concerns about how easy it is to take and share intimate images of a person without their consent and how difficult it is to remove such images from digital platforms (Powell & Henry, 2014; Powell, Henry, & Flynn, 2018). It is important to acknowledge, however, that while TMSI and sexting may increase the risk of intimate images being shared without consent, they are not a necessary prerequisite. The non-consensual taking (e.g., up-skirting, down-blousing, toileting) and creation (e.g., photoshopping) of intimate images mean that young people may experience the non-consensual sharing of intimate images even though they have not engaged in the consensual taking or sharing of intimate images. Although the mainstream media often use the term "revenge pornography," this chapter uses the term IBSA because it offers a more accurate and inclusive terminology for the taking and sharing (including threats to share) of intimate images of another person without their consent (McGlynn & Rackley, 2017; McGlynn, Rackley, & Houghton, 2017; Powell et al., 2018).

Extent and Nature of IBSA and Intimate Image Sharing

One of the first large-scale surveys to examine adolescent and adult (aged between 16 and 49 years) experiences of IBSA was conducted in Australia (Henry, Powell, & Flynn, 2017; Powell, Henry, Flynn, & Scott, 2019). Henry et al. (2017) found that 23% of respondents reported being a victim of at least one form of IBSA: 20% reported being a victim of the non-consensual taking of intimate images, 11% reported being a victim of the non-consensual sharing of intimate images, and 9% reported being a victim of threats to share intimate images. Although victimization rates were similar for males and females, younger respondents were more likely to report being a victim of IBSA (29% for respondents aged between 16 and 29 years) than older respondents (20% for respondents aged between 30 and 49 years). In the majority of instances, respondents reported that the perpetrator was male and someone they had known previously (Henry et al., 2017).

Further research examined the victimization experiences of college students (average age of 19 years) and found that 10% reported having an intimate image shared with someone beyond the intended recipient, often by a current or former partner (Branch, Hilinski-Rosick, Johnson, & Solano, 2017). Similarly, a recent meta-analysis of 39 studies found a prevalence rate of 8% for young people (under the age of 18 years) having been victims of the non-consensual sharing of intimate images (Madigan, Ly, Rash, Van Ouytsel, & Temple, 2018).

With regard to perpetration, Powell et al. (2019) found that 11% of respondents reported being a perpetrator of at least one form of IBSA: 9% reported being a perpetrator of the non-consensual taking of intimate images, 6% reported being a perpetrator of the non-consensual sharing of intimate images, and 5% reported being a perpetrator of threats to share intimate images. In contrast to victimization rates, males (14%) were more likely to report being a perpetrator of IBSA than females (7%). In the majority of instances, respondents reported that the victim was female and someone they had known previously (Powell et al., 2019).

Further research found that 23% of adults (aged between 21 and 75 years) who had received intimate images and 19% of adults (aged between 18 and 55 years) who had received private sexts reported sharing them with other people without their consent (Clancy, Klettke, & Hallford, 2019; Garcia et al., 2016). Garcia et al. (2016) also found that males (25%) were more likely than females (20%) to report the non-consensual sharing of intimate images and that those who did share intimate images shared them with an average of more than three other people (ranging from 1 to 25 other people). Finally, the aforementioned recent meta-analysis found a prevalence rate of 12% for young people (under the age of 18 years) having been perpetrators of the non-consensual sharing of intimate images (Madigan et al., 2018).

Although less attention has been given to the extent and nature of bystanders of intimate image sharing, Hudson, Fetro, & Ogletree (2014) found that 64% of undergraduate students (predominantly aged between 18 and 19 years) reported having a private intimate image shared with them. Fleschler Peskin et al. (2013) found a lower prevalence rate with school children (average age of 16 years), whereby 18% reported having a private intimate image shared with them. Interestingly, nearly a third of their respondents reported being both perpetrators of, and bystanders to, non-consensual intimate image sharing.

Impacts and Fears of Victims

Henry et al. (2017) found that the majority of adolescent and adult respondents who had experienced IBSA victimization had experienced levels of psychological distress that equated to a moderate-to-severe diagnosis of depression and/ or anxiety disorder (taken: 67%, shared: 75%, threatened: 80%). Respondents who had experienced IBSA victimization also reported being fearful for their safety (taken: 28%, shared: 39%, threatened: 46%), with females more likely than males to report being fearful (Henry et al., 2017). Furthermore, a qualitative study with 38 female adults (aged between 18 and 44 years) found that all victims experienced negative emotional responses when they discovered that they had been victims of IBSA (Office of the eSafety Commissioner, 2017). Common emotional responses included anger, embarrassment, and shame (see also, McGlynn et al., 2019, 2020). These victims also reported being anxious and fearful during and after the abuse, particularly with regard to the possibility of the intimate images resurfacing. Other impacts included lost friendships, reduced social media presence, and the need to take time off from school or work, or to leave school or work altogether (Office of the eSafety Commissioner, 2017). Similarly, research has shown that young people often experience negative emotional responses as a consequence of having intimate messages and/or images shared without their consent. For example, Stanley et al. (2018) found that 61% of females (aged between 14 and 17 years) who reported negative impacts of sexting had experienced a message being shared without their consent. In addition, Branch et al. (2017) found that 54% of college students felt angry at the person who shared the intimate images and 33% felt angry at themselves for initially sending the intimate images.

Motivations of Perpetrators

Clancy et al. (2019) found that the most common reasons for sharing private sext messages were that it was not a big deal and that it was a joke. Other motivations included the following: to get attention, to improve social status, in response to a request, in response to feeling pressured, and to get the recipient of the message in trouble. Overall, there were no gender differences in motivations to perpetrate IBSA, with the exception that males were more likely than females to be motivated by a desire to improve their social status (Clancy et al., 2019). Further research has analyzed the posts of male perpetrators on revenge pornography websites to examine how they justify the posting of intimate images (Henry & Flynn, 2019; Hall & Hearn, 2019). For example, Hall & Hearn found that all posts contained an element of victim blaming, and that the posting of intimate images was a form of "retaliation" for some past misdemeanor (e.g., infidelity) by their (ex)partner. They also suggested that the posting of intimate images allowed these male perpetrators to overcompensate, protect their manhood, and hurt the female (ex)partners they felt wronged by.

Reactions of Bystanders

The experiences and perspectives of bystanders have received much less attention in the research literature than those of victims and perpetrators. However, a recent qualitative study with 25 young adults (aged between 18 and 25 years) examined bystanders' experiences of viewing intimate images when they were not the intended recipient (Harder, 2020). Harder found that bystanders often experienced mixed feelings because of the excitement of seeing the intimate images and the moral obligation they felt toward the person in the images. Bystanders found these experiences weird or awkward, but generally did not want to risk challenging the group dynamics by saying anything. This reluctance was less apparent for females than males, with female bystanders being more likely to express their condemnation (Harder, 2020). These gender differences echo those of a previous quantitative study that reported on adolescents' (aged between 11 and 18 years) experiences of secondary sexting (i.e., forwarding images of others or being forwarded images of others; Del Rey et al., 2019). Del Rey et al. found that males were more likely than females to report positive emotional impacts of secondary sexting, whereas females were more likely than males to report negative emotional impacts.

Current Study

It is apparent from the research literature presented that further research is needed to increase knowledge regarding young people's experiences and perspectives of IBSA and intimate image sharing. Young people represent a vulnerable group due to their extensive engagement with technology, both generally and when engaging in TMSI, their developing sexual identities, and their greater rates of IBSA victimization compared to adults (Gassó et al., 2019; Henry, Flynn, & Powell, 2019a, 2019b; Henry et al., 2017, 2020). The current study explores the IBSA and intimate image sharing experiences of 293 Australian youth, aged between 16 and 20 years, and is the first of its kind to examine the experiences of young people from victim, perpetrator, and bystander perspectives. Specifically, it examines (1) the extent and nature of IBSA and intimate image sharing, (2) the impacts and fears of victims of IBSA, (3) the motivations of perpetrators of IBSA, and (4) the reactions of bystanders of intimate image sharing. Consideration will also be given to whether there are any gender differences in young people's experiences of IBSA and intimate image sharing.

METHODS

Respondents and Procedure

This chapter reports on a sample of 293 Australian youth, aged between 16 and 20 years, who represent a subsample of the 4,053 residents, aged between 16 and 49 years, who responded to a larger survey developed as part of a research grant examining experiences of IBSA (see Henry et al., 2017, 2019b). The survey was administered online, responses were anonymous, and respondents received a small monetary payment for completing the survey. Table 4.1 presents the demographic characteristics of the respondents.

Table 4.1 Demographic Characteristics of the Respondents

	Victim Group % (n)	Perpetrator Group % (n)	Bystander Group % (n)	All Respondents % (n)
Gender				
Female	68.7 (57)	65.5 (19)	71.1 (101)	69.6 (204)
Male	31.3 (26)	35.5 (10)	28.9 (41)	30.4 (89)
Age				
Mean	18.19	18.24	18.02	18.18
SD	1.35	1.38	1.36	1.39
Sexuality				
Heterosexual	77.1 (64)	86.2 (25)	79.6 (113)	83.3 (244)
Lesbian, gay, bisexual	22.9 (19)	13.8 (4)	20.4 (29)	16.7 (49)
Indigeneity				
Non-indigenous	92.8 (77)	86.2 (25)	95.8 (136)	96.9 (284)
Indigenous	7.2 (6)	13.8 (4)	4.2 (6)	3.1 (9)
Education				
Primary or secondary	68.7 (57)	69.0 (20)	78.9 (112)	78.2 (229)
Tertiary	31.3 (26)	31.0 (9)	11.3 (16)	21.8 (64)
Total	100.0 (83)	100 (29)	100.0 (142)	100.0 (293)

Note. The victim, perpetrator, and bystander groups are not mutually exclusive (i.e., the same respondents may have been victims, perpetrators, and/or bystanders).
Source: Data created by author study.

Respondents were recruited by Research Now, a global online sampling and data collection company, who distributed emails to panel members who resided in Australia. Quota sampling was used to ensure that the sample was reasonably representative of the Australian population (as per the Australian Bureau of Statistics census data) for certain key characteristics (gender, age, sexuality). All respondents were presented with an information letter before providing their informed consent and a debrief statement after completing the survey. They were informed that the survey examined attitudes and experiences of sex, technology, and relationships. The research was approved by a university human ethics committee following the guidelines prescribed by the Australian National Statement on Ethical Conduct in Human Research.

Measures

Respondents completed an online survey that comprised a series of measures relating to their demographic characteristics, as well as their experiences of IBSA and intimate image sharing from victim, perpetrator, and bystander perspectives. The measures reported in this chapter are described below.

Demographic Characteristics

Respondents were asked their gender (female, male), age (in years), sexuality (heterosexual, lesbian, gay, bisexual), indigeneity (non-Indigenous, Indigenous), and the highest level of education (high school or less, trade certificate, university/college, postgraduate/advanced degree).

Extent and Nature of IBSA and Intimate Image Sharing

Respondents were asked whether they had ever (since the age of 16 years) (1) had intimate images of themselves taken, shared, and/or threatened to be shared without their consent (victim); (2) taken, shared, and/or threatened to share intimate images of another person without their consent (perpetrator); and (3) been shown or sent intimate images of another person (bystander). Eight items related to the content of the images for each form of IBSA and intimate image sharing, specifically whether the person in the images (1) was partially clothed or semi-nude, (2) had their breasts, including nipples, visible, (3) was completely nude, (4) had their genitals visible, (5) was engaged in a sex act, (6) was showering, bathing or toileting, and whether the images were (7) up a skirt (up-skirting), and (8) of cleavage (down-blousing). All items were measured via single answer (yes, no) multiple-choice questions. For the purpose of analysis, eight composite measures were created for each form of IBSA and intimate image sharing ("any intimate images" in table 4.2).

Table 4.2 Extent of Image-Based Sexual Abuse and Intimate Image Sharing Behaviors across the Victim, Perpetrator, and Bystander Groups

	Victim Group			Perpetrator Group			Bystander Group	
	Taken % (n)	Shared % (n)	Threatened % (n)	Taken % (n)	Shared % (n)	Threatened % (n)	Shown % (n)	Sent % (n)
Partially clothed or semi-nude	16.4 (48)	10.9 (32)	7.8 (23)	4.1 (12)	3.8 (11)	1.4 (4)	34.8 (102)	14.0 (41)
Breasts, including nipples, visible	4.8 (14)	2.4 (7)	3.8 (11)	3.4 (10)	1.4 (4)	1.4 (4)	24.6 (72)	10.2 (30)
Completely nude	5.5 (16)	2.4 (7)	2.0 (6)	3.1 (9)	2.0 (6)	1.0 (3)	18.8 (55)	8.5 (25)
Genitals visible	6.8 (20)	2.7 (8)	2.7 (8)	1.7 (5)	2.4 (7)	1.0 (3)	26.3 (77)	13.3 (39)
Sex act	7.2 (21)	3.4 (10)	3.4 (10)	1.4 (4)	2.0 (6)	1.0 (3)	12.6 (37)	5.5 (16)
Showering, bathing or toileting	8.9 (26)	4.1 (12)	2.7 (8)	3.1 (9)	0.3 (1)	1.4 (4)	15.0 (44)	4.8 (14)
Up a skirt (up-skirting)	4.4 (13)	2.0 (6)	0.7 (2)	2.0 (6)	0.3 (1)	1.4 (4)	7.2 (21)	3.1 (9)
Of cleavage (down-blousing)	8.5 (25)	4.1 (12)	1.7 (5)	1.7 (5)	1.0 (3)	1.0 (3)	16.4 (48)	3.4 (10)
Any intimate image sharing	22.5 (66)	13.3 (39)	9.6 (28)	7.8 (23)	5.5 (16)	3.4 (10)	44.4 (130)	22.2 (65)

Note. The victim, perpetrator, and bystander groups are not mutually exclusive (i.e., the same respondents may have reported being victims, perpetrators and/or bystanders).
Source: Data created by author study.

Respondents who reported being victims of IBSA were asked about the gender of (male, female, both male and female, don't know), and their connection to (intimate partner or ex-partner, family member, friend, stranger, acquaintance, or don't know their identity), the perpetrator(s) for each form of IBSA. Similarly, respondents who reported being perpetrators of IBSA were asked about the gender of, and their connection to, the victim(s) for each form of IBSA. All items were measured via single-answer (select the choice that applies) multiple-choice questions. For the purpose of analysis, four composite measures were created for the gender and connection items across all three forms of IBSA. Respondents who reported being bystanders of intimate image sharing were asked whether they believed the person in the images had given their permission for each form of intimate image sharing. Both items were measured via single answer (yes because from commercial pornography, yes because I know the person gave permission, no I don't think the person gave permission, I don't know) multiple-choice questions. For the purpose of analysis, one composite measure was created for the permission item across both forms of intimate image sharing.

Impacts and Fears of Victims

Respondents who had been victims of IBSA were asked about their most recent experiences of having intimate images of themselves taken, shared, and/or threatened to be shared, specifically the impacts and their fears. Three items related to the impacts of each form of IBSA, and whether the experiences negatively impacted upon their (1) work or study performance, (2) relationships with friends and family, and (3) relationship with an intimate partner. Four items related to their fears regarding each form of IBSA, and whether they feared the discovery of the images by (1) friends and family, (2) a current or future employer, (3) a current or future intimate partner, and (4) current or future children. All items were measured via five-point scales ranging from 1 "not at all" to 5 "extremely" and were collapsed to create dichotomous "yes" (4 and 5) and "no" (1 to 3) responses. For the purpose of analysis, seven composite measures were created for the fears and impacts of victims across all three forms of IBSA ("all forms" in table 4.3).

Table 4.3 Impacts and Fears of Victims across the Different Forms of Image-Based Sexual Abuse

	Victim Group				Gender	
	Taken (n=66) % (n)	Shared (n=39) % (n)	Threatened (n=28) % (n)	All Forms (n=83) % (n)	Female (n=57) % (n)	Male (n=26) % (n)
Impacts						
Work or study performance	16.7 (11)	15.4 (6)	25.0 (7)	25.3 (21)	26.3 (15)	23.1 (6)
Relationships with friends and family	15.2 (10)	17.9 (7)	21.4 (6)	21.7 (18)	22.8 (13)	19.2 (5)
Relationship with an intimate partner	13.6 (9)	15.4 (6)	25.0 (7)	20.5 (17)	24.6 (14)[†]	11.5 (3)
Fears						
Discovered by friends and family	31.8 (21)	33.3 (13)	35.7 (10)	38.6 (32)	42.1 (24)[†]	30.8 (8)
Discovered by current or future employer	28.8 (19)	20.5 (8)	39.3 (11)	36.1 (30)	40.4 (23)[†]	26.9 (7)
Discovered by current or future intimate partner	18.2 (12)	30.8 (12)	42.9 (12)	30.1 (25)	35.1 (20)[†]	19.2 (5)
Discovered by current or future children	27.3 (18)	28.2 (11)	35.7 (10)	30.1 (25)	36.8 (21)[†]	15.4 (4)

Note. Respondents could select multiple impacts and fears, and the different forms of IBSA are not mutually exclusive (i.e., the same respondents may have had intimate images of themselves taken, shared, and/or threatened to be shared).
[†] Difference of 10.0% or more with a minimum of a small effect size (i.e., a noteworthy gender difference).
Source: Data created by author study.

Motivations of Perpetrators

Respondents who had been perpetrators of IBSA were asked about their most recent experiences of taking, sharing, and/or threatening to share intimate images of another person, specifically their motivations. Nine items related to their motivations for each form of IBSA, and whether they believed it was (1) funny, (2) sexy or flirty, and whether they desired to (3) get back at the person, (4) impress friends, (5) embarrass the person, (6) control the person, (7) humiliate the person, (8) trade the images for other images, and (9) trade the images for money. All items were measured via multiple answer (select all choices that apply), multiple-choice questions. For the purpose of analysis, nine composite measures were created for the motivations of perpetrators across all three forms of IBSA ("all forms" in table 4.4).

Reactions of Bystanders

Respondents who had been bystanders of intimate image sharing were asked about their most recent experiences of being shown or sent intimate images of another person, specifically their reactions. Six items related to their reactions to each form of intimate image sharing, and whether they (1) felt uncomfortable, (2) felt embarrassed, (3) were bothered but did not say anything, (4) were okay with it, (5) were bothered and said something, and (6) thought it was funny. All items were measured via five-point scales ranging from 1 "not at all" to 5 "extremely" and were collapsed to create dichotomous "yes" (4

Table 4.4 **Motivations of Perpetrators across the Different Forms of Image-Based Sexual Abuse**

	Perpetrator Group				Gender	
	Taken (n=23) % (n)	Shared (n=16) % (n)	Threatened (n=10) % (n)	All Forms (n=29) % (n)	Female (n=19) % (n)	Male (n=10) % (n)
Thought it was funny	30.4 (7)	25.0 (4)	10.0 (1)	37.9 (11)	36.8 (7)	40.0 (4)
Thought it was sexy or flirty	34.8 (8)	12.5 (2)	20.0 (2)	34.5 (10)	31.6 (6)	40.0 (4)
To get back at the person	13.0 (3)	12.5 (2)	60.0 (6)	27.6 (8)	31.6 (6)†	20.0 (2)
To impress friends	17.4 (4)	18.8 (3)	20.0 (2)	20.7 (6)	26.3 (5)†	10.0 (1)
To embarrass the person	4.3 (1)	12.5 (2)	20.0 (2)	17.2 (5)	15.8 (3)	20.0 (2)
To control the person	8.7 (2)	12.5 (2)	10.0 (1)	13.8 (4)	21.1 (4)†	0.0 (0)
To humiliate the person	13.0 (3)	6.3 (1)	20.0 (2)	13.8 (4)	5.3 (1)†	30.0 (3)
Trade images for other images	8.7 (2)	6.3 (1)	10.0 (1)	6.9 (2)	5.3 (1)	10.0 (1)
Trade images for money	4.3 (1)	6.3 (1)	0.0 (0)	3.4 (1)	5.3 (1)	0.0 (0)

Note. Respondents could select multiple motivations, and the different forms of IBSA are not mutually exclusive (i.e., the same respondents may have taken, shared, and/or threatened to share intimate images of another person).
† Difference of 10.0% or more with a minimum of a small effect size (i.e., a noteworthy gender difference).
Source: Data created by author study.

Table 4.5 Reactions of Bystanders across the Different Forms of Intimate Image Sharing

	Bystander Group			Gender	
	Shown (n=130) % (n)	Sent (n=65) % (n)	Both Forms (n=142) % (n)	Female (n=101) % (n)	Male (n=41) % (n)
Uncomfortable	40.0 (52)	44.6 (29)	43.7 (62)	45.5 (46)	39.0 (16)
Embarrassed	35.4 (46)	32.3 (21)	39.4 (56)	45.5 (46)*	24.4 (10)
Bothered but did not say something	25.4 (33)	30.8 (20)	31.0 (44)	30.7 (31)	31.7 (13)
Okay with it	24.6 (32)	27.7 (18)	31.0 (44)	29.7 (30)	34.1 (14)
Bothered and said something	20.8 (27)	29.2 (19)	25.4 (36)	25.7 (26)	24.4 (10)
Funny	9.2 (12)	13.8 (9)	14.8 (21)	9.9 (10)*	26.8 (11)

Note. Respondents could select multiple reactions, and the different forms of intimate image sharing are not mutually exclusive (i.e., the same respondents may have been shown and/or sent intimate images of another person).
* p < .05 (i.e., a significant gender difference).
Source: Data created by author study.

and 5) and "no" (1 to 3) responses. For the purpose of analysis, six composite measures were created for the reactions of bystanders across both forms of IBSA ("both forms" in table 4.5).

Analysis

Descriptive analyses were performed to examine the extent and nature of IBSA and intimate image sharing, as well as the impacts and fears of victims, the motivations of perpetrators, and the reactions of bystanders. Chi-square analyses were also performed to explore whether there were any significant gender differences in the extent of IBSA and intimate image sharing, the nature of intimate image sharing, and the reactions of bystanders. Unfortunately, small sample sizes precluded chi-square analyses from being performed for the nature of IBSA, the impacts and fears of victims, and the motivations of perpetrators. However, potentially noteworthy gender differences (i.e., differences of 10.0% or more with a minimum of small effect size) are reported, given the exploratory nature of the current study. Effect size was measured using phi (φ) for analyses involving two dichotomous variables and Cramer's V (φ_c) for analyses involving one dichotomous variable and one non-dichotomous variable. The analyses used the eight composite measures for the extent of IBSA and intimate image sharing, the five composite measures for the nature of IBSA and intimate image sharing, the seven composite measures for the impacts and fears of victims, the nine composite measures for the motivation of perpetrators, and the six composite measures for the reactions of bystanders. Significant and noteworthy gender differences are reported in the text (%, n), with the associated test statistics (chi-square analyses only) and effect sizes.

RESULTS

Extent and Nature of IBSA and Intimate Image Sharing

Overall, 28.3% (n=83) of respondents reported being victims of IBSA, 9.9% (n=29) reported being perpetrators of IBSA, and 48.5% (n=142) reported being bystanders of intimate image sharing. However, it is important to acknowledge that the victim, perpetrator, and bystander groups were not mutually exclusive. For example, 74.7% (n=62) of respondents who reported being victims of IBSA were also perpetrators of IBSA and/or bystanders of intimate image sharing; 96.6% (n=28) of respondents who reported being perpetrators of IBSA were also victims of IBSA and/or bystanders of intimate image sharing; and 47.2% (n=67) of respondents who reported being bystanders of intimate image sharing were also victims and/or perpetrators of IBSA. Table 4.2 presents the extent of IBSA and intimate image sharing behaviors across the victim, perpetrator, and bystander groups.

Table 4.2 shows that respondents were most likely to report being bystanders of intimate image sharing (shown: 44.4%, n=130, sent: 22.2%, n=65) and least likely to report being perpetrators of IBSA (taken: 7.8%, n=23, shared: 5.5%, n=16, threatened: 3.4% n=10). With regard to the different forms of IBSA and intimate image sharing, respondents who reported being victims of IBSA were most likely to have had images taken (22.5%, n=66), respondents who reported being perpetrators of IBSA were most likely to have taken images (7.8%, n=23), and respondents who reported being bystanders of intimate image sharing were most likely to have been shown images (44.4%, n=130). Chi-square analyses of the eight composite measures (any intimate image sharing) revealed that there were no significant gender differences in the extent of IBSA or intimate image sharing across any of the victim, perpetrator, or bystander groups.

Respondents who reported being victims of IBSA were most likely to be targeted by male perpetrators (53.0%, n=44), followed by female perpetrators (24.1%, n=20). The remaining 22.9% (n=19) of respondents were targeted by both male and female perpetrators or did not know the gender of the perpetrators. The vast majority of respondents were targeted by people they had previous close relationships with (81.9%, n=28), such as intimate partners or ex-partners, family members, and/or friends. Comparatively, few were targeted by strangers, acquaintances, multiple perpetrators, or perpetrators with whom they did not know the identity (18.1%, n=15). Analyses of the two victim composite measures revealed that the gender of, and respondents' connection to, the perpetrator(s) of IBSA were similar irrespective of respondents' gender.

Respondents who reported being perpetrators of IBSA were most likely to target female victims (44.8%, n=13), followed by male victims (31.0%, n=9). The remaining 24.1% (n=7) of respondents targeted both male and female victims or did not know the gender of their victims. The vast majority of respondents targeted people they had previous close relationships with (75.9%, n=22), and comparatively few respondents targeted strangers, acquaintances, multiple victims, or victims with whom they did not know the identity (24.1%, n=7). Analyses of the two perpetrator composite measures revealed two noteworthy, but non-significant, gender differences. Males were more likely than females to target female victims (60.0%, n=6 vs. 36.8%, n=7), whereas females were more likely than males to target both male and female victims or to not know the gender of their victims (31.6%, n=6 vs. 10.0%, n=1; φ_c = .266). In addition, males were more likely than females to target strangers or victims with whom they did not know the identity (20.0%, n=2 vs. 10.5%, n=2), whereas females were more likely than males to target multiple victims (15.8%, n=3 vs. 0.0%, n=0; φ_c = .265).

Finally, respondents who reported being bystanders of intimate image sharing were similarly likely to believe the person in the images had (33.1%, n=47) and had not (29.6%, n=42) given their permission. The remaining respondents believed some of the people in the images had given their permission, whereas others had not (11.3%, n=16) or did not know if the person in the images had given their permission (26.1%, n=37). Chi-square analysis of the bystander composite measure revealed a statistically significant gender difference. Males were more likely than females to believe the person in the images had given their permission (51.2%, n=21 vs. 25.7%, n=26), whereas females were more likely than males to believe the person in the images had not given their permission (33.7%, n=34 vs. 9.5%, n=8) or to believe some of the people in the images had given their permission, whereas others had not (14.9%, n=15 vs. 2.4%, n=1; χ^2 = 11.69, p = .009, φ_c = .287).

Impacts and Fears of Victims

Respondents who reported being victims of IBSA experienced negative impacts on their work or study performance (25.3%, n=21), on their relationships with friends and family (21.7%, n=18), and on their relationship with an intimate partner (20.5%, n=17). Furthermore, respondents feared the images being discovered by friends and family (38.6%, n=32), by a current or future employer (36.1%, n=30), by a current or future intimate partner (30.1%, n=25), and by their current or future children (30.1%, n=25). Table 4.3 presents the impacts and fears of victims across the different forms of IBSA.

Analyses of the three composite measures (all forms) revealed that IBSA had similar impacts on respondents irrespective of their gender. There was just one noteworthy, but non-significant, exception: females were more likely than males to experience negative impacts on their relationship with an intimate partner (24.6%, n=14 vs. 11.5%, n=3; $\varphi = -.150$). With regard to the fears of victims, analyses for the four composite measures (all forms) revealed that there were four noteworthy, but non-significant, gender differences. Females were more likely than males to fear the images being discovered by friends and family (42.1%, n=24 vs. 30.8%, n=8; $\varphi = -.108$), by a current or future employer (40.4%, n=23 vs. 26.9%, n=7; $\varphi = -.130$), by a current or future intimate partner (35.1%, n=20 vs. 19.2%, n=5; $\varphi = -.160$), and by their current or future children (36.8%, n=21 vs. 15.4%, n=4; $\varphi = -.217$).

Motivations of Perpetrators

Respondents who reported being perpetrators of IBSA were most likely to be motivated by the belief that it was funny (37.9%, n=11) and/or sexy or flirty (34.5%, n=10), followed by the desire to get back at the person (27.6%, n=8) or impress friends (20.7%, n=6). Fewer respondents were motivated by the desire to embarrass (17.2%, n=5), control, or humiliate the person (both 13.8%, n=4). Fewer respondents still were motivated by the desire to trade the images for other images (6.9%, n=2) or money (3.4%, n=1). Table 4.4 presents the motivations of perpetrators across the different forms of IBSA.

Analyses of the nine composite measures (all forms) revealed that there were four noteworthy, but non-significant, gender differences. Females were more likely than males to be motivated by the desire to get back at a person (31.6%, n=6 vs. 20.0, n=2; $\varphi = -.123$), to impress friends (26.3%, n=5 vs. 10.0, n=1; $\varphi = -.191$), and to control the person (21.1%, n=4 vs. 0%, n=0; $\varphi = -.290$). In contrast, males were more likely than females to be motivated by the desire to humiliate the person (30.0%, n=3 vs. 5.3%, n=1; $\varphi = .341$).

Reactions of Bystanders

Respondents who reported being bystanders of intimate image sharing were most likely to feel uncomfortable (43.7%, n=62) and/or embarrassed (39.4%, n=56). Fewer respondents were bothered but did not say something or were okay with it (both 31.0%, n=44). Fewer respondents still were bothered and said something (25.4%, n=36) or thought it was funny (14.8%, n=21). Table 4.5 presents the reactions of bystanders across the different forms of intimate image sharing.

Chi-square analyses of the six composite measures (both forms) revealed that respondents' reactions to intimate image sharing were similar irrespective of their gender. There were just two statistically significant exceptions: females were more likely than males to feel embarrassed (45.5%, n=46 vs. 24.4%, n=10; χ^2 = 5.46, p = .019, φ = −.196), and males were more likely than females to find it funny (26.8%, n=11 vs. 9.9%, n=10; χ^2 = 6.63, p = .010, φ = .216).

DISCUSSION

This chapter presents survey findings relating to the IBSA and intimate image sharing experiences of 293 Australian youth, aged between 16 and 20 years, from victim, perpetrator, and bystander perspectives. Specifically, it examined (1) the extent and nature of IBSA and intimate image sharing, (2) the impacts and fears of victims of IBSA, (3) the motivations of perpetrators of IBSA, and (4) the reactions of bystanders of intimate image sharing.

Overall, 1 in 4 respondents had been victims of IBSA, 1 in 10 had been perpetrators of IBSA, and 1 in 2 had been bystanders of intimate image sharing. The non-consensual taking of intimate images was the most frequent form of IBSA for both victims and perpetrators, followed by the sharing and threats to share intimate images. Bystanders were more likely to be shown, rather than sent, intimate images. There were no gender differences with regard to the extent of IBSA and intimate image sharing. These findings are generally consistent with previous research that has examined victimization (Branch et al., 2017; Henry et al., 2017; Madigan et al., 2018) and perpetration (Powell et al., 2019) rates with both adolescent and adult respondents. However, there were a few notable differences. For example, some of the perpetration rates reported by previous research for the non-consensual sharing of intimate images are considerably higher than those reported in the current study (Clancy et al., 2019; Garcia et al., 2016). These discrepancies may reflect methodological differences. The current study only examined the non-consensual sending and uploading of intimate images, whereas previous research also examined the non-consensual showing of intimate images. Irrespective, these findings highlight the need for educational programs to make it clear that all forms of non-consensual intimate image taking and sharing (including threats to share) are IBSA.

The lack of any gender differences in victimization rates is consistent with previous research with both adolescent and adult respondents (Henry et al., 2017; Henry et al., 2019). However, the lack of any gender differences in perpetration rates contrasts with previous research that has found perpetration rates to be higher for males compared to females (Garcia et al., 2016; Powell et al., 2019). Nevertheless, the perpetrators of respondents who reported being victims of IBSA were more likely to be male than female, and the victims of respondents who reported being perpetrators of IBSA were more likely to be female than male. In addition, most respondents who reported being victims and/or perpetrators were targeted by, or targeted, people they had previous close relationships with. These findings are consistent with previous research examining offline sexual violence (e.g., rape and sexual assault; Kelly, Lovett, & Regan, 2005) and IBSA (Henry et al., 2017; Powell et al., 2019). They also highlight the need for educational programs to teach young people about healthy intimate relationships and the importance of consent in the context of intimate image taking and sharing.

With regard to the impacts and fears of victims, about 1 in 4 respondents reported that IBSA victimization impacted upon their work or study performance, and about 1 in 5 reported that it impacted upon their relationships with friends, family, and intimate partners. Furthermore, about 1 in 3 respondents feared that the intimate images would be discovered by friends and family, as well as current or future employers, intimate partners, and children. These findings are consistent with previous research that found IBSA victimization impacted upon the school performance and relationships of young people and caused fear during and after the abuse (Office of the eSafety Commissioner, 2017). However, the comparatively low frequencies for impacts and fears in the current study, compared with previous research (Henry et al., 2017; Office of the eSafety Commissioner, 2017), are concerning. They suggest that a proportion of youth do not consider the potential risks associated with intimate image sharing. It is important, therefore, that young people are made aware of these impacts and fears and that schools, colleges, and universities develop processes to minimize the potential repercussions of IBSA.

Gender comparisons revealed that females were more likely than males to experience negative impacts on their relationship with an intimate partner and to fear that the intimate images would be discovered by friends and family, as well as current and future employers and children. These findings are consistent with previous research that found females tended to express more negative emotional responses to sexting than males (Del Rey et al., 2019; Gassó et al., 2019). They are also consistent with pervasive societal views that shame and judge females, but reward males, for their expressions of sexual desire and agency (Allen, 2005; Fine & McClelland, 2006; Holland, Ramazanoglu, Sharpe, & Thomson, 1998; Powell, 2010).

With regard to the motivations of perpetrators, about 1 in 3 respondents reported that they thought it was funny, sexy, or flirty and about 1 in 5 reported that they wanted to impress friends. Between about 1 in 10 and 1 in 5 respondents reported that they wanted to get back at, embarrass, control and/or humiliate the person. Finally, less than 1 in 10 respondents reported that they wanted to trade the images for other images or money. These findings are consistent with previous research (Clancy et al., 2019). Although it is possible that sexy and flirty motivations are a consequence of respondents rationalizing their behavior, it is also possible that a proportion of young people genuinely fail to comprehend the negative impacts of IBSA. For example, previous research has shown that motivations for IBSA often reflect a lack of awareness regarding the severity of the behavior (Clancy et al., 2019). From an educational perspective, the latter interpretation of the findings is preferable because it should be easier to challenge frequently occurring "non-criminal" motivations than less frequently occurring "criminal" motivations. Finally, these findings support the view that "revenge pornography" is an inadequate term because it fails to encompass the broad range of motivations associated with the non-consensual taking and sharing (including threats to share) of intimate images. In the current study, revenge was not the sole motivation, nor was it the most common.

Gender comparisons revealed that females were more likely than males to report perpetrating IBSA to impress friends, as well as to get back at and/or control the person. Males, by comparison, were more likely than females to report perpetrating IBSA to humiliate the person. These findings suggest motivations may vary according to gender. Therefore, further research needs to explore these and other potential group differences to better understand the underlying motivations for IBSA.

With regard to the reactions of bystanders, just under 1 in 2 respondents who received intimate images felt uncomfortable and just over 1 in 3 felt embarrassed. A similar proportion of respondents (about 1 in 3) were bothered but did not say something or were okay with it. Finally, about 1 in 4 respondents were bothered and said something, and about 1 in 7 thought it was funny. These findings are consistent with previous research that suggests bystanders may not say anything because of the endorsement of peer norms and an aversion to challenging group dynamics (Harder, 2020). Therefore, further research needs to examine if and why bystanders of IBSA are reluctant to intervene. This is particularly important given the role that bystanders may have in the prevention of this form of abuse.

It is interesting, although not surprising, that only a small proportion of bystanders thought intimate image sharing was funny given that a large proportion of perpetrators believed IBSA was funny, sexy, and/or flirty. From an educational perspective, it may be beneficial to encourage young people to engage in open and honest discussions about their thoughts regarding, and experiences of, receiving intimate images, especially non-consensually shared images. These discussions would not only highlight the importance of consent in the context of intimate image taking and sharing but also help challenge the social norms that minimize or condone IBSA (see Powell, 2014). Furthermore, it would be beneficial to provide practical advice about when and how to intervene.

Gender comparisons revealed that bystander reactions were generally similar irrespective of gender, although males were more likely to find incidents funny, and females were more likely to find incidents embarrassing. These findings are consistent with previous research (Del Rey et al., 2019) and suggest that males may be less likely to appreciate the potential negative impacts of IBSA. Further research is needed to better understand variations in young people's reactions so that educational programs can be tailored accordingly.

Implications, Limitations, and Further Research

It is encouraging that this chapter has been included in a book relating to interpersonal violence, as it represents an important step in recognizing that the non-consensual taking and sharing (including threats to share) of intimate images is a form of sexual violence rather than just "revenge pornography" or "sexting gone wrong." The current study certainly suggests that the extent and nature of IBSA, as well as the impacts and fears of victims, are not adequately represented by either of these terms. Given that legislation and policy do not recognize IBSA as a form of sexual violence (McGlynn et al., 2017), being able to frame IBSA as part of the continuum of sexual violence has important implications for the support offered to victims of this form of abuse. Framing IBSA in this way also helps ensure that educational programs, victim support services, and law and policy responses are coherent and form part of the overall strategy to prevent sexual violence (McGlynn & Rackley, 2017; McGlynn et al., 2017). It is vitally important that research continues to challenge the current victim blaming and harm minimization rhetoric associated with IBSA and intimate image sharing. Instead, IBSA needs to be conceptualized as a breach of trust and a violation of sexual autonomy, for which the perpetrator, rather than the victim, is responsible (Bothamley & Tully, 2018).

It is important to acknowledge that the current study used a non-generalizable community subsample of Australian residents recruited via a global online sampling and data collection company. Although the original sample was substantial, the subsample of youth was limited. Consequently, it was not possible to explore intersectionality in young people's experiences of IBSA and intimate image sharing, and the gender comparisons presented in this chapter must be interpreted with caution. The limited sample also resulted in the experiences and perspectives of victims, perpetrators, and bystanders being examined separately. Finally, although the current study examined whether young people had been shown or sent intimate images it did not distinguish between images that had been shown or sent consensually or non-consensually. Consequently, it was not possible to examine the experiences and perspectives of bystanders of the non-consensual sharing of intimate images only. Further research is needed, therefore, to examine the range of intersectional contexts in which IBSA occurs, to unpack the interrelated nature of the different forms of IBSA, and to examine the experiences and perspectives of bystanders of IBSA.

CONCLUSION

This chapter presented findings relating to the IBSA and intimate image sharing experiences of 293 Australian youth, aged between 16 and 20 years, from victim, perpetrator, and bystander perspectives. Overall, 1 in 4 respondents had been victims of IBSA, 1 in 10 had been perpetrators of IBSA, and 1 in 2 had been bystanders of intimate image sharing. Importantly, these groups are not mutually exclusive and the same respondents may have been victims, perpetrators, and/or bystanders. These findings highlight the need for evidence-based educational programs that promote the development of healthy intimate relationships and challenge the non-consensual taking and sharing (including threats to share) of intimate images. Further research is needed to develop a more complete understanding of IBSA and intimate image sharing among young people to help prevent this form of abuse and the associated negative emotional responses.

REFERENCES

Allen, L. (2005). *Sexual subjects: Young people, sexuality and education*. London: Palgrave MacMillan.

Anderson, M., & Jiang, J. (2018). *Teens, social media & technology 2018*. Retrieved from: https://www.pewresearch.org/internet/2018/05/31/teens-social-media-technology-2018/

Barter, C., Stanley, N., Wood, M., Lanau, A., Aghtaie, N., Larkins, C., & Øverlien, C. (2017). Young people's online and face-to-face experiences of interpersonal violence and abuse and their subjective impact across five European countries. *Psychology of Violence, 7*, 375–384. doi: 10.1037/vio0000096

Bond, E. (2010). The mobile phone = bike shed? Children, sex and mobile phones. *New Media & Society, 13*, 587–604. doi: 10.1177/1461444810377919

Bothamley, S., & Tully, R. J. (2018). Understanding revenge pornography: Public perceptions of revenge pornography and victim blaming. *Journal of Aggression Conflict and Peace Research, 10*, 1–10. doi: 10.1108/JACPR-09-2016-0253

Branch, K., Hilinski-Rosick, C. M., Johnson, E., & Solano, G. (2017). Revenge porn victimization of college students in the United States: An exploratory analysis. *International Journal of Cyber Criminology, 11*, 128–142. doi: 10.5281/zenodo.495777

Clancy, E. M., Klettke, B., & Hallford, D. J. (2019). The dark side of sexting – Factors predicting the dissemination of sexts. *Computers in Human Behavior, 92*, 266–272. doi: 10.1016/j.chb.2018.11.023

Courtice, E. L., & Shaughnessy, K. (2017). Technology-mediated sexual interaction and relationships: A systematic review of the literature. *Sexual and Relationship Therapy, 32,* 269–290. doi: 10.1080/14681994.2017.1397948

Crofts, T., Lee, M., McGovern, A., & Milivojevic, S. (2016). *Sexting and young people.* London: Palgrave MacMillan.

Del Rey, R., Ojeda, M., Casas, J. A., Mora-Merchán, J. A., & Elipe, P. (2019). Sexting among adolescents: The emotional impact and influence of the need for popularity. *Frontiers in Psychology, 10,* 1–11. doi: 10.3389/fpsyg.2019.01828

Drouin, M., Coupe, M., & Temple, J. R. (2017). Is sexting good for your relationship? It depends …. *Computers in Human Behavior, 75,* 749–756. doi: 10.1016/j.chb.2017.06.018

Fine, M., & McClelland, S. I. (2006). Sexuality education and desire: Still missing after all these years. *Harvard Educational Review, 76,* 297–338. doi: 10.17763/haer.76.3.w5042g23122n6703

Fleschler Peskin, M., Markham, C. M., Addy, R. C., Shegog, R., Thiel, M., & Tortolero, S. R. (2013). Prevalence and patterns of sexting among ethnic minority urban high school students. *Cyberpsychology, Behavior, and Social Networking, 16,* 454–459. doi: 10.1089/cyber.2012.0452

Garcia, J. R., Gesselman, A. N., Siliman, S. A., Perry, B. L., Coe, K., & Fisher, H. E. (2016). Sexting among singles in the USA: Prevalence of sending, receiving, and sharing sexual messages and images. *Sexual Health, 13,* 428. doi: 10.1071/SH15240

Gassó, A. M., Klettke, B., Agustina, J. R., & Montiel, I. (2019). Sexting, mental health, and victimization among adolescents: A literature review. *International Journal of Environmental Research and Public Health, 16,* 2364. doi: 10.3390/ijerph16132364

Henry, N., & Flynn, A. (2019). 'Image-based sexual abuse: Online distribution channels and illicit communities of support', *Violence Against Women, 25,* 1932–1955. doi.org/10.1177/1077801219863881

Henry, N., Flynn, A., & Powell, A. (2019a). 'Image-based abuse: Victimisation and perpetration of non-consensual sexual or nude imagery', *Trends and Issues in Crime and Justice, 572.*

Hall, M., & Hearn, J. (2019b). Revenge pornography and manhood acts: A discourse analysis of perpetrators' accounts. *Journal of Gender Studies, 28,* 158–170. doi: 10.1080/09589236.2017.1417117

Harder, S. K. (2020). The emotional bystander – Sexting and image-based sexual abuse among young adults. *Journal of Youth Studies.* Advance online publication. doi: 10.1080/13676261.2020.1757631

Henry, N., Flynn, A., & Powell, A. (2019). *Responding to 'revenge pornography': Prevalence, nature and impacts.* Canberra: Australian Research Council.

Henry, N., McGlynn, C., Flynn, A., Johnson, K., Powell, A., & Scott, A.J. (2020). *Beyond revenge porn: Gender, justice and image-based sexual abuse.* Abingdon: Routledge.

Henry, N., Powell, A., & Flynn, A. (2017). *Not just 'revenge pornography': Australians' experiences of image-based abuse: A summary report.* Melbourne: RMIT University.

Holland, J., Ramazanoglu, C., Sharpe, S., & Thomson, R. (1998). *The male in the head: Young people, heterosexuality and power.* London: Tufnell Press.

Hudson, H. K., Fetro, J. V., & Ogletree, R. (2014). Behavioral indicators and behaviors related to sexting among undergraduate students. *American Journal of Health Education; Reston, 45,* 183–195. doi: 10.1080/19325037.2014.901113

International Telecommunications Union. (2017). ICT facts and figures 2017. Retrieved from https://www.itu.int/en/ITU-D/Statistics/Pages/facts/default.aspx

Kelly, L., Lovett, J., & Regan, L. (2005). *A gap or a chasm? Attrition in reported rape cases.* London: Home Office. Retrieved from https://webarchive.nationalarchives.gov.uk/20110218141141/http://rds.homeoffice.gov.uk/rds/pdfs05/hors293.pdf

Lenhart, A. (2015). *Teens, social media & technology overview 2015.* Retrieved from https://www.pewresearch.org/internet/2015/04/09/teens-social-media-technology-2015/

Madigan, S., Ly, A., Rash, C. L., Van Ouytsel, J., & Temple, J. R. (2018). Prevalence of multiple forms of sexting behavior among youth: A systematic review and meta-analysis. *JAMA Pediatrics, 172,* 327. doi: 10.1001/jamapediatrics.2017.5314

Maheux, A. J., Evans, R., Widman, L., Nesi, J., Prinstein, M. J., & Choukas-Bradley, S. (2020). Popular peer norms and adolescent sexting behavior. *Journal of Adolescence, 78,* 62–66. doi: 10.1016/j.adolescence.2019.12.002

McGlynn, C., & Rackley, E. (2017). Image-based sexual abuse. *Oxford Journal of Legal Studies, 37,* 534–561. doi: 10.1093/ojls/gqw033

McGlynn, C., Rackley, E., & Houghton, R. (2017). Beyond 'revenge porn': The continuum of image-based sexual abuse. *Feminist Legal Studies, 25,* 25–46. doi: 10.1007/s10691-017-9343-2

McGlynn, C., Rackley, E., Johnson, K., Henry, N., Gavey, N., Flynn, A. & Powell, A. (2020). "'It's torture for the soul': The harms of image-based sexual abuse", *Social & Legal Studies,* online first, doi.org/10.1177/0964663920947791.

McGlynn, C., Rackley, E., Johnson, K., Henry, N., Flynn, A., Powell, A., Gavey, N. & Scott, A.J. (2019). *Shattering lives and myths: A report on image-based sexual abuse.* United Kingdom: Durham University.

Mori, C., Temple, J. R., Browne, D., & Madigan, S. (2019). Association of sexting with sexual behaviors and mental health among adolescents: A systematic review and meta-analysis. *JAMA Pediatrics, 173,* 770–779. doi: 10.1001/jamapediatrics.2019.1658

Office of the eSafety Commissioner. (2017). *Image-based abuse: Qualitative research summary.* Retrieved from https://www.esafety.gov.au/about-us/research/image-based-abuse

Powell, A. (2010). *Sex, power and consent: Youth culture and the unwritten rules.* Melbourne: Cambridge University Press.

Powell, A. (2014). Shifting upstream. In N. Henry & A. Powell (Eds.) *Preventing sexual violence: Interdisciplinary approaches to overcoming a rape culture* (pp. 189–207). London: Palgrave Macmillan.

Powell, A., & Henry, N. (2014). Blurred lines? Responding to 'sexting' and gender-based violence among young people. *Children Australia, 39,* 119–124. doi: 10.1017/cha.2014.9

Powell, A., Henry, N., & Flynn, A. (2018). Image based sexual abuse. In W.S. DeKeseredy & M. Dragiewicz (Eds.) *Routledge Handbook of Critical Criminology* (2nd ed., pp. 305–315). Abingdon: Routledge.

Powell, A., Henry, N., Flynn, A., & Scott, A. J. (2019). Image-based sexual abuse: The extent, nature, and predictors of perpetration in a community sample of Australian residents. *Computers in Human Behavior, 92*, 393–402. doi: 10.1016/j.chb.2018.11.009

Reed, L. A., Boyer, M. P., Meskunas, H., Tolman, R. M., & Ward, L. M. (2020). How do adolescents experience sexting in dating relationships? Motivations to sext and responses to sexting requests from dating partners. *Children and Youth Services Review, 109*, 104696. doi: 10.1016/j.childyouth.2019.104696

Stanley, N., Barter, C., Wood, M., Aghtaie, N., Larkins, C., Lanau, A., & Överlien, C. (2018). Pornography, sexual coercion and abuse and sexting in young people's intimate relationships: A European study. *Journal of Interpersonal Violence, 33*, 2919–2944. doi: 10.1177/0886260516633204

Sudan, M., Olsen, J., Sigsgaard, T., & Kheifets, L. (2016). Trends in cell phone use among children in the Danish national birth cohort at ages 7 and 11 years. *Journal of Exposure Science & Environmental Epidemiology, 26*, 606–612. doi: 10.1038/jes.2016.17

Symons, K., Ponnet, K., Walrave, M., & Heirman, W. (2018). Sexting scripts in adolescent relationships: Is sexting becoming the norm? *New Media & Society, 20*, 3836–3857. doi: 10.1177/1461444818761869

Wincentak, K., Connolly, J., & Card, N. (2017). Teen dating violence: A meta-analytic review of prevalence rates. *Psychology of Violence, 7*, 224–241. doi: 10.1037/a0040194

Ybarra, M. L., Espelage, D. L., Langhinrichsen-Rohling, J., Korchmaros, J. D., & Boyd, D. (2016). Lifetime prevalence rates and overlap of physical, psychological, and sexual dating abuse perpetration and victimization in a national sample of youth. *Archives of Sexual Behavior, 45*, 1083–1099. doi: 10.1007/s10508-016-0748-9

Yeung, T. H., Horyniak, D. R., Vella, A. M., Hellard, M. E., & Lim, M. S. C. (2014). Prevalence, correlates and attitudes towards sexting among young people in Melbourne, Australia. *Sexual Health, 11*, 332–339. doi: 10.1071/SH14

Chapter 5

Cyberbullying

Its Social and Psychological Harms among Schoolers[1]

Hyeyoung Lim[2] and Hannarae Lee

Bullying has been one of the top social and health issues for children and adolescents worldwide (see Zych, Ortega-Ruiz, & Del Rey, 2015; also see stop-bullying.org). The term *bullying* was initially interpreted as school violence, which is intentional and repetitive aggression against a student by his/her peer(s) at school environments. Since the term has been more broadly used, bullying has been referred to as not only school violence among peer groups but also some workplace violence among employees. Also, living in the current internet and high-tech era, the place of bullying moves from a physical place to cyberspace. Due to the complications in defining the term, it was not until the early 2010s to have a consensus and commonly adopted bullying definition. Although the target subject has been expanded from schoolers to adults, the current study focuses on school bullying, especially cyberbullying and its social and psychological harms.

The initial school bullying was studied in Scandinavia in the 1970s (Heinemann, 1972; Olweus, 1973; cited in Zych et al., 2015). Since then, studies have been conducted on the bully (Li, 2006, 2007; Mishna, Cook, Gadalla, Daciuk, & Solomon, 2010; Slonje & Smith, 2008), bully-bullied (Mishna, Khoury-Kassabri, Gadalla, & Daciuk, 2012; Mishna et al., 2020; Vieno, Gini, & Santinello, 2011), the bullied (victims) (Chen et al., 2018; Fredrick & Demaray, 2018; Mishna, Cook, Gadalla, Daciuk, & Solomon, 2010), and bystanders such as teachers, parents, caregivers, and/or social support groups who might control, prevent, and assist the bully and the bullied (Bastiaensens et al., 2014; Pozzoli & Gini, 2019). Those studies also have examined the effect of school and social systems on school bullying, including physical security and safety systems, crime reporting systems, and school justice systems as well as social justice systems. In particular, the studies examined the bullied and their physical, social, and psychological damage and distress reveal that many peer victims internalize and/or externalize problems such as suicidal ideation and behavior, depression, drug and/or alcohol use, emotional and sleeping problem, and more. These symptoms were identified among the victims of both traditional and cyberbullying. Relatively few studies, however, have examined what treatments or assistance are effective for peer victims reducing and recovering from their suffering.

To bridge the research gap, the current study reviews the definitions of the term *cyberbullying* and operationalizes it for this study purposes. And then, using the datasets of the NCVS-SCS in 2011 and 2013, the present study examines the effects of adult and peer support for adolescent cyberbullying victims on social harm and psychological harm, where other variables are controlled. Discussions and policy implications are made based on the study findings.

LITERATURE REVIEW

The Definitions of Cyberbullying

To defining the term *cyberbullying*, it is necessary to review how the term *bullying* has been defined (e.g., Beran, Rinaldi, Bickham, & Rich, 2012; Hinduja & Patchin, 2013; Inchley et al., 2016; Lessne & Cidade, 2016; Li, 2006, 2007; Litwiller & Brausch, 2013; Rice et al., 2015; Slonje & Smith, 2008; Slonje, Smith, & Frisén, 2013; Smith et al., 2008; Tokunaga, 2010; Watts, Wagner, Velasquez, & Behrens, 2017). In existing bullying literature, the term had been inconsistently defined for individual study purposes until the U.S. federal government agencies developed a uniform definition of bullying in 2014 (see Gladden Gladden, Vivolo-Kantor, Hamburger, & Lumpkin, 2014). Through a process of consulting with bullying experts and practitioners as well as the people from the federal partner agencies such as the Centers for Disease Control and Prevention (CDC), the National Center for Injury Prevention and Control, and the Department of Education (ED), the term *bullying* was defined as the following:

> Any unwanted aggressive behavior(s) by another youth or group of youths who are not siblings or current dating partners that involves an observed or perceived power imbalance and is repeated multiple times or is highly likely to be repeated. Bullying may inflict harm or distress on the targeted youth including physical, psychological, social, or educational harm. (see Gladden et al., 2014, p. 7)

In this definition, youth are school-aged individuals 5 to 18 years of age; the term *unwanted* means the targeted youth want to stop perpetrator(s)' intentional use of *aggressive behavior* to harm against him or her, regardless of threatened or actual; the term *harm* means any physical, psychological, social and/or educational negative experiences or injuries including physical pain, feelings of distress, social damage of self-reputation at school, and/or limits or damages to educational opportunities (see Gladden et al., 2014, p. 8). According to this definition, cyberbullying was not directly defined or considered as a different type of bullying, but a subcategory of bullying locations occurred in cyberspace using electronic devices (see Gladden et al., 2014, p. 55).

In addition, the term *bullying* is somewhat differently defined in the three commonly used national surveys to measure the prevalence of bullying: (1) the Health Behaviors in School-age Children (HBSC), (2) the Youth Risk Behavior Survey (YRBS), and (3) the SCS. For example, HBSC sees bullying as

> a student is being bullied when another student, or a group of students, say or do nasty and unpleasant things to him or her. It is also bullying when a student is teased repeatedly in a way he or she does not like or when he or she is deliberately left out of things. But it is not bullying when two students of about the same strength or power argue or fight. It is also not bullying when a student is teased in a friendly and playful way. (Inchley et al., 2016, p. 197)

On the other hand, the YRBS defines bullying

> when 1 or more students tease, threaten, spread rumors about, hit, shove, or hurt another student over and over again. It is not bullying when 2 students of about the same strength or power argue or fight or tease each other in a friendly way. (CDC, 2019, p. 7)

Finally, in the SCS, bullying happens

> when one or more students tease, threaten, spread rumors about, hit, shove or hurt another student. It is not bullying when students of about the same strength or power argue or fight or tease each other in a friendly way. Bullies are usually stronger, or have more friends or more money, or some other power over the student being bullied. Usually, bullying happens over and over, or the student being bullied thinks it might happen over and over. (United States Department of Justice, 2013, p. 9)

Starting in 2015, the SCS started to include the follow-up questions on repetition and power imbalance to estimate the percentage of bullying experience as outlined in the CDC uniform definition (Lessne & Cidade, 2016).

Instead of developing a new definition for cyberbullying, early studies placed space restriction from traditional bullying to cyberspace where one can access using electronic communication tools (Li, 2006, 2007; Slonje & Smith, 2008; Smith et al., 2008). Consequently, several bullying characteristics have been adopted to the cyberbullying definition such as the repetition of the act, the power imbalance, and the intent of embarrassing or damaging other individuals (Beran et al., 2012; Hinduja & Patchin, 2013; Rice et al., 2015; Slonje et al., 2013). In addition, cyberbullying most often involves abusive or hurtful texts, emails, posts, images, and videos, as well as deliberately excluding others online and gossiping or spreading rumors in an attempt to imitate and humiliate targeted individuals (Tokunaga, 2010; Watts et al., 2017).

Due to the unique characteristics of cyberspace, such as no space and time restriction and perceived anonymity (Kowalski, Morgan, & Limber, 2012), defining cyberbullying is a challenging task. At the same time, such characteristics also led scholars to agree that cyberbullying can occur at any time in any place. Therefore, based on previous literature, the current study defines cyberbullying as any intentional harm delivered through electronic media, including emails, instant messaging or chat, texts, online gaming, and posts from social media, which may inflict psychological, social, educational, and/or physical harm to the targeted youth.

Someone may wonder how cyberbullying can physically harm the youth. There might be no pushing, shoving, or tripping by others in cyberbullying cases, but victims can inflict self-harm as a response to their victimization. For example, from a large risk-behavior screening study with a sample of 4,693 public high school students, Litwiller & Brausch (2013) found that both cyberbullying and traditional bullying victims showed problems with substance use, violence, and unsafe sexual behavior. More importantly, both bullying victims also showed suicidal behavior after victimization. Hinduja & Patchin (2010) also found that students who experienced both traditional and cyberbullying showed suicidal ideation or attempted to commit suicide. In cyberbullying cases, victims were almost twice more likely to have attempted suicide than those who were not cyberbullying victims.

Cyberbullying Literature since the Mid-2000s

Since its inception, many cyberbullying studies have compared the demographic characteristics of bullies and victims of both school bullying (a.k.a., traditional bullying) and cyberbullying (Baldry, Farrington, & Sorrentino, 2017; Li, 2006, 2007; Erdur-Baker, 2010; Slonje & Smith, 2008; Vieno, Gini, & Santinello, 2011; Waasdorp & Bradshaw, 2015), while others focused on psychological characteristics of bullies and victims of both school bullying and cyberbullying such as depression symptoms and suicidal ideation (Bauman et al., 2013; Gradinger et al., 2009; Kubiszewski et al., 2015; Pabian & Vandebosch, 2016). Besides, physical characteristics such as aggression (Gradinger et al., 2009; Mishna et al., 2020) and presence of coping or preventive factors, including peer influence, adult influence, and school safety measures (Charalampous et al., 2018; Meter & Bauman, 2018), were also examined by scholars in various fields.

Cyberbullying literature tends to focus on children and adolescent populations, but some studies also utilized college populations to demonstrate the impacts and factors of cyberbullying (Francisco, Simão, Ferreira, & das Dores Martins, 2015; Gaffney, Ttofi, & Farrington, 2019; Goodboy & Martin, 2015; Menesini & Salmivalli, 2017). For example, according to the HBSC 2013/2014 data (Inchley et al., 2019), 10.6% out of 176,185 students experienced cyberbullying through messages (e.g., instant messages, emails, text messages) and unflattering or inappropriate pictures as well as by posting them online without permission (8.4% out of 178,935 participants). Furthermore, since cyberbullying is not an issue that is confined to one country, scholars worldwide demonstrated their interests and examined factors, impact, and prevention mechanisms regarding cyberbullies and victims. Such a trend of focusing on cyberbullies and victims then expanded to include bully-victims who experienced both spectra of bullying (Del Rey, Elipe, & Ortega-Ruiz, 2012; Vieno, Gini, & Santinello, 2011; Wang et al., 2019).

Even though the majority of cyberbullying literature is focused on the characteristics and factors surrounding bullies and victims, two different areas have emerged. First, widespread use of social networking services and innovative techniques in automated prediction led scholars to develop cyberbullying prediction models using automated detection programs incorporating personality traits and psychological features (Balakrishnan, Khan & Arabnia, 2020; Del Rey, Mora-Merchán, Casas, Ortega-Ruiz, & Elipe, 2018; Fazil & Abulaish, 2018; Rosa et al., 2019). The use of a prediction model is a new area of research that requires rigorous and continuous development as well as evaluation. Second, there is also an emerging trend of focusing on the bystander effects of cyberbullying (Pazzoli & Gini, 2020; Song & Oh, 2018). Studies on bystander effects focus on psychological and situational factors surrounding the bystander. Findings from these two areas are still in their infancy to generalize and require further assessment.

Social and Psychological Harm

As defined by Gladden et al. (2014), it is obvious that the bullied suffer from social, educational, and psychological distress along with physical harms. Existing literature demonstrates how bullying inflicts harm or distress on the victim as well as what mechanisms effectively assist victims in being recovered from such distresses. Several studies have found that bullying victimization is related to externalizing and/or internalizing problems (Cook et al., 2010; Reijntjes et al. 2011). For instance, bullying increases suicidal ideation and behavior (Holt et al., 2015; Kowalski et al., 2014; van Geel et al., 2014), depression (Hawker & Boulton, 2000; Kowalski et al., 2014; Trofi et al., 2014), anxiety (Kowalski et al., 2014), psychotic/psychosomatic/ psychological symptoms (Albdour, Hong, Lewin, & Yarandi, 2019; Cunningham et al., 2015; Gini & Pozzoli, 2013; Van Dam et al., 2012), stress (Kowalski et al., 2014), drug and alcohol use (Kowalski et al., 2014; Trofi et al., 2011), emotional (Kowalski et al., 2014) and sleeping problems (van Geel et al., 2016). Additionally, bullying decreases self-esteem (Hawker & Boulton, 2000; Kowalski et al., 2014; Tsaousis, 2016), social esteem (Hawker & Boulton, 2000), and academic achievement (Nakamoto & Schwartz, 2009).

Table 5.1 summarizes selected studies that test the impacts of emotional and psychological distresses on the victims of cyberbullying for the purpose of the current study. For example, Albdour, Hong, Lewin, & Yarandi (2019) examined a convenient sample of 150 Arab American adolescents on their cyberbullying experience and its impact on their health. Using the Children's Somatization Inventory (CSI-24) and the Kassler Psychological Distress Scale (K10), they tested the severity of non-specific somatic symptoms, anxiety levels, and depression symptoms experienced by the adolescents who had cyberbullied (perpetrators) and/or had been cyberbullied (victims). Albdour et al. (2019) found that both cyberbullying perpetration and victimization were positively correlated with both physical complaints and psychological distress. However, by controlling the demographic variables, physical complaints were significantly related to cyberbullying perpetrators only ($B = 11.02$, $p<.001$), and psychological distress was only significantly associated with victimization ($B = 3.69$, $p<.05$). Tsaousis (2016) also found that peer victimization was negatively significant with self-esteem through analyzing 121 existing bullying studies published by June 2014. This study also found a significant relationship between bullying behavior and self-esteem, but the degree of association was very low. That is, the victims' self-esteem is more lowered by peer aggression and bullying than the perpetrators' self-esteem. With the fact that interpersonal and intrapersonal factors are more likely to influence self-esteem in its development, it is crucial to consider the robust study finding in the development of a victim assistance program for peer victimizations and how other individual characteristics and qualities play a role in bullying and its victimization (Tsaousis, 2016).

To assess if the strength of the association between peer victimization (bullying and peer aggression) and psychosomatic health problems relies on how to measure bullying or peer aggression, Hellström and her colleagues (2017)

Table 5.1 Selected Multivariate Studies on Physical and Psychological Impacts of Cyberbullying

Source	Sample Region/Sampling Design	Age Range	Method (n)	Types	Symptoms
Albdour et al. (2019)	Midwest, USA/convenience	12–16 years	Regression (n=150)	Cyber victimization Cyber perpetrator	Psychological distress (+) Physical complaints (+)
Bauman et al. (2013)	Canada/two-stage cluster sampling	Grade 9–12	Structural equation modeling (n=1,491)	Cyberbullying Cyber Victimization	Suicide attempt (+) Depression (+)
Bonanno & Hymel (2013)	Canada/ recruitment	Grade 8–10	Hierarchical multiple regression analyses (n=399)	Cyberbullying	Depressive symptomatology (+) suicidal ideation (+)
				Cyberbullying victimization	Depressive symptomatology (+) Suicidal Ideation (+)
Brewer & Kerslake (2015)	The North West of England/recruitment	16–18 years	Multiple regression (n=90)	Cyber perpetrators	Empathy (–) self-esteem (–)
				Cyber victimization	Self-esteem (–)
Chen et al. (2018)	China/a two-stagedstratified sampling method	15–17 years	Multinomial logistic regressions (n=18,341)	Cyber victimization (internet victimization)	Symptoms of PTSD (+),depression (+), self-harm (+)
Fredrick & Demaray (2018)	Midwest, USA/school-wide social-emotional assessment	13–16 years	Path analysis (n=403)	Cyber victimization	Depressive symptoms (+) suicidal ideation (+)
Hay & Meldrum (2010)	Southeastern USA/recruitment	10–21 years	Ordinary least squares (n=426)	Cyberbullying victimization	Negative emotions (anxiety, depression, low self-worth) (+) self-harm (+) suicidal behavior (+)
Landoll et al. (2015)	Southeastern, USA/recruitment	14–18 years	Confirmatory factor analyses (n=839)	Cybervictimization	Social anxiety (–) Depressive symptoms from the Center for Epidemiological Studies- Depression Scale (+)
Mishna et al. (2010)	Canada/ a stratified, clustered random sampling	Grade 6, 7, 10, and 11	Chi-square test (n= 2,186)	Cyberbullying	Fun, popular and powerful but with remorse
				Cyberbullying victimization	Anger (+) sadness (+) depression (+)

(Continued)

Table 5.1　Selected Multivariate Studies on Physical and Psychological Impacts of Cyberbullying (Continued)

Source	Sample Region/Sampling Design	Age Range	Method (n)	Types	Symptoms
Spears et al. (2009)	Australia/convenience and purposive sampling	20 students (12–18 years) 10 teachers 6 counselors	Narrative and thematic analyses (n=36)	Cyberbullying victimization	Negative feelings and emotions (e.g., fear, helplessness, unnerving, demeaning, inescapable, unsafe, vulnerable feeling, loneliness, disruption to and dislocation from participant's relationship) (+)
Wang et al. (2010)	The U.S. Sample from the 2005/2006 Health Behaviour in School-aged Children (HBSC)/ A complex survey design*	Grade 6–10	Latent class analyses (n=7,475)	Cyberbullying	Depression (+) medically attended injuries (+) medicine use (+)

*See Currie et al. (2009) for more details regarding the HBSC sampling methods. Currie, C., Gabhainn, S. N., & Godeau, E. (2009). The Health Behaviour in School-aged Children: WHO Collaborative Cross-National (HBSC) study: origins, concept, history and development 1982–2008. *International journal of public health, 54*(2), 131-139.
Source: Data created by author study.

analyzed 2,578 Swedish adolescents aged 13 to 15 years and found that adolescent victims have more significant psychosomatic problems than non-victims. While the impacts on psychosomatic health problems with each measure (bullying, occasional peer aggression, and frequent peer aggression) were not significantly different, the adolescents victimized by both measures (bullying plus occasional peer aggression; and bullying plus frequent peer aggression) showed higher levels of psychosomatic health problems (Hellström et al., 2017).

Several studies on bullying treatment and assistance focus on coping mechanisms, including the effect of *social or emotional support* (Collins & Laursen, 2004; House, 1981; Moss, 1973). Moss (1973) defined the term *social support* as the subjective feelings of being cared for, accepted, loved, needed, and belonged. House (1981) described emotional support as the perception of support conveyed to others, such as the provision of acceptance, reassurance, and encouragement in times of stress or difficulty. It is a widely known fact that positive parental supports and the perceptions of supportive relationships with parents are essential keys to adolescents' well-being (Collins & Laursen, 2004). Parental support, however, may not be the most significant factor to prevent and reduce peer victimizations and to support adolescent victims because bullying and/or peer aggression most frequently occur in school settings. That is, other emotional and social support groups are needed for the victims in a school setting such as adult (e.g., teacher and school staff) and/or peer support groups.

A paucity of studies has examined the importance of emotional support groups for adolescent victims seeking help, particularly for the victims of cyberbullying. Yeung and Leadbeater (2010) examined the moderation effect of the three adult emotional support groups (father, mother, and teacher) on the relations between peer victimization and maladaptive outcomes (emotional and behavioral problems) with a total of 664 adolescents over a two-year period (N=664) in the first survey (2003, T1) and N=580 in the follow-up survey (2005, T2). The results showed that both physical and relational (i.e., peers tell lies about the victim) victimizations were positively significant on both emotional and behavioral problems among adolescents. And it was found that females were more emotionally and behaviorally distressed by victimizations than male adolescents (Yeung & Leadbeater, 2010). Particularly, the behavioral problems among female adolescents were positively significant with the relational victimization in T2. In other words, the study found that behavioral problems are caused by relational bullying experiences in later years, especially among female victims. One interesting finding of the study was that the higher emotional support from father lowers adolescents' emotional and behavioral problems both in T1 and T2, while their mothers' emotional support significantly moderated their children's emotional problems only in T1. Moreover, teachers' emotional support significantly lowered adolescents' relational problems in T1 and T2, while its significant moderation effects on emotional problems were found in T2. Yeung and Leadbeater (2010) constructed the temporal ordering from bullying to emotional and behavioral harms inflicted on adolescents. They also demonstrated moderated effect of fathers' and teachers' supports on reducing the harm caused by bullying.

Current Study

The current study extends previous research on cyberbullying victimization among youth by examining the impact of the presence of adult and peer support on the level of social and psychological harms. According to the NCVS-SCS data between 2011 and 2013, cyberbullying victims experience social harm 1.5 times more than traditional bullying victims and experience twice more psychological harm compared to traditional bullying victims (NCVS-SCS, 2011; 2013). The literature on causes and preventive methods on reducing both social and psychological harm, however, is limited. Therefore, under the assumption that adult and peer support can reduce the level of both social and psychological harm, the current study hypotheses the following:

> Hypothesis 1: Cyberbullying victims are less likely to experience social harm with adult support.
> Hypothesis 2: Cyberbullying victims are less likely to experience social harm with peer support.
> Hypothesis 3: Cyberbullying victims are less likely to experience psychological harm with adult support.
> Hypothesis 4: Cyberbullying victims are less likely to experience psychological harm with peer support.

Methods

Data

The data used in the current study are from the NCVS-SCS. Every year, NCVS interviews each household member who is aged 12 years and older. SCS, as a supplement to the annual NCVS, started collecting data in 1989, then again in 1995. Beginning 1999, NCVS-SCS has been collected every two years. SCS interviews each household member aged 12 to 18 who attends a primary or secondary education program (Bureau of Justice Statistics, 2015). The NCVS-SCS dataset first introduced questions regarding cyberbullying in 2011. Starting in 2015, the NCVS-SCS removed eight cyberbullying-related questions and included one question asking the place of bullying to capture whether the bullying occurred online or by text. Thus, we used the 2011 and 2013 data only for the current study purpose. To include students who experienced cyberbullying, the current study included respondents who indicated experiencing cyberbullying using the cyberbullying-related questions. The questions include posting hurtful information about the victim; purposely sharing private information, photos, or videos on the internet or mobile phones; threatened or insulted victims through email, instant messaging, chat, text message, online gaming; or excluding victims from online communications. We also cross-referenced victims using one question asking the frequency of all these questions. This procedure classified 498 cyberbullying victims from 2011 and 325 cyberbullying victims from 2013 (N=823).

Dependent Variables

Social Harm

In the current study, social harm was measured through students' answers on whether or not they were staying away from seven different places in school (e.g., school entrance, hallways and stairs, cafeteria, restrooms, parking lot, other school building, or other school ground) or route to school, as well as avoiding any online activities. Dichotomized response options for the nine items were summed across the items to reflect the severity of social harm as a count variable. An index reliability of Cronbach's alpha is 0.78, and the higher numbers represent the higher severity of social harm.

Psychological Harm

Psychological harm was measured with four dichotomized questions (0 = no, 1 = yes) and three 4-point Likert scale questions (0 = never, 1 = almost never, 2 = sometimes, and 3 = most of the time). The dichotomized questions were the following: (1) Did you avoid any activities at your school because you thought someone might attack or harm you? (2) Did you avoid any class at your school because you thought someone might attack or harm you? (3) Did you stay home from school because you thought someone might attack or harm you? and (4) During the last four weeks, did you skip any classes? The three Likert scale questions were (1) How often are you afraid that someone will attack or harm you on a school building/property? (2) How often are you afraid that someone will attack or harm you on a school bus or on the way to and from school? and (3) Besides the times you are on school property or going to or from school, how often are you afraid that someone will harm you? Three Likert scale questions were re-coded to represent no experience (0 =

never and almost never) and experience of psychological harm (1 = sometimes and most of the time) prior to summing across seven items to reflect
the severity of psychological harm as a count variable. An index reliability
of Cronbach's alpha is 0.73, and the higher number represents more severe
psychological harm.

Independent Variables

Adult Support

Adult support was measured with six 5-point Likert scale questions that
asked the support from adult figures in school, including teachers who cared,
noticed, listened, told positive stuff, wished the best, and believed the students (e.g., "There is an adult at school who believes that you will be . . ." or
"Teachers care about students"; strongly negative = 0, negative = 1, neutral =
2, positive=3, strongly positive = 4). All Likert scale questions were summed
across six items and then divided by six to reflect the severity of adult supports from strongly negative (= 0) to strongly positive (= 4). An index reliability of Cronbach's alpha is 0.83, and the higher number represents more
support from adult figures in school.

Peer Support

Peer support was measured with one 4-point Likert scale question that
asked the presence of friends whom the respondent can talk to, cares about
feelings, and what happened to the students (i.e., "Would you agree, at
school, you have a friend you can talk to, who cares about your feelings
and what happens to you"; strongly disagree = 0, disagree = 1, agree = 2,
strongly agree = 3).

Control Variables

School Experience and Safety Features

To capture the impact of negative experiences in school, the current study
utilized victimization report questions regarding hate-related words on race,
religion, ethnicity, disability, gender, and sexual orientation (e.g., "Were any
of the hate-related words related to you race?"). Those who reported any one
of the above victimizations were coded as 1 and 0 otherwise. The physical
atmosphere of the school can also influence students' social and psychological harm. Thus, the study utilized a dichotomized question regarding the presence of hate symbols in school (0 = no, 1 = yes). In a similar vein, the study
also included the nine dichotomized safety features at school (e.g., the

presence of security guards or assigned police officers, metal detectors, visitor sign-in process, security cameras, and the code of student conduct) to represent none (0) to high (9) physical safety levels.

Demographic Features

The current study included three demographic variables as covariates: gender (0 = male, 1 = female), age (12–18), and ethnicity (0 = others, 1= Caucasian).

Analytical Strategies

The two dependent variables for the current study, *social* and *psychological harm*, are the count variables. Although the Linear Regression Model (LRM) has often been applied to count outcomes, this can result in inefficient, inconsistent, and biased estimates. Even though there are situations in which the LRM provides reliable results, it is much safer to use models designed explicitly for count variable outcomes.

By utilizing count models, the current study assumed that every bullying victim has a positive probability of experiencing any given level of social and/or psychological harm. Depends on individual characteristics, the probability of being a victim may differ across victims, but all victims have some probability of experiencing harm. To run count models, the study began with the Poisson Regression Model (PRM). Both social harm and psychological harm variable, however, contained strong evidence of over-dispersion (social harm: $G^2 = 1275.79$, $p = 0.001$; $X^2 = 2121.42$, $p = 0.001$ and psychological harm: $G^2 = 959.02$, $p = 0.001$; $X^2 = 1555.81$, $p = 0.001$). Thus, instead of applying the PRM, we ran the Negative Binomial Regression Model (NBRM) for both models. The NBRM improves upon the underprediction of zeros in the PRM by increasing the conditional variance without changing the conditional mean. The NBRM allows examining the over-dispersed portion of the count variable, which indicates that the variance exceeds the mean, and the distribution of outcomes is determined by both random and non-random (i.e., risk heterogeneity and/or event dependence) processes (Park & Eck, 2013; Winkelmann, 2008).

Results

Table 5.2 presented the descriptive statistics of measures utilized in the current study. Among 823 cyberbullying victims aged 12 to 18 in public and private schools in the United States, approximately 24% of students expressed experiencing some level of social harm (26% of females; 20% of males), while approximately 19% experienced some level of psychological

Table 5.2   Descriptive Statistics

Variable	N	Mean	St.d.	Min	Max
Social harm	823	0.51	1.25	0	9
Psychological harm	823	0.38	0.95	0	6
Adult support	823	3.27	0.55	1	4
Peer support	823	3.43	0.79	0	4
Hate words	823	0.30	0.46	0	1
Hate symbols in school	823	0.52	0.50	0	1
Presence of safety features	823	5.88	1.38	0	9
Caucasian	823	0.66	0.47	0	1
Gender (female=1, male=0)	823	0.61	0.49	0	1
Age	823	14.88	1.81	12	18

Note. St.d. = Standard Deviation.
Source: Data created by author study.

harm (22% of females; 15% of males). The current data contained 66% of White students compared to other races, and most of the schools on the data showed at least one safety feature in school. The majority of cyberbullying victims in the current data did not experience hate words in school (70%), but approximately half of students (52%) saw hate-related words or symbols written in his or her school.

Social Harm

Table 5.3 showed the outcome of NBRM for cyberbullying victims with social harm.

Findings from table 5.3 supported hypothesis one, the presence of adult support reduces the level of social harm by cyberbullying victims. The results also supported hypothesis two—the presence of peer support reduced the level of social harm. When students felt substantial support from adult figures in school, their rate for social harm would be expected to decrease by a factor of 0.64 while holding all other variables in the mode constant. For example, when a student has no adult support, his/her/their social harm is equal to 100. If the student has some peer support (1 unit increases), that student's social harm would down to 64 from 100, indicating a 36% decrease. When students felt the more substantial support by their peers, their rate for social harm would be expected to decrease by a factor of 0.73, while holding all other variables in the model constant. We further discussed this issue in the next section.

The current study also included measures of hate words and hate symbols because of the possibility for cyberbullying victims to experience social harm due to negative school experiences. The findings indicated that cyberbullying victims who heard hate-related words were 2.76 times more likely to experi-ence social harm. Seeing signs of hate symbols in school also increased social

Table 5.3 Negative Binomial Regression Model for Cyberbullying Victims with Social Harm

	β	(Std. Err)	IRR	(Std. Err)
Adult support	−0.45**	0.14	0.64**	0.09
Peer support	−0.32***	0.10	0.73***	0.07
Hate words	1.02***	0.17	2.76***	0.48
Hate symbols in school	0.43*	0.18	1.54*	0.27
Presence of safety features	0.03	0.06	1.03	0.07
Caucasian	−0.20	0.17	0.82	0.14
Female	−0.28	0.17	1.33	0.23
Age	−0.14**	0.05	0.87**	0.04
Constant	2.97	0.91	19.49	3.78

Notes. Std. Err = Standard Error; IRR = Incident-Rate Ratios.
* $p<0.05$, ** $p<0.01$, *** $p<0.001$.
Source: Data created by author study.

Table 5.4 Negative Binomial Regression Model for Cyberbullying Victims with Psychological Harm

	β	(Std. Err)	IRR	(Std. Err)
Adult Support	−0.37*	0.16	0.69*	0.11
Peer Support	−0.33**	0.11	0.72**	0.08
Hate Words	1.20***	0.19	3.32***	0.65
Hate Symbols in School	0.06	0.19	1.06	0.21
Presence of Safety Features	−0.01	0.07	1.00	0.07
Caucasian	−0.15	0.19	0.85	0.17
Female	0.58**	0.19	1.78**	0.35
Age	−0.14**	0.05	0.87**	0.04
Constant	2.49	1.01	12.04	12.18

Notes. Std. Err = Standard Error; IRR = Incident-Rate Ratios.
* $p<0.05$, ** $p<0.01$, *** $p<0.001$.
Source: Data created by author study.

harm by 1.54 times. The level of social harm by cyberbullying victims was reduced for every additional year in school by 13%. Unlike previous literature, we did not find any statistical significance between male and female cyberbullying victims' level of social harm, as well as differences in race.

Psychological Harm

Table 5.4 indicated the outcome of PRM for cyberbullying victims with psychological harm. As shown in table 5.4, the presence of both adult and peer support reduced the level of psychological harm. Cyberbullying victims experienced less psychological harm by the presence of adult support (31%) and peer support (28%). These findings supported hypotheses three and four of the current study. Unlike social harm, cyberbullying victims with psychological harm were not significantly affected by negative school experiences and environments, such as hearing hate words or seeing hate-related symbols on school property.

Besides, victims with psychological harm were 78% more likely to be female. Similar to social harm model, the finding also indicated that the level of psychological harm among cyberbullying victims was reduced for every additional year in school by 13%.

DISCUSSIONS

The current study examined the effects of adult and peer support on social and psychological harm among adolescent victims of cyberbullying aged 12 to 18 using the NCVS-SCS data in 2011 and 2013. As found, almost all victims reported that they experienced certain degrees of social and psychological distress from their cyberbullying victimization. The results supported the four research hypotheses that assumed the negative relationship between two types of harms (social and psychological harm) and two emotional support groups (peer and adult). First, we found that peer support lowered not only the levels of social harm but also psychological harm among adolescent victims of cyberbullying. It is not surprising that most students have at least one close friend at school. Although we would like to capture a more versatile measure of peer support, we were unable to provide a more sophisticated measure of peer support due to the distribution of the measure and lack of peer support variables in the dataset. Several existing studies found that peer support has a positive impact on students' experience at school by creating a socio-emotional climate and providing social and emotional support and functions as school bullying intervention and prevention (Cowie, 2011; Naylor & Cowie, 1999; Cowie & Olafsson, 2000; Tzani-Pelpelasi et al., 2019; Yin et al., 2017). Although these studies did not test peer support directly on cyberbullying victimization, it is clear that peers and fellow students play critical roles to the bullied to overcome their social and psychological damage and distress from the peer bullies. There is a common phrase used in South Korea: *Wounds from people are eventually healed by people.* In other words, social and psychological harms from peers at school are healed by peers. The current study clearly demonstrated such proverb.

Second, we found a positive effect of adult support on both social and psychological harms among adolescent victims of cyberbullying. That is, adult support alleviates the levels of social and psychological distress suffering among peer victims. Yeung & Leadbeater (2010) found that adult emotional support moderates the association between peer victimization and emotional and behavioral problems among adolescents. In particular, the higher father and teacher's emotional support, the lower the adolescent victims' emotional and behavioral problems caused by both physical and relational victimization concurrently and across time (Yeung & Leadbeater, 2010). Although Yeung & Leadbeater (2010) did not separately measure cybervictimization from physical and relational victimization, it was obvious that adult support moderates emotional and behavioral maladaptive outcomes among adolescent victims of peer aggression and harassment.

According to Mitchell and her colleagues (2016), adolescent victims had the most emotional harm by mixed harassment incidents (in-person and technology involved) because of being victimized in multiple places such as school, home, and cyberspace. To our knowledge, the current study is the first study that empirically examined the effects of adult and peer support on social and psychological harm among adolescent victims of cyberbullying, as well as the first study finding the positive impacts of adult and peer support on cyber victimization. The result of the current study also supports the finding of Yeung and Leadbeater's study (2010) that adult support makes a difference for peer-victimized adolescents.

Third, it was not our main focus but worth to mention the important finding of the relationships between both hate words and hate symbols in school and the levels of social harm. It was not a surprising finding that adolescent victims were not only physically but also verbally abused by their peers, using hate words related to various personal factors. However, it is necessary to pay good attention to the positive relationship between hate symbols in school and social harm. Neutrality in the school environment has been highly emphasized by many scholars and teachers, especially in public schools, in order to provide a safer and better learning environment by eliminating any confusion or animosity for students on polarized opinions on any controversial topics in social justice (see Hart, 1964; Kelly, 2001; and Kyritsis & Tsakyrakis, 2013). The finding of the current study lets us rethink about the carelessness, negligence, or insensitivity on hate symbols among teachers and/or school administrators as well as the pain of the adolescent victims caused by inattentive and/or unintentional hazardous school climates. Besides, it implies the importance of school justice systems and disciplines against any violations of human rights. As described earlier, however, both variables, hate words and the presence of hate symbols in school, were measured with one dichotomized item, so it is recommended for future studies to measure them with more sophisticated items to investigate the impacts of hate on perpetrators and victims.

There are several limitations to the current study concerning the data. Similar to many other self-reported survey data, the NCVS-SCS contains issues regarding sampling error. Even though the NCVS-SCS collects data from the nationally representative samples, any given NCVS-SCS student sample may differ from estimates that would have been produced from other student samples. In addition, the NCVS-SCS asks on an entire year of school victimization in every two years. Thus, at the response process stage, students may forget an event or telescope forward or backward. Since 2011, there were a total of four NCVS-SCS datasets that include cyberbullying-related items. Starting in 2015, NCVS-SCS substituted the eight cyberbullying-related questions to one question that asks the place of bullying with an option to choose online or by text. For this reason, we used the 2011 and 2013 datasets only in the current study. It is recommended for future studies to examine the 2015 and 2017 datasets for the comparison purpose. The current study combined two NCVS-SCS data to demonstrate the relationship between peer and adult support on bullying victims. Due to the data limitation, we cannot control or examine the temporal ordering between bullying and support from adults and peer groups. Instead, this study assumed the more significant impact of adult and peer support on bullying victims. Therefore, future studies should address the issue of the temporal ordering between bullying and supports.

Another concern in this study is that there is no way to identify whether the findings of this study are the result of the adult and/or peer support programs already being effective. There is no such question indicating whether or not individual participants' school has such programs in the NCVS-SCS questionnaire. As stated, we measured peer and adult support regardless of the existence of such support programs. Hence, the findings of this study should be cautiously interpreted, and it is also recommended for future studies to address and/or resolve the issue of a black-box approach, caused by the limitation of using secondary data. Furthermore, the current study only includes both adult and peer support at school. Since it is plausible to obtain both supports from outside school boundaries, expanding the scope to include support from other adults and peers is also encouraged for further assessment.

According to Yeung & Leadbeater (2010), teachers' emotional support could reduce emotional and behavioral problems among adolescents. Unfortunately, the NCVS-SCS data did not allow us to differentiate the emotional support from teachers only. There were three items asking students' experiences with teachers, but those items asked overall perceptions of teachers rather than personal experience with teachers. Therefore, the current study was unable to demonstrate the impact of teacher support separately from adult support. Lastly, due to the data restriction, we were unable to construct a robust measure that represents peer support. Unlike the adult support measure that draws from six items, the peer support measure came from one item. Aforementioned, there is no other nationally representative dataset containing cyberbullying victimization and various adult and peer support items to the authors' knowledge, so we recommend adding more cyber victimization and peer support items on the NCVS-SCS or constructing another nationally representative platform data that specify cyber victimization of students.

CONCLUSION

The important thing in human relations is consideration, respect, and concern for others. However, if these concerns and considerations are distorted and appear as violence, no one will want to engage. With the development of technological civilization, many people are changing to a society that places indirect contact over a face-to-face, personal work rather than collaboration, and anonymity rather than naming. As Aristotle said, however, humans are social animals (see Loard, 2013); we seek the meaning of our existence under constant relationships with others. Because of this, violence in relations forces to leave more profound and fatal wounds on the victim. In particular, bullying victimizations during the sensitive adolescence period may place unforgettable scars on the victim's remaining life. This current study empirically demonstrated the possibility that such wounds, *social and psychological harms*, can be alleviated and restored by the support of adults and peers. Moreover, the current study indicates that psychological harm is more prevalent among cyberbullying victims compared to social harm, which warrants intervention and prevention programs to mediate existing psychological harm and reduce future harm by cyberbullying. Even though the percentage of experiencing social harm is relatively lower compared to psychological harm, the presence of social harm also cannot be ignored and warrants intervention and prevention. Based on these findings, we believe that developing new adult- and peer-supporting programs or enhancing existing assisting programs can be vital methods to help distressed students' recovery process, while enhancing knowledge on cyberbullying: prevention and danger. It is people who cause problems, and it is also people who solve the problems. Perhaps being wounded by a person and healed by another person is a way that we live in society. There is growing evidence of the effectiveness of peer supporting programs across the literature (Adickes et al. 2013; Tzani-Pelpelasi et al., 2019. Williford et al., 2012; Yerger & Gehret 2011). The sustainability of such programs, however, needs to be carefully managed with surrounding factors within the school environment and students' characteristics.

NOTES

1. This article originally appreated in *International Journal of Cybersecurity Intelligence & Cybercrime* (IJCIC), 4(1), 2021, pp. 25-45. doi: 10.52306/04010321KNSZ7360. Revised and reprinted with permission.
2. Corresponding author.

REFERENCES

Adickes, J., Worrell, K., Klatt, C., Starks, J., Vosicky, A., & Moser, C. S. (2013). Bullying. *Journal of Occupational Therapy, Schools, and Early Intervention, 6*(1), 1–13. httl://doi.org/10.1080/19411243.2013.771099

Albdour, M., Hong, J., Lewin, L., & Yarandi, H. (2019). The impact of cyberbullying on physical and psychological health of Arab American adolescents. *Journal of Immigrant and Minority Health, 21*, 706–715.

Aristole (2013). *Aristotle's politics*, 2nd ed. (Carnes Lord, Trans.) Chicago, IL: University of Chicago Press (Original work written 350 B.C.E.).

Balakrishnan, V., Khan, S., & Arabnia, H. R. (2020). Improving cyberbullying detection using twitter users' psychological features and machine learning. *Computers & Security, 90*, 101710.

Baldry, A. C., Farrington, D. P., & Sorrentino, A. (2017). School bullying and cyberbullying among boys and girls: Roles and overlap. *Journal of Aggression, Maltreatment & Trauma, 26*(9), 937–951.

Bastiaensens, S., Vandebosch, H., Poels, K., Van Cleemput, K., DeSmet, A., & De Bourdeaudhuij, I. (2014). Cyberbullying on social network sites. An experimental study into bystanders' behavioural intentions to help the victim or reinforce the bully. *Computers in Human Behavior, 31*, 259–271.

Bauman, S., Toomey, R. B., & Walker, J. L. (2013). Associations among bullying, cyberbullying, and suicide in high school students. *Journal of Adolescence, 36*(2), 341–350.

Bonanno, R., & Hymel, S. (2013). Cyber bullying and internalizing difficulties: Above and beyond the impact of traditional forms of bullying. *Journal of Youth Adolescence, 42*, 685–697.

Brewer, G., & Kerslake, J. (2015). Cyberbullying, self-esteem, empathy and loneliness. *Computers in Human Behavior, 48*, 255–260.

Campbell, M. A., Slee, P. T., Spears, B., Butler, D., & Kift, S. (2013). Do cyberbullies suffer too? Cyberbullies' perceptions of the harm they cause to others and to their own mental health. *School Psychology International, 34*(6), 613–629. https://doi.org/10.1177/0143034313479698

Campbell, M., Spears, B., Slee, P., Butler, D., & Kift, S. (2012). Victims' perceptions of traditional and cyberbullying, and the psychosocial correlates of their victimisation. *Emotional and Behavioural Difficulties, 17*(3–4), 389–401.

Cantor, D., & Lynch, J. P. (2000). Self-report surveys as measures of crime and criminal victimization. *Criminal Justice, 4*, 85–138.

Centers for Disease Control and Prevention (2018). Youth risk behavior surveillance—United States, 2017. *Morbidity and Mortality Weekly Report--Surveillance Summaries, 67*(8), 1–478. Retrieved from https://www.cdc.gov/healthyyouth/data/yrbs/pdf/2017/ss6708.pdf

Centers for Disease Control and Prevention (2019). Youth Risk Behavior Surveillance System (YRBSS): 2019 National Youth Risk Behavior Survey Questionnaire. Retrieved from https://www.cdc.gov/healthyyouth/data/yrbs/pdf/2019/2019_YRBS-National-HS-Questionnaire.pdf

Charalampous, K., Demetriou, C., Tricha, L., Ioannou, M., Georgiou, S., Nikiforou, M., & Stavrinides, P. (2018). The effect of parental style on bullying and cyber bullying behaviors and the mediating role of peer attachment relationships: A longitudinal study. *Journal of Adolescence, 64*, 109–123.

Chen, Q., Lo, C., K. M., Zhu, Y., Cheung, A., Chan, K. L., & Ip, P. (2018). Family poly-victimization and cyberbullying among adolescents in a Chinese school sample. *Child Abuse & Neglect, 77*, 180–187.

Cohen, S., & Willis, T. A. (1985). Stress, social support, and the buffering hypothesis. *Psychological Bulletin, 98*(2), 310–357.

Cowie, H. (2011). Peer support as an intervention to counteract school bullying: Listen to the children. *Children & Society, 25*, 287–292.

Cowie, H., & Olafsson, R. (2000). The role of peer support in healing the victims of bullying in a school with high levels of aggression. *School Psychology International, 21*(1), 79–95.

Del Rey, R., Elipe, P., & Ortega-Ruiz, R. (2012). Bullying and cyberbullying: Overlapping and predictive value of the co-occurrence. *Psicothema, 24*(4), 608–613.

Del Rey, R., Mora-Merchán, J. A., Casas, J. A., Ortega-Ruiz, R., & Elipe, P. (2018). 'Asegúrate' program: Effects on cyber-aggression and its risk factors. *Comunicar: Media Education Research Journal, 26*(56), 39–48.

Ditzen, B., & Heinrichs, M. (2014). Psychobiology of social support: The social dimension of stress buffering. *Restorative Neurology and Neuroscience, 32*(1), 149–162.

Erdur-Baker, Ö. (2010). Cyberbullying and its correlation to traditional bullying, gender and frequent and risky usage of internet-mediated communication tools. *New Media & Society, 12*(1), 109–125.

Fazil, M., & Abulaish, M. (2018). A hybrid approach for detecting automated spammers in twitter. *IEEE Transactions on Information Forensics and Security, 13*(11), 2707–2719.

Francisco, S. M., Simão, A. M. V., Ferreira, P. C., & das Dores Martins, M. J. (2015). Cyberbullying: The hidden side of college students. *Computers in Human Behavior, 43*, 167–182.

Fredrick, S. S., & Demaray, M. K. (2018). Peer victimization and suicidal ideation: The role of gender and depression in a school-based sample. *Journal of School Psychology, 67*, 1–15.

Gaffney, H., Ttofi, M. M., & Farrington, D. P. (2019). Evaluating the effectiveness of school-bullying prevention programs: An updated meta-analytical review. *Aggression and Violent Behavior, 45*, 111–133.

Gini, G., & Pozzoli, T. (2009). Association between bullying and psychosomatic problems: A meta-analysis. *Pediatrics, 123*(3), 1059–1065.

Gini, G., & Pozzoli, T. (2013). Bullied children and psychosomatic problems: A meta analysis. *Pediatrics, 132*, 720–729.

Gladden, R. M., Vivolo-Kantor, A. M., Hamburger, M. E., & Lumpkin, C. D. (2014). *Bullying surveillance among youths: Uniform definitions for public health and recommended data elements, version 1.0.* Atlanta, GA; National Center for Injury

Prevention and Control, Centers for Disease Control and Prevention, and U.S. Department of Education.

Glanz, K., & Schwartz, M. D. (2008). Stress, coping, and health behavior. In Karen Glanz, Barbara K. Rimer, and K. Viswanath (Eds.), *Health behavior and health education: Theory, research, and practice*, 4th ed. (pp. 211–236). San Francisco, CA: John Wiley & Sons, Inc.

Goodboy, A. K., & Martin, M. M. (2015). The personality profile of a cyberbully: Examining the Dark Triad. *Computers in Human Behavior, 49*, 1–4.

Google, Inc. (2020). Google scholar. Retrieved from https://scholar.google.com/intl/en/scholar/help.html

Gradinger, P., Strohmeier, D., & Spiel, C. (2009). Traditional bullying and cyber-bullying: Identification of risk groups for adjustment problems. *Zeitschrift für Psychologie/Journal of Psychology, 217*(4), 205–213.

Hard, R. L. (1964, November). Must schools be neutral? *Educational Leadership.* Retrieved from http://www.ascd.org/ASCD/pdf/journals/ed_lead/el_196411_hart.pdf

Hay, C., & Meldrum, R. (2010). Bullying victimization and adolescent self-harm: Testing hypotheses from general strain theory. *Journal of Youth Adolescence, 39*, 446–459.

Hawker, D. S. J., & Boulton, M. J. (2000). Twenty years' research on peer victimization and psychosocial maladjustment: A meta-analytic review of cross-sectional studies. *Journal of Child Psychology and Psychiatry, 41*, 441–455.

Heaney, C. A., & Israel, B. A. (2008). Social networks and social support. In Karen Glanz, Barbara K. Rimer, and K. Viswanath (Eds.) *Health behavior and health education: Theory, research, and practice*, 4th ed. (pp. 189–210). San Francisco, CA: John Wiley & Sons, Inc.

Hellström, L., Beckman, L., & Hagquist, C. (2017). Does the strength of the association between peer victimization and psychosomatic health problems depend on whether bullying or peer aggression is measured? *Child Indicator Research, 10*, 447–459.

Hinduja, S., & Patchin, J. W. (2010). Bullying, cyberbullying, and suicide. *Archives of Suicide Research, 14*(3), 206–221.

Holt, M. K., Vivolo-Kantor, A. M., Polanin, J. R., Holland, K. M., DeGue, S., Matjasko, J. L., et al. (2015). Bullying and suicidal ideation and behaviors: A meta-analysis. *Pediatrics, 135*(2), 496–509. http://dx.doi.org/10.1542/peds.2014-1864

House, J. S. (1981). *Work stress and social support.* Reading, MA: Addison-Wesley.

Inchley, J., Currie,, D., Young, T., Samdal, O., Torsheim, T., Augustson, L., Mathison, D., Aleman-Diaz, A., Molcho, M., Weber, M., & Barnekow, V. (2019). Growing up unequal: Gender and socioeconomic differences in young people's health and well-being. *Health Behaviour in School-aged Children (HBSC) Study: International Report from the 2013/2014 Survey.* Copenhagen, WHO Regional Office for Europe, 2016 (Health Policy for Children and Adolescents, No. 7). Retrieved from http://www.euro.who.int/__data/assets/pdf_file/0003/303438/HSBC-No.7-Growing-up-unequal-Full-Report.pdf?ua=1

Jayaratne, S., & Ches, W. A. (1984). The effects of emotional support on perceived job stress and strain. *Journal of Applied Behavioral Science, 20*(2), 141–153.

Kowalski, R. M., Morgan, C. A., & Limber, S. P. (2012). Traditional bullying as a potential warning sign of cyberbullying. *School Psychology International, 33*(5), 505–519.

Kowalski, R. M., Giumetti, G. W., Schroeder, A. N., & Lattanner, M. R. (2014). Bullying in the digital age: A critical review and meta-analysis of cyberbullying research among youth. *Psychological Bulletin, 140*, 1073–1137.

Kubiszewski, V., Fontaine, R., Potard, C., & Auzoult, L. (2015). Does cyberbullying overlap with school bullying when taking modality of involvement into account? *Computers in Human Behavior, 43*, 49–57.

Kyritsis, D., & Tsakyrakis, S. (2013). Neutrality in the classroom. *International Journal of Constitutional Law, 11*(1), 200–217.

Landoll, R. R., La Greca, A. M., Lai, B. S., Chan, S. F., & Herge, W. M. (2015). Cyber victimization by peers: Prospective associations with adolescent social anxiety and depressive symptoms. *Journal of Adolescence, 42*, 77–86.

Leiner, B. M., Cerf, V. G., Clark, D. D., Kahn, R. E., Kleinrock, L., Lynch, D. C., … & Wolff, S. (2009). A brief history of the internet. *ACM SIGCOMM Computer Communication Review, 39*(5), 22–31.

Lessne, D., & Cidade, M. (2016). Split-half administration of the 2015 school crime supplement to the national crime victimization survey: Methodology report. NCES 2017–004. *National Center for Education Statistics.*

Li, Q. (2006). Cyberbullying in schools: A research of gender differences. *School Psychology International, 27*(2), 157–170.

Li, Q. (2007). New bottle but old wine: A research of cyberbullying in schools. *Computers in Human Behavior, 23*(4), 1777–1791.

Litwiller, B. J., & Brausch, A. M. (2013). Cyber bullying and physical bullying in adolescent suicide: The role of violent behavior and substance use. *Journal of Youth and Adolescence, 42*(5), 675–684.

Menesini, E., & Salmivalli, C. (2017). Bullying in schools: The state of knowledge and effective interventions. *Psychology, Health & Medicine, 22*(sup1), 240–253.

Mishna, F., Cook, C., Gadalla, T., Daciuk, J., & Solomon, S. (2010). Cyber bullying behaviors among middle and high school students. *American Journal of Orthopsychiatry, 80*(3), 362–374.

Mishna, F., Khoury-Kassabri, M., Gadalla, T., & Daciuk, J. (2012). Risk factors for involvement in cyber bullying: Victims, bullies and bully–victims. *Children and Youth Services Review, 34*(1), 63–70.

Mishna, F., Schwan, K. J., Birze, A., Van Wert, M., Lacombe-Duncan, A., McInroy, L., & Attar-Schwartz, S. (2020). Gendered and sexualized bullying and cyber bullying: Spotlighting girls and making boys invisible. *Youth & Society, 52*(3), 403–426.

Mitchell, K. J., Jones, L. M., Turner, H. A., Shattuck, A., & Wolak, J. (2016). The role of technology in peer harassment: Does it amplify harm for youth? *Psychology of Violence, 6*(2), 193–204.

Moss, E. G. (1973). *Illness, immunity, and social interaction.* New York: John Wiley and Sons.

Naylor, P., & Cowie, H. (1999). The effectiveness of peer support systems in challenging school bullying: The perspectives and experiences of teachers and pupils. *Journal of Adolescence, 22*(4), 467–479.

Pabian, S., & Vandebosch, H. (2016). An investigation of short-term longitudinal associations between social anxiety and victimization and perpetration of traditional bullying and cyberbullying. *Journal of Youth and Adolescence, 45*(2), 328–339.

Park, S, M., & Eck, J. E. (2013). Understanding the random effect on victimization distribution: A statistical analysis of random repeat victimizations. *Victims & Offenders, 8*(4), 399–415.

Pozzoli, T., & Gini, G. (2019). Behavior during cyberbullying episodes: Initial validation of a new self-report scale. *Scandinavian Journal of Psychology, 61,* 22–29.

Reijntjes, A., Kamphuis, J. H., Prinzie, P., Boelen, P. A., van der Schoot, M., & Telch, M. J. (2011). Prospective linkages between peer victimization and externalizing problems in children: A meta-analysis. *Aggressive Behavior, 37,* 215–222.

Rosa, H., Pereira, N., Ribeiro, R., Ferreira, P. C., Carvalho, J. P., Oliveira, S., Coheur, L., Paulino, P., Veiga Simão, A. M., & Trancoso, I. (2019). Automatic cyberbullying detection: A systematic review. *Computers in Human Behavior, 93,* 333–345.

Sarason, I. G., & Sarason, B. R. (2009). Social support: Mapping the construct. *Journal of Social and Personal Relationships, 26*(1), 113–120.

Slavin, L. A., & Rainer, K. L. (1990). Gender differences in emotional support and depressive symptoms among adolescents: A prospective analysis. *American Journal of Community Psychology, 18*(3), 407–421.

Slonje, R., & Smith, P. K. (2008). Cyberbullying: Another main type of bullying? *Scandinavian Journal of Psychology, 49*(2), 147–154.

Smith, P. K., Mahdavi, J., Carvalho, M., Fisher, S., Russell, S., & Tippett, N. (2008). Cyberbullying: Its nature and impact in secondary school pupils. *Journal of Child Psychology and Psychiatry, 49*(4), 376–385.

Song, J., & Oh, I. (2018). Factors influencing bystanders' behavioral reactions in cyberbullying situations. *Computers in Human Behavior, 78,* 273–282.

Spears, B., Slee, P., Owens, L., & Johnson, B. (2009). Behind the scenes and screens: Insights into the human dimension of covert and cyberbullying. *Journal of Psychology, 217*(4), 189–196.

Thoits, P. A. (1995). Stress, coping, and social support processes: Where are we? What next? In *Special issue: Forty years of medical sociology: The state of the art and directions for the future.* Edited by Mary L. Fennell. *Journal of Health and Social Behavior* 35 (extra issue): 53–79.

Tokunaga, R. S. (2010). Following you home from school: A critical review and synthesis of research on cyberbullying victimization. *Computers in Human Behavior, 26,* 277–287.

Tsaousis, I. (2016). The relationship of self-esteem to bullying perpetration and peer victimization among schoolchildren and adolescents: A meta-analytic review. *Aggression and Violent Behavior, 31,* 186–199.

Ttofi, M. M., Farrington, D. P., Lösel, F., & Loeber, R. (2011a). Do the victims of school bullies tend to become depressed later in life? A systematic review and meta-analysis of longitudinal studies. *Journal of Aggression, Conflict and Peace Research, 3,* 63–73.

Tzani-Pelpelasi, C., Ioannou, M., Synnott, J., & McDonnell, D. (2019). Peer support at schools: The buddy approach as prevention and intervention strategy for school bullying. *International Journal of Bullying Prevention, 1,* 111–123.

United States Department of Justice. Office of Justice Programs. Bureau of Justice Statistics. (2011). *National crime victimization survey: School crime supplement.* Ann Arbor, MI: Inter-university Consortium for Political and Social Research [distributor], 2013-03-26. https://doi.org/10.3886/ICPSR33081.v1

United States Department of Justice. Office of Justice Programs. Bureau of Justice Statistics. (2013). *National crime victimization survey: School crime supplement.* Ann Arbor, MI: Inter-university Consortium for Political and Social Research [distributor]. 2014-12-2. https://doi.org/10.3886/ICPSR34980.v1

van Dam, D. S., van der Ven, E., Velthorst, E., Selten, J. P., Morgan, C., & de Haan, L. (2012). Childhood bullying and the association with psychosis in non-clinical and clinical samples: A review and meta-analysis. *Psychological Medicine, 42,* 2463–2474.

van Geel, M., Goemans, A., & Vedder, P. H. (2016). The relation between peer victimization and sleeping problems: A meta-analysis. *Sleep Medicine Reviews, 27,* 89–95. http://dx.doi.org/10.1016/j.smrv.2015.05.004

Vieno, A., Gini, G., & Santinello, M. (2011). Different forms of bullying and their association to smoking and drinking behavior in Italian adolescents. *Journal of School Health, 81*(7), 393–399.

Waasdorp, T. E., & Bradshaw, C. P. (2015). The overlap between cyberbullying and traditional bullying. *Journal of Adolescent Health, 56*(5), 483–488.

Wang, J., Ianotti, R. J., Luk, J. W., & Nansel, T. R. (2010) Co-occurrence of victimization from five subtypes of bullying: Physical, verbal, social exclusion, spreading rumors, and cyber. *Journal of Pediatric Psychology, 35*(10), 1103–1112.

Watts, L. K., Wagner, J., Velasquez, B., & Behrens, P. I. (2017). Cyberbullying in higher education: A literature review. *Computers in Human Behavior, 69,* 268–274.

Williford, A., & Depaolis, K. J. (2016). Predictors of cyberbullying intervention among elementary school staff: The moderating effect of staff status. *Psychology in the Schools, 53*(10), 1032–1044. http://doi.org/10/1022/pits.21973.

Winkelmann, R. (2008). *Econometric analysis of count data.* Heidelberg: Springer Science & Business Media

Winkelmann, R. (2008). *Econometric analysis of count data.* Heidelberg: Springer Science & Business Media

Yerger, W., & Gehret, C. (2011). Understanding and dealing with bullying in schools. *The Educational Forum, 75*(4), 315–326. https://doi.org/10.1080 /00131725.2011.602468.

Yeung, R., & Leadbeater, B. (2010). Adults make a difference: The protective effects of parent and teacher emotional support on emotional and behavioral problems of peer-victimized adolescents. *Journal of Community Psychology, 38*(1), 80–98.

Yin, X., Wang, L., Zhang, G., Liang, X., Li, J., Zimmerman, M. A., & Wang, J. (2017). The promotive effects of peer support and active coping on the relationship between bullying victimization and depression among Chinese boarding students. *Psychiatry Research, 256,* 59–65.

Zych, I., Ortega-Ruiz, R., & Del Rey, R. (2015). Scientific research on bullying and cyberbullying: Where have we been and where are we going. *Aggression and Violent Behavior, 24,* 188–198.

Zych, I., Ortega-Ruiz, R., & Rey, R. D. (2015). Systematic review of theoretical studies on bullying and cyberbullying: Facts, knowledge, prevention, and intervention. *Aggression and Violent Behavior, 23,* 1–21.

Chapter 6

Technology-Facilitated Crimes against Children

The Scope of the Problem and Interventions

Ashley L. Boal, Kyung-shick Choi,
Lisa M. Jones, Li Sian Goh, Hannarae
Lee, Pamela MacDougall, and Anthony Petrosino

Technology-facilitated crimes against children have become an increasing area of concern for law enforcement. According to the United Nations (2019), online child sexual exploitation and the sale of children as commodities, both within and across national borders, has grown at an alarming rate. The National Center for Missing and Exploited Children (NCMEC) reports that the CyberTipline, a central repository for online exploitation of children reports, has received more than 57 million reports of potential child exploitation using the internet since its inception in 1998, including more than 18.4 million in 2018 alone (NCMEC, 2020). Most of the reported incidents involve abusive images of children, online enticement, child sex trafficking, and child sexual molestation. In addition to increasing reports of child exploitation, the number of offenders arrested for these crimes has also increased over time. Specifically, arrests for all types of technology-facilitated crimes against children nearly tripled from 2,577 in 2000 to 7,010 in 2006 and continued to increase to 8,144 in 2009 (Wolak et al., 2012a). In fiscal year 2019, the ICAC task force network, a government-funded and collaborative collection of law enforcement personnel tasked with investigating these crimes in the United States, carried out more than 9,500 arrests for various technology-facilitated crimes against children (Office of Juvenile Justice and Delinquency Prevention [OJJDP], 2019).

Rapid technological advancement in communication and information-sharing online enables offenders to connect and more easily share encrypted information with one another. Essentially, these technological developments help to increase efficiency while lowering the potential risks. By utilizing the "Dark Net," these offenders also present increased challenges for law enforcement to stop them. Given these rapid changes in technology, the dynamics of the crimes change quickly, and the global, and often anonymous, context of the internet complicates efforts to apprehend offenders and protect children. Although many aspects of online crimes against children are new, these crimes have a great deal of overlap with traditional, in-person crimes, and law enforcement has also evolved to use new technology to collect evidence and prosecute offenders.

This chapter aims to serve as an introduction to technology-facilitated crimes against children and the ways in which law enforcement responds to these crimes. A review of the research literature in these areas, coupled with publicly available documentation about these crimes and interventions for these crimes, is presented to serve as a foundation for understanding the current state of information related to technology-facilitated crimes against children. Information compiled through this chapter may serve as a useful resource for researchers, policymakers, and practitioners to better understand the current state of the field, notable gaps in the research, and considerations from related fields that might be helpful in thinking about how to address this problem moving forward. We begin this chapter by defining technology-facilitated crimes against children and narrowing our focus to briefly review what is known about technology-facilitated sexual exploitation of children. Next, we provide a description of offender typologies and current approaches to investigating and prosecuting these crimes, both within the United States and globally. We end the chapter with an overview about what is currently known regarding training to support those involved in technology-facilitated crimes investigation.

DEFINING TECHNOLOGY-FACILITATED CRIMES AGAINST CHILDREN

Although there may be stereotypical incidents that come to mind when using the term technology-facilitated crimes against children, defining this category of crimes can be difficult given that a large proportion of all crimes increasingly has some element of online communication. Many crimes against children occur through a mix of both online and offline components, such as attempts at grooming victims and the production of child sexual abuse images (Wolak et al., 2012a). In some cases, the use of new technology to carry out the crime is minor compared to the in-person elements of the crime. An option for clarifying this definitional issue is to outline some distinctions about how much technology involvement is required to label something as a technology-facilitated crime. It may be helpful, for example, to distinguish these crimes by organizing them around two types: (a) crimes in which the child and the offender met online or (b) crimes in which all or the majority of the offense involved online interactions or activities. Although there may be multiple categories of crimes that meet this definition (e.g., internet fraud involving child victims), most of the concerns have focused on crimes involving technology-facilitated child sexual exploitation. Below, we focus our attention on reviewing what is known about the scope and dynamics of three of these categories: technology-facilitated sexual solicitation of children, child sex trafficking, and child sexual abuse image production and distribution.

Scope and Dynamics of Technology-Facilitated Crimes against Children

Online Sexual Solicitation of Children

Public concern about technology-facilitated sexual solicitation of children is often generated by the scenario of a young child being unwittingly solicited by an adult sex offender while communicating on social media or playing online games. However, surveys of youth and law enforcement show the dynamics of most of these crimes to be somewhat at odds with widely held stereotypes (Bergen et al., 2014; Black et al., 2015; Winters et al., 2017; Wolak et al., 2008). In a survey of a national sample of 10- to 17-year-olds, approximately 2%–3% of youth described receiving aggressive or distressing online sexual solicitations (Jones et al., 2012). Most of these youth, however, were older adolescents who had received unwanted sexual solicitations from peers and not adults. Law enforcement and perpetrator-focused data about online sexual solicitation crimes also suggest that older adolescents are the most typical victim type. Studies of online sex crimes against children found that most of the victims were age 12 or older (Katz, 2013; Winters et al., 2017; Wolak et al., 2012a). Additionally, in these cases, most of the arrestees were not online strangers, but acquaintances from face-to-face environments who used technology to further build relationships with youth and then used those relationships to facilitate the crime (Black et al., 2015; Wolak & Finkelhor, 2013; Wolak et al., 2012a). There were few differences in the dynamics comparing online-meeting and face-to-face/online perpetrators: the majority of cases for both involved statutory rape (i.e., non-forcible illegal sexual activity with underage youth) and noncontact offenses such as child pornography production or sexual solicitation of a minor.

Generally, both youth and law enforcement surveys asking about adult online sexual solicitation of youth find that deceptions about identity and sexual motives are not the dominant offender strategies (Black et al., 2015; Winters et al., 2017). Rather, like in-person victimization, the typical victims are teens who are drawn into romantic and sexual relationships with older partners for various reasons, such as feeling flattered and thinking they had found someone who cared about them. Understanding these data helps illuminate discrepancies between stereotypes about these crimes and actual victimization experiences. Further, these findings suggest there is likely considerable overlap and similarity between internet-mediated and more conventional forms of child sexual abuse and statutory rape.

Technology-Facilitated Child Sex Trafficking

Child sex trafficking (or commercial sexual exploitation of children) has received increased attention in recent years by policymakers in the United States. There appears to be an assumption that all forms of formerly offline child sex trafficking and sex tourism have moved into the technology domain in recent years, but this has not been quantified (Latonero et al., 2012) and current data regarding the use of technology to facilitate sex trafficking are sparse. In 2006 law enforcement data for the United States, about a third of sex-trafficking arrests could be connected to some online facilitation (Mitchell et al., 2011). Thus, while child sex trafficking is a concern for those combating technology-facilitated crimes against children, the approach to investigating these crimes may overlap considerably with investigating child sex trafficking in general. Although guesstimates are widely cited, there are no accepted scientifically informed estimates of the extent of sex-trafficking and sex-tourism problems (Finkelhor et al., 2017). In fact, most of the research done in this area has focused on reviewing offender behavior and describing subtypes of technology-facilitated child-trafficking cases (Gallagher et al., 2006; Hargreaves-Cormany et al., 2016; Mitchell et al., 2010). The literature primarily focuses on discussing child trafficking activity that is organized by pimps or facilitators with some distinction between organized commercial activity and more informal facilitator-managed crimes. Technology is often cited as facilitating the exploitation, but some emphasis is also given to the tools and opportunities that technology has created for law enforcement (Latonero et al., 2012).

Production and Distribution of Child Sex Abuse Images

According to estimates based on the volume of reports that ISP and the public make to the CyberTipline, an estimated minimum of 1 million images or videos of child sexual abuse imagery were accessed or exchanged each month globally in 2017 (Bursztein et al., 2019). Another systematic study looking at the peer-to-peer Gnutella network in 2011 observed 776,000 computers worldwide that shared known child sexual exploitation content, including 245,000 in the United States (Wolak et al., 2014). This study also found evidence of 140,000 distinct files (related to the number of distinct different images) having been distributed.

Research that directly measures how child sexual abuse image production crimes are changing over time is limited, and updated studies are needed. The National Juvenile Online Victimization (NJOV) surveys collected data from law enforcement agencies in the United States in 2000, 2006, and 2009 and found that over this timeframe there were increases in cases involving teenage victims and cases involving youth-produced sexual images (Wolak et al., 2011, 2012b). Police also increasingly used technology as a part of proactive tactics to combat child sexual abuse image possession and distribution, and close to 10% of such cases in 2009 identified offline child molesters who probably would not have otherwise been detected. A fourth NJOV study is currently underway that will collect data from 2020. Findings from the NJOV studies demonstrate the rapid changes that occur in these cases over a relatively short period of time and highlight the need for studies that track this volatile environment over shorter time periods in order to best inform law enforcement efforts to respond.

Consequences for Victims of Technology-Facilitated Sexual Exploitation

Given the overlap between online and conventional sexual exploitation, the extremely large body of research confirming the extensive short- and long-term physical and emotional harm of child sexual abuse is relevant to understanding the impact of technology-facilitated sex crimes on children. Child sexual abuse images are generated, for the most part, by acts of adult sexual abuse of children (Seto, 2013). Because of these and other issues, victim harm, treatment, and prevention related to technology-facilitated crimes against children overlap considerably with findings and conclusions about sexual abuse in general. There is a voluminous literature base about the impact of childhood sexual abuse that shows it to be a major risk factor for later social, mental, and physical health problems (see for example reviews: Hailes et al., 2019; Maniglio, 2009; Sanci, 2019). Research has also shown that victims of sex trafficking are at high risk for multiple physical and mental health problems including substance use, sexually transmitted diseases, pregnancy, sexual and physical assault trauma, PTSD, depression, suicidality, aggression, and oppositional behavior (Greenbaum et al., 2015).

However, there may be additional negative impacts for victims related to new technology. Some interviews with survivors and their therapists highlight the aggravating feature of having to constantly worry about the use and resurfacing of images (von Weiler et al., 2010). However, there are methodological and conceptual challenges in trying to disentangle the effects of the image production and circulation from those of the original abuse and its disclosure and management for child victims (Seto, 2013). Given the profound impacts that technology-facilitated crimes against children have on those who are victimized, like all child sexual victimization, a strong understanding of offenders, as well as how to prevent and investigate these crimes, is vital.

TECHNOLOGY-FACILITATED CRIMES AGAINST CHILDREN OFFENDER TYPOLOGY

Understanding offender typologies is important as typologies can be used to better understand offender strategies and motivations, which can be useful when making decisions about investigations, sentencing, treatment, and supervision (Simons, 2015). Therefore, this section provides an overview of different typologies that have been proposed by various scholars.

Typology Based on Behaviors and Motivations of Offenders

Prior to the advent of the internet, Hartman et al. (1984) identified four behavioral types of individuals who collect sexually abusive images of children: closet, isolated, cottage, and commercial collectors. Closet collectors are offenders who secretly collect abusive images of children without contact. Isolated collectors collect abusive images in conjunction with the contact offenses, while cottage collectors share their collection and experiences with like-minded others, primarily for the validation that the act provides. Commercial collectors are those who seek financial benefits from their collection.

Although the typology proposed by Hartman & colleagues (1984) predates the internet era, similar behavior and motivational drives are utilized to describe the offenders who commit technology-facilitated crimes against children. For example, Sullivan & Beech (2004) suggested three types of abusive image collection behaviors. Within their typology, type 1 offenders are those who collect images as a part of a larger pattern of sexual offending, which includes offline meetings for sexual offending, that is, contact offending. Type 2 offenders collect images to feed a developing sexual interest in children, which has potential to escalate and crossover to contact offending.

Type 3 offenders collect images out of curiosity and rarely engage in contacting children for sexual relationships.

Based on the results from a collaborative program between the Australian Institute of Criminology and the Australian High-Tech Crime Centre, Krone (2004) demonstrated a more in-depth version of typology based on the seriousness of three online behavioral factors. The three factors used to inform subtype assignment are (a) the nature of the abuse being either indirect or direct; (b) the level of networking by the offenders; and (c) the level of security offenders employ to avoid detection. Using these factors, Krone (2004) classified nine groups of offenders to examine offenders' progression from the use of abusive online images to the crossover and the commission of offenses. These nine offender groups included browser, private fantasy, trawler, non-secure collector, secure collector, groomer, physical abuser, producer, and distributor. According to Krone (2004), each offender type has a unique pattern of behaviors, with the groomer, physical abuser, and producer being involved in direct abuse as opposed to indirect abuse.

In the 2010s, several scholars provided more behavioral- and motivational-based typologies developed using specific cases (Briggs et al., 2011), interviews with offenders (Webster et al., 2012), and official reports (DeHart, 2017; Tener et al., 2015). Briggs & colleagues (2011) classified internet-initiated sex offenders who used an internet chat room to either tempt or entice an adolescent into a sexual relationship. While studying the internet chat room, the authors identified two subgroups: a contact-driven group and a fantasy-driven group. As the name suggests, a contact-driven group is motivated to engage in offline sexual behavior with minors. In contrast, a fantasy-driven group engages in online cybersex without an expressed intent to meet offline. Webster & colleagues (2012) identified three types of offenders using a qualitative analysis of interviews with 36 men convicted of offenses in the United Kingdom: intimacy seeking, adaptable, and hyper-sexual. Unlike previous typologies, which mainly focused on sexual behavior or motivations of offenders, their classifications focused on not only offenders' motivation but also the use of deception, indecent images of children, and the intention to meet child victims.

While Webster & colleagues (2012) conducted their study based on the interview with offenders, DeHart & colleagues (2017) identified different typologies by utilizing case files involving offender chat logs, email threads, and social networking posts gathered from state and local ICAC task forces. From a sample of 200 offenders, the study categorized the offenders into four groups: cybersex-only offenders, schedulers, cybersex/schedulers, and buyers. According to the authors (2017), cybersex-only offenders engaged in online abuse only (e.g., prolonged online interactions, sought sexually explicit photos), while schedulers, cybersex/schedulers, and buyers engaged in or planned to engage in direct, in-person abuse. The offender characteristics of each category (e.g., demographic information, common behaviors) were also introduced.

From 75 reports made by law enforcement officers, Tener et al. (2015) present 4 groups of offenders who utilize online communications to commit sex crimes against children: the expert, the cynical, the affection-focused, and the sex-focused. Each category of offenders is characterized by specific patterns demonstrated in their online communications, offline and online identity, relationship dynamics with the victims, and level of sex crime expertise. By utilizing the official reports, the previous criminal history of similar cases and the victim-offender relationship information played a key role demonstrating the typology.

Even though there are numerous ways that scholars have proposed to classify and understand the characteristics of online child sex offenders, many studies contain, either in part or in entirety, four criteria to delineate offenders into subgroups: (a) curiosity and impulse-based without physical contact; (b) fulfillment of sexual fantasies without contact; (c) grooming and facilitation of the contact; and (d) production and distribution of abusive images for the financial gain.

Examining the Criteria Commonly Used in Offender Typologies

There is always a first time for everything. A person may access abusive images of children out of curiosity or impulsivity. If the action stops there, and he or she reports the act to authorities, that action may not even qualify as one indicative of an online child sex offense. If the act persists even sporadically, and a person saves the file, however, they may be eligible to be included in an online child sex offenders' typology. For example, Krone's (2004) browser type who responded to spam or accidentally hit on suspected site material and knowingly saved the file would qualify for this criterion, along with Sullivan & Beech's (2004) type 3 offenders. Because most of the typologies are based on interviews of offenders and law enforcement officers or reliant on secondary data from law enforcement agencies, not all the introduced typologies described in the above section contain the first criterion.

However, with the exception of the typologies described by Webster et al. (2012) and Tener et al. (2015), all of the typologies include the second and third criteria (i.e., fulfillment of sexual fantasy without contact and the grooming and facilitation of the contact). Those two typologies specifically targeted either online groomers or those convicted of internet-related child sexual exploitation crimes. Thus, they did not include the fantasy-driven offenders who do not engage in physical contact. For the second criterion, Krone's

(2004) private fantasy, trawler, non-secure collector, and secure collector and Briggs & colleagues' (2011) subgroup classification of a fantasy-driven group would qualify for the fulfillment of sexual fantasies without contact, as well as the cybersex offender group of DeHart & colleagues' (2017) study. Due to the seriousness of the act and the impact on children, all of the above typologies included grooming behaviors or facilitation of physical contact as part of their classification.

The commercial aspects have also been noted in various typologies separately (Krone, 2004) or in conjunction with other typologies (Clevenger et al., 2016). Interestingly, Clevenger et al. (2016) explored differences among those who possessed child pornography, those who attempted or committed an offense of sexually exploiting a minor, and those who produced or distributed child pornography using the internet. Their findings indicate the differences among the three groups, which include but are not limited to the level of self-control, substance abuse, and history of violence. According to their findings, distributors and producers have the least amount of self-control compared to other groups. They were also more likely to have substance abuse issues and a history of violence compared to those who attempted or committed an offense of sexually exploiting a minor (Clevenger et al., 2016).

Other Typologies

While many scholars articulated various typologies based on the behavioral characteristics of offenders, other scholars classify offenders based on how offenders utilize the internet. Alexy et al. (2005) suggested three behavioral uses of the internet by online sex offenders: traders, travelers, and trader-travelers. Traders are those who use the internet to supply the market with abusive images of children through collections and trafficking. Travelers are those who use the internet to lure children into an offline sexual relationship. Trader-travelers are those who use the internet for the collection and distribution of abusive images while manipulating children for the sexual relationship.

While the typology created by Alexy et al. (2005) focused on both the use of the internet and the intention of offenders, Beech et al. (2008) placed greater emphasis on the different uses of the internet and proposed three groups based on reviews of the literature up to 2006. Those three groups are (a) using the internet as a dissemination tool of sexually abusive images of children for personal and/or commercial reasons; (b) using the internet as a communication tool with other individuals who have a sexual interest in children; and (c) using the internet as a tool to maintain and develop online pedophilic networks.

This section covered a voluminous literature base and intended to provide an overview on the vast range of typologies available within the field.

Different authors developed different typologies based on distinct samples and collected data on crime types in different periods. Because this is an evolving area of study, determining the most valuable typology is not yet possible and future research is needed to examine the utility of these typologies in guiding successful investigations and interventions.

INTERVENTIONS FOR TECHNOLOGY-FACILITATED CRIMES AGAINST CHILDREN

In efforts to prevent further technology-facilitated crimes against children and to identify and prosecute offenders, various intervention approaches have emerged. These approaches include those at global and national levels. Additionally, private organizations have joined the efforts to address the issue of technology-facilitated crimes against children. These interventions seek to provide those involved in this field with a deeper understanding of the issue, as well as the tools and expertise needed to prevent victimization and identify and prosecute offenders when victimization has occurred. Thus, the following section covers international, domestic (United States), and private approaches from the past to the current.

International Approaches

Historically, laws do not consider children as the bearers of rights who require legal protection. Over the course of the last century, however, many countries have recognized children as either a deserving party or a special protection party for legal codes. Furthermore, several international guidance documents require countries to implement strategies to protect children from abuse and exploitation while engaging in international cooperation in the investigation and prosecution of crimes against children (United Nations, 2015). For example, the United Nations Convention on the Rights of the Child (CRC), a nearly universally ratified human rights treaty, sets the minimum protection standard of harmful influences, abuse, and exploitation of children (United Nations, 1989, 2015).

While the CRC sets the standard, in 2002, the Optional Protocol to the Convention on the Rights of the Child on the Sale of Children, Child Prostitution, and Child Pornography (OPSC) emphasized the importance of adopting and implementing criminal legislation on child sexual abuse and exploitation. This resolution requires countries that have ratified or acceded the OPSC to not only implement criminal code for crimes but also establish criminal, civil, or administrative accountability of legal persons with regard to child sexual abuse and exploitation (United Nations, 2002).

In addition to the CRC and the OPSC, the United Nations Office on Drugs and Crime's (UNODC) Convention Against Transitional Organized Crime considers penal matters and a range of provisions concerning international cooperation against transnational organized crime, including the use of information and communication technology (UNODC, 2003). The United Nations Economic and Social Council also adopted the Guidelines on Justice in Matters involving Child Victims and Witnesses of Crime (United Nations, 2015) to ensure full respect for the rights of child victims and witnesses of crime. The ramifications of these international approaches to national legal implementations, however, vary among countries.

For example, the UNODC study (2013) on cybercrime indicated that while 80% of countries in Europe report sufficient criminalization of cybercrime acts, 60% of countries in other regions of the world report insufficiency of criminal code regarding cybercrime. The issue is prevailing in the case of the production of child sexual abuse material. Many countries criminalized the crime; however, there is no gold standard on the definition of the term child, and the elements of the crime are not concrete (UNODC, 2013). In the United States, the legal term of child or minor varies by state between 16 and 18. According to Beaulieu (2008), each country's definition of child or minor in the case of sexual crime (i.e., the age of consent) varies from 13 years (Japan and Spain) to 18 years (El Salvador and Egypt). The elements of crime also suffer the same definitional issue raging from kissing to sexual intercourse (Beaulieu, 2008). Furthermore, because many technology-facilitated crimes against children overlap with existing crimes (i.e., trafficking, cyber-grooming, cyber-solicitation, cyber-stalking, cyber-harassment, and exposure to harmful content), many countries apply more general criminal offenses rather than implementing cyber-specific criminal laws.

There is also an international task force composed of a select cadre of 53 online child sexual exploitation investigators and law enforcement experts representing 48 countries. This task force is known as the Violent Crimes against Children International Task Force (VCACITF), which was formerly known as the Innocent Images International Task Force (FBI, 2019). The VCACITF serves as the largest task force of its kind in the world and is tasked with formulating and delivering a dynamic global response to online child exploitation. This coalition approach enables the task force to coordinate and operate strategically through the extensive use of liaison and operational support (FBI, 2019).

U.S. Approaches

Within the United States, the ICAC task force program, the Federal Bureau of Investigation (FBI), and NCMEC jointly collaborate to identify, investigate, prosecute, and prevent crimes against children online. The ICAC task force program, which is funded by the OJJDP within the United States Department of Justice (USDOJ), has funded ICAC task forces since the late 1990s. This funding stream represents a significant investment over the past two decades. The OJJDP currently supports 61 task forces across the United States representing over 4,500 federal, state, and local law enforcement and prosecutorial agencies focused on investigating and prosecuting persons involved in cybercrimes against children (OJJDP, 2019).

In general, the ICAC task forces and their affiliates initiate their investigation when the task forces receive complaints of technology-facilitated crimes against children through CyberTipline reports. The CyberTipline was created by the NCMEC, which is a private, non-profit organization designated by Congress to serve as a national clearinghouse on issues related to missing and exploited children and works in cooperation with the USDOJ and other federal, state, and local law enforcement agencies, as well as education and social service agencies, families, and the public (USDOJ, 2016).

The ICAC task force network has contributed to numerous investigations into, and arrests of, technology-facilitated crimes against children perpetrators. According to the USDOJ's 2016 report to Congress regarding child exploitation prevention and interdiction, there were a total of 344,801 complaints filed between the fiscal years of 2010 and 2015 across all ICAC task forces. Among the lead agencies for the task forces, ten agencies filed more than 10,000 complaints of potential technology-facilitated child sexual abuse during the six-year period examined. The highest number of complaints was filed within the purview of the California-Los Angeles Police Department (15,208), followed by Ohio-Cuyahoga County Prosecutor's office (13,772), Pennsylvania-Delaware County District Attorney's Office (13,613), Michigan-Michigan State Police (11,423), Hawaii-Hawaii Department of Attorney General (11,176), and New York-State Police (11,102).

Once a complaint is filed through the CyberTipline, NCMEC staff review the case, analyze the content, add relevant publicly available information, and make the report available to law enforcement agencies for independent review and possible investigation (USDOJ, 2016). In fiscal year 2019, the ICAC task force network carried out more than 81,000 investigations (OJJDP, 2019). According to Mitchell and Boyd (2014), who conducted a survey of 144 investigators from ICAC task forces and affiliate agencies, the majority of respondents initiated investigations using the manual and human-centric nature of using technological tools, as opposed to more automated approaches. For instance, investigators start their investigation by tracking known websites such as online classifieds, niche websites, and search engines. They also monitor specific characteristics of websites or advertisements that fit the characteristics of a targeted crime such as using specific photos or buzzwords.

Because the perpetrators of technology-facilitated child sexual exploitation do not solely rely on one type of technology, investigators also utilize a variety of different technologies to identify the victim or the perpetrator. Investigators inspect a wide range of everyday communication platforms such as social networking sites, instant messaging, email, SMS or text messaging, and underground communication channels like the Dark Net. Even though it was not the case for the majority, some investigators initiate their examination using more sophisticated technologies like face recognition programs (Mitchell & Boyd, 2014).

On top of the initial investigation, ICAC task forces and their affiliates also perform forensic examinations. Between the years of 2010 and 2014, ICAC investigators in all 50 states performed forensic examinations on 253,778 cases (USDOJ, 2016) and in fiscal year 2019 alone the ICAC task force network carried out more 85,700 forensic exams (OJJDP, 2019). Investigators also conducted in-person interviews with victims when it was necessary. According to Roby and Vincent (2017) the majority of the children and adolescents who have been exploited in commercial sex acts have experienced prior abuse, neglect, or other forms of trauma. Therefore, investigators are also trained to work with the victims through various training opportunities, often provided by non-profit organizations.

After investigations by each agency, a total of 41,851 arrests were made between 2010 and 2015 and in fiscal year 2019 the ICAC task force network carried out more than 9,500 arrests (OJJDP, 2019). Once an arrest is made, ICAC task forces can refer these cases for further investigation to their state legal system or to the United States Attorneys' Offices for prosecutions. Recently, the coordinated operation known as *Broken Heart* resulted in the arrest of more than 2,300 suspected online child sex offenders between March and May in 2018, and more than 1,700 suspected online child sex offenders between April and May in 2019. According to the USDOJ (2018, 2019), the operation targeted suspects who

- produce, distribute, receive, and possess child pornography;
- engage in online enticement of children for sexual purposes;
- engage in the sex trafficking of children; or
- travel across state lines or to foreign countries and sexually abuse children.

During the two iterations of this operation, the ICAC task forces investigated more than 25,200 and 18,500 complaints, respectively. Considering the highest number of filed complaints between 2010 and 2015 was 86,390 complaints in 2015, the *Broken Heart* operation also represents a drastic increase in the use of the CyberTipline and a higher number of arrests within a short time frame of the operation periods.

Private Sector Approaches

Given that regulating the flow of content on the internet is impractical to any government, assistance from the private sector is critical to combat technology-facilitated child sexual exploitation. In order to offend, these perpetrators require internet access to commit any sort of crime involving a child. Therefore, participation of internet service providers (ISP) in prevention and regulation approaches is crucial. Though several countries, including the United States, mandate ISPs to report any identified sites that contain child sexual abuse materials to the police within a reasonable period of time, many countries do not have the policies that help to regulate ISPs' behavior (UNODC, 2015). The UNODC (2015) also revealed that the ISP industry itself is moving toward drafting a formal code of conduct that requires members to refrain from "knowingly accepting illegal content on their sites and to expediently remove content when they are alerted to its existence" (p.50).

Other private sector organizations also willingly install specific types of programs that aim to disrupt the spread of known child sexual abuse images online, such as PhotoDNA technology. Microsoft donated PhotoDNA technology to help online service providers and others disrupt the spread of known child sexual abuse images online in 2009 (USDOJ, 2016). The technology works by creating a unique signature, like a fingerprint, for a digital photograph. Once a signature, also known as a hash, is created, the signature will contain the essential characteristics of the image. Generally, a hash can be altered once a simple change like resizing of the file occurs. The hash created by PhotoDNA, however, can consistently match the signature across extensive datasets regardless of alternations. Currently, NCMEC has the legal rights to sublicense the technology for free to domestic and foreign email service providers who are interested in taking proactive steps to identify and eliminate child pornography from their servers.

In addition, there are several international coalitions of private sector partners that aim to disrupt and dismantle technology-facilitated child sexual exploitation. The International Center for Missing and Exploited Children's (ICMEC) Technology Collections is a voluntary collaboration of nine major internet companies in a bid to develop and execute plans for technology-based solutions to identify, disrupt, and possibly dismantle child exploitation criminal enterprises (UNODC, 2015). Similarly, ICMEC's Financial Coalitions against Child Sexual Exploitation (2020) consists of numerous leading banks, credit card companies, electronic payment networks, third-party payment companies, and internet service companies to identify, disrupt, and curb the economics of commercial child sexual abuse materials. Furthermore, according to the UNODC (2015), many private sector organizations implemented a wide range of internal policies and external obligations concerning domestic and foreign law enforcement data requests. For instance, to protect the privacy of consumers while cooperating with investigations, most of the major social media companies enable public access to law enforcement guidelines, which specify procedures to request information regarding a target of the investigation (Choi, 2015).

TRAINING TO SUPPORT THE INVESTIGATION AND PROSECUTION OF TECHNOLOGY-FACILITATED CRIMES AGAINST CHILDREN

Given the frequency and impact of technology-facilitated crimes against children, investigating these crimes has been, and continues to be, a great area of focus for law enforcement. However, investigating technology-facilitated crimes against children can present unique challenges. For example, although personal victimization (occurring offline) presents its own challenges, police usually have a single event, a perpetrator and victim in a unique time and space to investigate, discrete evidentiary clues to assess, and training in traditional law enforcement strategies that can be used to pursue the perpetrator. In the case of technology-facilitated crimes against children, the perpetrators can "hide" in cyberspace with their identity disguised, can be located anywhere in the world, can victimize hundreds of youth simultaneously and the "cyber clues" represent a different kind of evidence for which traditional law enforcement may not have training or experience (Wolak et al., 2006). These challenges can be compounded when law enforcement agencies have limited resources and technical capacity as investigators work to keep up with new means of offending. The complexity of these cases necessitates high-quality, ongoing training to ensure investigators have the knowledge, skills, and resources required to conduct thorough and appropriate investigations.

One way to support the delivery of training for technology-facilitated crimes against children investigators within the United States is through the ICAC task force program. In addition to funding the task forces, this funding stream also provides resources and access to relevant training for task force affiliates. Since the ICAC program began in 1998, over 732,000 law enforcement officers, prosecutors, and other professionals have received training related to technology-facilitated crimes against children (OJJDP, 2019). In fiscal year 2019 alone, more than 39,570 law enforcement personnel, 3,770 prosecutors, and 13,120 other professionals received training through the ICAC program (OJJDP, 2019). Although the ICAC task force program provides training to many individuals, training may also occur through other channels such as other government-funded training programs (e.g., grant-funded training on internet crime prevention), private organizations, or universities or technical schools.

Although training on the investigation and prosecution of technology-facilitated crimes against children is crucial to ensure law enforcement have the required knowledge and skills to be successful and it is clear that training is currently being delivered (e.g., through the ICAC task force program), very little is currently known about what training entails or the utility of training activities. Given the scarcity of information on this topic, this section aims to compile what is currently known about training for law enforcement investigating these crimes, as well as information from the broader learning literature to unpack what high-quality training in this area might look like. Because little is known about training content or quality, this section does not draw conclusions about the quality or impact of training activities, nor how training content aligns with information about offender typologies. However, this section provides an overview of what is known that may be a helpful starting point for researchers interested in studying training for technology-facilitated crimes against children investigators or training developers interested in creating content to support this field.

Technology-facilitated Crimes against Children Training

Training for law enforcement around technology-facilitated crimes against children is important due to the complex nature of investigating and prosecuting these types of crime, but little is known about the content or quality of these trainings. Like all law enforcement training, training for technology-facilitated crimes against children investigators is sensitive. Publicly sharing the strategies and techniques to investigate these crimes may provide offenders with information that allows them to evade law enforcement or develop new ways to exploit children without detection. Given the sensitive nature of this topic and the significant implications of making training content public, it is not surprising that there is little information publicly available about the content of these trainings.

Despite the limited availability of information on training content, several publicly available resources are helpful to better understand the range of topics that may be covered in these trainings. For example, a conference paper focused on technology-facilitated crimes against children in the state of Florida sheds some light on the types of information that were shared within one training offered to law enforcement in the state. Topics included providing a basic understanding of investigation competencies; an introduction to technology-facilitated crimes against children and child exploitation investigation; an orientation to computer technology, including hardware and software; and an overview of legal issues surrounding investigations such as judicial subpoenas, search warrants, and recent court rulings (Breeden & Mulholland, 2006). Additionally, the OJJDP currently funds five organizations to provide training and technical assistance to ICAC task forces and examining the description of their offerings highlights major topics covered in training for task force participants. These training providers focus on topics such as investigative techniques, undercover operations, use of different technological platforms and approaches (e.g., social-networking sites, cell phone technology, peer-to-peer file sharing), other issues related to missing and exploited children, and mental health and wellness for those working in the field (OJJDP, 2019).

Given the sensitivity of these topics and limited availability of information on training content, the lack of information on the quality and impacts of these trainings is not unsurprising. However, the limited research on the impact of training for individuals working on these cases suggests that training matters. For example, a 2011 survey of 59 ICAC task forces across the United States found that the number of trained personnel in each task force was positively correlated with the number of computer forensic examinations conducted by the task force in the past year (Marcum & Higgins, 2011). Training may be especially important when the characteristics of those receiving training are considered. Holt & Bossler (2012) conducted a study to identify the characteristics of law enforcement personnel most interested in cybercrime training broadly. This study did not identify any demographic correlates to officer interest in cybercrime training and found that previous computer training was not associated with interest in future cybercrime training. Rather, law enforcement personnel most likely to indicate interest in cybercrime training showed attitudinal differences from the survey population: they had higher self-reported computer skills than their colleagues and believed that cybercrime investigations were valuable (Holt & Bossler, 2012). Thus, although those who engage in training may be interested in the topic, they may not bring expertise from formal training, which may contribute to diverse levels of expertise that must be addressed in training environments.

Learning from Related Fields to Develop High-Quality Training Experiences

In the face of such limited research directly examining the content, quality, and impact of training related to technology-facilitated crimes against children, it is helpful to draw on insights from related fields and domains to identify topics that should be covered and strategies that should be utilized in high-quality trainings. The purpose of this section is to provide those who develop and deliver training with insight into how to best design trainings to support those who investigate these crimes.

Training Topics

Literature suggests that training for law enforcement should focus on useful tactics and digital forensics, with an emphasis on strategies to investigate offenders who present the greatest danger to children. Given how quickly technology evolves it is clear that any training content for technology-facilitated crimes against children investigators must be constantly updated and investigators must engage in ongoing training experiences to stay up to date (Mitchell et al., 2010). Valuable non-technical training topics may include an introduction to technology-facilitated crimes against children and offender characteristics and/or typologies, legal issues related to these types of investigations, and specific investigative strategies to investigate these crimes. In addition to research aimed at categorizing offenders discussed previously, researchers have also attempted to examine the constellation of offender and crime characteristics, coupled with online behaviors, to provide law enforcement with guidance to prioritize cases (Dwyer et al., 2016). In particular, Dwyer & colleagues (2016) argue that cases should be prioritized when they involve the (a) production rather than possession/distribution of child pornography, (b) online luring for the purpose of meeting the minor versus offenders who exclusively seek online sexual contact, and (c) cases involving offenders with a known history of committing contact sexual offenses against children rather than those with no known history. Learning to prioritize cases that cause the most harm may be especially important given that the scale of technology-facilitated crimes against children and number of offenders far exceeds the amount of resources law enforcement authorities are able to expend on investigations. Further, different investigative strategies might be more appropriate for specific offender subgroups. For example, one common strategy that may be appropriate in some situations involves law enforcement personnel posing as juveniles online. Mitchell & colleagues' (2005) study of such investigations suggested that this was an effective strategy in terms of apprehension: arrests following such tactics represented 25% of all technology-facilitated crimes against children arrests and produced high rates of guilty pleas. In addition, such tactics allowed law enforcement to intervene before a youth was victimized. Legal issues that investigators should be aware of include topics such as the applicable laws surrounding rules of evidence for computer-generated and computer-stored information, the applicable legal challenges to obtaining and utilizing cyber data, and privacy and liability issues relating to cloud computing and suspension of networked computing services respectively (Brown, 2015).

In considering necessary training regarding digital forensics, Brown (2015) provides an overview of the technical competencies and digital forensic skills required to effectively investigate online crime, much of which is applicable to technology-facilitated crimes against children. In addition to possessing hard skills such as the ability to conduct research, investigators should also possess an awareness of developments in information security, maintain strict compliance with established processes for demonstrating chain of custody when handling electronically stored information, have a practical understanding of the Open System Interconnection model, and comprehend the function of communication technologies in the storage and transmission of data. In addition, they should be able to conduct forensic imaging; structured, unstructured, and semi-structured data analysis; reverse engineering; programming and scripting; virtualization; and technical reporting. Personnel should also be knowledgeable about hardware and file systems.

Beyond the technical training topics to support this work, the vast literature on offender typologies may be valuable to help law enforcement understand offender behaviors and motivations, as well as prioritize cases. Understanding which offenders fit into specific typologies may facilitate law enforcement understanding about which offenders are most likely to carry out in-person abuse or to share child abuse imagery with a large volume of individuals. Given the incredible volume of technology-facilitated crimes against children tips and cases, being able to evaluate which offenders are likely to cause the greatest harm is vital for determining which investigations are most urgent.

Finally, there has been some discussion in the literature regarding secondary traumatic stress among personnel working in the field of technology-facilitated crimes against children. Bourke & Craun (2014) suggest that because seeing an abused child ranks as one of the top stressors found in policing. Investigators for these cases are particularly at risk for negative outcomes associated with working in this field if they are regularly exposed to disturbing images of child sexual exploitation. A survey of 600 ICAC investigators found that about one-quarter of respondents faced significant secondary traumatic stress, although slightly over half of respondents seemed to cope well, citing strong social support as an important coping mechanism (Bourke & Craun, 2014). These findings suggest that officer wellness should be an integral component of training for these investigators

Approach to Training

Regardless of the training topic, engaging adult learners may require different strategies than those commonly used with children. Advanced by Malcolm Knowles in the 1970s and 1980s, the theory of andragogy proposes five assumptions vital to adult learning (Knowles, 1984). First, adult learners should play a prominent role in directing their own learning. Second, adult learners bring personal and professional experience with them that should be used throughout the learning experience. Third, instruction should be relevant to their current experience. Fourth, adult learners should focus on solving problems rather than just absorbing content. Fifth, adult learners should be motivated to learn by internal rather than external factors. These assumptions are supported by neuroscientific findings of neural networks related to memory and cognition (Hagen & Park, 2016) and are commonly implemented across disciplines such as criminal justice, medicine, education, and management (Bedi, 2004; Birzer, 2004; Bolton, 2006; Chan, 2010; Forrest & Peterson, 2006). Given adult learners' preference for active involvement in the learning process (Caffarella & Daffron, 2013), this offers direct implications for training related to technology-facilitated crimes against children, in that trainings that are more hands-on and self-directed are preferable. In addition to the implications of adult learning principles, insights from digital forensics instruction in university settings are helpful to further understand the most effective approaches when teaching digital forensics to adult learners. Studies evaluating digital forensics courses in university settings suggest that introducing students to useful resources, ensuring content is current, fostering collaborative learning environments through group exercises, and utilizing problem-based assignments focused on real-world problems are valuable for adult learners navigating digital forensics content (Kessler & Haggerty, 2010).

CONCLUSION

Since the mid-1990s, changing technology has posed challenges for law enforcement agencies requiring them to confront situations not anticipated in existing criminal statutes, master new technical capabilities, and develop new investigative techniques. Child sexual abuse image possession and transmission is considered criminal in most countries but not everywhere globally. Many countries have had to enact new statutes to cover some of the digital solicitation and communication behaviors that are key elements when technology is used in sexual exploitation (Bulger et al., 2017). Legislators in the United States have created new statutes that encompass technology-facilitated offenses, including enhanced penalties, and chartered a clearinghouse for reports about technology-facilitated crimes against children—the CyberTipline operated by the NCMEC. Additionally, ICAC task forces, developed to identify, investigate, and prosecute online offenders, grew from 30 agencies to 61 between 2000 and 2015, with over 4,500 affiliated federal, state, and local law enforcement and prosecutorial agencies to date (OJJDP, 2019). ICAC task forces are now present in all 50 states (USDOJ, 2007).

Beyond the policy shifts that have occurred, considerable efforts characterized by international and private-public agency collaboration have also been undertaken. These efforts have focused on categorizing sexual abuse image materials and offender activities and examining their relevance to legal issues of criminality and dangerousness (Quayle, 2008; Seto, 2013; Taylor et al., 2001). There is an international review of legal responses with recommendations for harmonization of approaches (Akdeniz, 2016). The most widely implemented strategies involve laws and websites that promote the reporting of images when detected by ISPs and other users, combined with intensive policing, prosecution, and publicity to deter users.

A growing research base on technology-facilitated crimes against children has been developing over this time as well, but definitional ambiguity and rapid changes in both the nature of the crimes and policymakers' attention to them have limited the impact of existing research on policy and investigation practices. Although strategies to prevent and address in-person sexual abuse of children can be used to inform the investigation and prosecution of technology-facilitated crimes against children, new policies and investigation strategies are also needed to reduce and prevent accessing and disseminating of child sexual abuse images (Wortley & Smallbone, 2012).

The shifting nature of online child exploitation cases and the challenge they pose to investigative resources make it particularly important to monitor trends and developments in the nature of offenses investigated and methods used by offenders. Yet, the cost of failing to improve the response to these crimes is even higher. The cost of child sexual exploitation is substantial (Letourneau et al., 2018) and ineffective responses impose additional costs when untrained and underresourced investigators exacerbate victims' distress through repeated or insensitive interviewing, or poor investigative practices fail to bring perpetrators to justice and thus endanger other children. Taken together, the need for continued and current information driven by sound research methodology is critical for informing existing training opportunities for law enforcement and others working with this highly vulnerable population.

Increasing numbers of law enforcement personnel have received training to investigate technology-facilitated child sexual exploitation crimes (OJJDP, 2019). Unfortunately, resource constraints among law enforcement personnel drive an ongoing and unmet training and technical assistance need to combat technology-facilitated crimes against children. In a recent law enforcement survey, funding and manpower constraints were cited as limiting access to training to address these pressing issues (International Association of Chiefs of Police, 2011).

Due to an exponential rate of evolution in technology and the rise of technological availability to children, efforts to effectively and comprehensively combat technology-facilitated crimes against children will require a collective approach. As Merdian, Perkins, Webster, and McCashin (2019) suggested, it is also critical to invest in resources that can help to address the knowledge gaps that are currently limiting the ability for individuals associated with online or transnational child sexual abuse. The process of combating such crimes requires the active involvement of children, families, communities, governments, members of civil society, and private sectors. As we learn more about technology-facilitated crimes against children and how to investigate and prevent these crimes, training for law enforcement is critical. Developing and sustaining high-quality training that is up to date and prepares law enforcement to identify, investigate, and prosecute perpetrators requires ongoing monitoring and feedback, making evaluation of these trainings a key component in ensuring law enforcement receive the knowledge and skills they need to be successful.

REFERENCES

Akdeniz, Y. (2016). *Internet child pornography and the law: National and international responses*. London: Routledge.

Alexy, E. M., Burgess, A. W., & Baker, T. (2005). Internet offenders: Traders, travelers, and combination of trader-travelers. *Journal of Interpersonal Violence, 20*, 804–812. https://doi.org/10.1177/0886260505276091

Beaulieu, C. (2008). *Strengthening laws addressing child sexual exploitation: A practical guide*. https://www.ecpat.org/wp-content/uploads/2016/04/Legal_Instrument_En_Final.pdf

Bedi, A. (2004). An andragogical approach to teaching styles. *Education for Primary Care, 15*, 93–108.

Beech, A. R., Elliott, I. A., Birgden, A., & Findlater, D. (2008). The Internet and child sexual offending: A criminological review. *Aggression and Violent Behavior, 13*, 215–228. https://doi.org/10.1016/j.avb.2008.03.007

Bergen, E., Davidson, J., Schulz, A., Schuhmann, P., Johansson, A., Santtila, P., & Jern, P. (2014). The effects of using identity deception and suggesting secrecy on the outcomes of adult-adult and adult-child or -adolescent online sexual interactions. *Victims & Offenders, 9*(3), 276–298. https://doi.org/10.1080/15564886.2013.873750

Birzer, M. L. (2004). The theory of andragogy applied to police training. *Policing: An International Journal of Police Strategies and Management, 26*(1), 29–42. https://doi.org/10.1108/13639510310460288

Black, P. J., Wollis, M., Woodworth, M., & Hancock, J. T. (2015). A linguistic analysis of grooming strategies of online child sex offenders: Implications for our understanding of predatory sexual behavior in an increasingly computer-mediated world. *Child Abuse & Neglect, 44*, 140–149. https://doi.org/10.1016/j.chiabu.2014.12.004

Bolton, F. C. (2006). Rubrics and adult learners: Andragogy and assessment. *Assessment Update, 18*(3), 5–6.

Bourke, M. L., & Craun, S. W. (2014). Secondary traumatic stress among internet crimes against children task force personnel: Impact, risk factors, and coping strategies. *Sexual Abuse, 26*(6), 586–609. https://doi.org/10.1177/1079063213509411

Breeden, B., & Mulholland, J. (2006, April). *Investigating 'Internet Crimes Against Children' (ICAC) cases in the state of Florida* [Paper presentation]. Proceedings of the 2006 ACM Symposium on Applied Computing (pp. 288–292). https://doi.org/10.1145/1141277.1141345

Briggs, P., Simon, W. T., & Simonsen, S. (2011). An exploratory study of internet-initiated sexual offenses and the chat room sex offender: Has the internet enabled a new typology of sex offender? *Sexual Abuse: A Journal of Research and Treatment, 23*(1), 72–91. https://doi.org/10.1177/1079063210384275

Brown, C. S. (2015). Investigating and prosecuting cyber crime: Forensic dependencies and barriers to justice. *International Journal of Cyber Criminology, 9*(1), 55–119. https://doi.org/10.5281/zenodo.22387

Bulger, M., Burton, P., O'Neill, B., & Staksrud, E. (2017). Where policy and practice collide: Comparing United States, South African and European Union approaches to protecting children online. *New Media & Society, 19*(5), 750–764.

Bursztein, E., Bright, T., DeLaune, M., Elifff, D. M., Hsu, N., Olson, L., Shehan, J., Thakur, M., & Thomas, K. (2019, May 13–17). *Rethinking the detection of child sexual abuse imagery on the Internet* [Paper presentation]. The World Wide Web Conference, San Francisco, CA, United States. https://doi.org/10.1145/3308558.3313482

Caffarella, R. S., & Daffron, S. R. (2013). *Planning programs for adult learners: A practical guide.* John Wiley & Sons.

Chan, S. (2010). Applications of andragogy in multi-disciplined teaching and learning. *Journal of Adult Education, 39*(2), 25–35.

Choi, K. S. (2015). *Cybercriminology and digital investigation.* LFB Scholarly Publishing.

Clevenger, S. L., Navarro, J. N., & Jasinski, J. L. (2016). A matter of low self-control? Exploring differences between child pornography possessors and child pornography producers/distributors using self-control theory. *Sexual Abuse, 28*(6), 555–571. https://doi.org/10.1177/1079063214557173

DeHart, D., Dwyer, G., Seto, M. C., Moran, R., Letourneau, E., & Schwarz-Watts, D. (2017). Internet sexual solicitation of children: A proposed typology of offenders based on their chats, e-mails, and social network posts. *Journal of Sexual Aggression, 23*(1), 77–89. https://doi.org/10.1080/13552600.2016.1241309

Dwyer, R. G., Seto, M., DeHart, D., Letourneau, E., McKee, T., & Moran, R. (2016). *Protecting children online: Using research-based algorithms to prioritize law enforcement internet investigations, technical report.* United States Department of Justice, Office of Juvenile Justice and Delinquency Prevention. https://www.ncjrs.gov/pdffiles1/ojjdp/grants/250154.pdf

Federal Bureau of Investigation. (2019, September 3). *Inside the FBI: Violent crimes against children international task force expands.* [Audio File]. https://www.fbi.gov/audio-repository/inside-podcast-vcac-international-task-force-090319.mp3/view

Finkelhor, D., Vaquerano, J., & Stranski, M. (2017). Sex trafficking of minors: How many juveniles are being prostituted in the US? http://www.unh.edu/ccrc/pdf/ CV279_Revised_Sex_Trafficking_Bulletin.pdf

Forrest, S. P., III, & Peterson, T. O. (2006). It's called andragogy. *Academy of Management Learning and Education, 5*(1), 113–122. https://doi.org/10.5465/amle .2006.20388390

Gallagher, B., Fraser, C., Christmann, K., & Hodgson, B. (2006). *International and internet child sexual abuse and exploitation.* University of Huddersfield, Huddersfield, U.K. http://eprints.hud.ac.uk/id/eprint/461/1/GallagherInt.pdf

Greenbaum, J., Crawford-Jakubiak, J. E., & Committee on Child Abuse and Neglect. (2015). Child sex trafficking and commercial sexual exploitation: Health care needs of victims. *Pediatrics, 135*(3), 566–574. https://doi.org/10.1542/peds.2014 -4138

Hagen, M., & Park, S., (2016). We knew it all along! Using cognitive science to explain how andragogy works. *European Journal of Training and Development, 40*(3), 171–190. https://doi.org/10.1108/EJTD-10-2015-0081

Hailes, H. P., Yu, R., Danese, A., & Fazel, S. (2019). Long-term outcomes of child-hood sexual abuse: An umbrella review. *The Lancet Psychiatry, 6*(10), 830–839. https://doi.org/10.1016/S2215-0366(19)30286-X

Hargreaves-Cormany, H. A., Patterson, T. D., & Muirhead, Y. E. (2016). A typology of offenders engaging in the sex trafficking of juveniles (STJ): Implications for risk assessment. *Aggression and Violent Behavior, 30*, 40–47. https://doi.org/10.1016 /j.avb.2016.06.011

Hartman, C. R., Burgess, A. W., & Lanning, K. V. (1984). Typology of collectors. In A. W. Burgess & M. L. Clark (Eds.) *Child pornography and sex rings* (pp. 90–109). New York, NY: Lexington Books.

Holt, T. J., & Bossler, A. M. (2012). Predictors of patrol officer interest in cybercrime training and investigation in selected United States police depart-ments. *Cyberpsychology, Behavior, and Social Networking, 15*(9), 464–472. https://doi.org/10.1089/cyber.2011.0625

International Association of Chiefs of Police. (2011). *2011 Juvenile justice training needs assessment.* http://www.iacp.org/portals/0/pdfs/2011JuvenileJusticeTraining NeedsAssessmentHighlights.pdf

International Center for Missing and Exploited Children. (2020) *Financial coalitions against child sexual exploitation.* https://www.icmec.org/financial -coalitions/

Jones, L. M., Mitchell, K. J., & Finkelhor, D. (2012). Trends in youth Internet victim-ization: Findings from three youth Internet safety surveys, 2000–2010. *Journal of Adolescent Health, 50*, 179–186. https://doi.org/10.1016/j.jadohealth.2011.09.015

Katz, C. (2013). Internet-related child sexual abuse: What children tell us in their testimonies. *Children and Youth Services Review, 35*, 1536–1542. https://doi.org /10.1016/j.childyouth.2013.06.006

Kessler, G. C., & Haggerty, D. A. (2010). An online graduate program in digital investigation management: Pedagogy and overview. *Journal of Digital Forensic Practice, 3*(1), 11–22. https://doi.org/10.1080/15567280903357771

Knowles, M. and Associates (1984). *Andragogy in action: Applying modern principles of adult learning.* San Francisco: Jossey-Bass. https://doi.org/10.22230/cjc .1986v12n1a376

Krone, T. (2004). A typology of online child pornography offending. *Trends and Issues in Crime and Criminal Justice, 279,* 1–6.

Latonero, M., Musto, J., Boyd, Z., Boyle, E., Bissel, A., Gibson, K., & Kim, J. (2012). *The rise of mobile and the diffusion of technology-facilitated trafficking.* Los Angeles, CA: University of Southern California, Center on Communication Leadership. https://doi.org/10.2139/ssrn.2177556

Letourneau, E. J., Brown, D. S., Fang, X., Hassan, A., & Mercy, J. A. (2018). The economic burden of child sexual abuse in the United States. *Child Abuse & Neglect, 79,* 413–422. https://doi.org/10.1016/j.chiabu.2018.02.020

Maniglio, R. (2009). The impact of child sexual abuse on health: A systematic review of reviews. *Clinical Psychology Review, 29*(7), 647–657. https://doi.org/10.1016/j .cpr.2009.08.003

Marcum, C. D., & Higgins, G. E. (2011). Combating child exploitation online: Predictors of successful ICAC task forces. *Policing: A Journal of Policy and Practice, 5*(4), 310–316. https://doi.org/10.1093/police/par044

Merdian, H. L., Perkins, D. E., Webster, S. D., & McCashin, D. (2019). Transnational child sexual abuse: Outcomes from a roundtable discussion. *International Journal of Environmental Research and Public Health, 16*(2), 1–14. https://doi.org/10.3390 /ijerph16020243

Mitchell, K. J., & Boyd, D. (2014). *Understanding the role of technology in the commercial sexual exploitation of children: The perspective of law enforcement.* Crimes against Children Research Center, University of New Hampshire: Durham, NH. https://scholars.unh.edu/cgi/viewcontent.cgi?article=1036&context=ccrc

Mitchell, K. J., Finkelhor, D., Jones, L. M., & Wolak, J. (2010). Growth and change in undercover online child exploitation investigations, 2000–2006. *Policing & Society, 20*(4), 416–431. https://doi.org/10.1080/10439463.2010.523113

Mitchell, K. J., Finkelhor, D., & Wolak, J. (2010). Conceptualizing juvenile prostitution as child maltreatment: Findings from the National Juvenile Prostitution Study. *Child Maltreatment, 15*(1), 18–36. https://doi.org/10.1177/1077559509349443

Mitchell, K. J., Jones, L. M., Finkelhor, D., & Wolak, J. (2011). Internet-facilitated commercial sexual exploitation of children: Findings from a nationally representative sample of law enforcement agencies in the United States. *Sexual Abuse: A Journal of Research & Treatment, 23*(1), 43–71. https://doi.org/10.1177 /1079063210374347

Mitchell, K. J., Wolak, J., & Finkelhor, D. (2005). Police posing as juveniles online to catch sex offenders: Is it working? *Sexual Abuse: A Journal of Research and Treatment, 17*(3), 241–267. https://doi.org/10.1177/107906320501700302

National Center for Missing & Exploited Children. (2020). *Exploited children statistics.* http://www.missingkids.com/footer/media/keyfacts

Office of Juvenile Justice & Delinquency Prevention. (2019). *Internet crimes against children task force program.* https://ojjdp.ojp.gov/programs/internet-crimes -against-children-task-force-program

Quayle, E. (2008). The COPINE project. *Irish Probation Journal, 5,* 65–111.

Roby, J. L., & Vincent, M. (2017). Federal and state responses to domestic minor sex trafficking: The evolution of policy. *Social Work, 62*(3), 201–210. https://doi.org /10.1093/sw/swx026

Sanci, L. (2019). Understanding and responding to the long-term burdens of child-hood sexual abuse. *The Lancet Psychiatry, 6*(10), 795–797. https://doi.org/10.1016 /S2215-0366(19)30329-3

Seto, M. C. (2013). *Internet sex offenders.* Washington, DC: American Psychological Association. https://doi.org/10.1037/14191-000

Simons, D. A (2015). *Adult sex offender typologies.* United States Department of Justice, Office of Justice Programs. https://smart.ojp.gov/sites/g/files/xyckuh231/ files/media/document/adultsexoffendertypologies.pdf

Sullivan, J., & Beech, A. R. (2004). Assessing Internet sex offenders. In M. C. Calder (Ed.), *Child sexual abuse and the internet: Tackling the new frontier* (pp.69–83). Lyme Regis, UK: Russell House.

Taylor, M., Quayle, E., & Holland, G. (2001). Child pornography, the internet and offending. *Isuma - Canadian Journal of Policy Research, 2*(2), 94–100.

Tener, D., Wolak, J., & Finkelhor, D. (2015). A typology of offenders who use online com-munications to commit sex crimes against minors. *Journal of Aggression, Maltreatment & Trauma, 24*(3), 319–337. https://doi.org/10.1080/10926771.2015.1009602

United Nations. (1989). *Convention on the Rights of the Child adopted by the General Assembly of the United Nations.* https://www.ohchr.org/en/professionalinterest/ pages/crc.aspx

United Nations. (2002). *Optional protocol to the convention on the rights of the child on the sale of children, child prostitution and child pornography.* https://www .ohchr.org/EN/ProfessionalInterest/Pages/OPSCCRC.aspx

United Nations. (2005). *Guidelines on justice in matters involving child victims and witnesses of crime.* https://www.un.org/en/ecosoc/docs/2005/resolution%202005 -20.pdf

United Nations. (2019). *Guidelines regarding the implementation of the Optional Protocol to the Convention on the Rights of the Child on the sale of children, child prostitution and child pornography.* https://www.ohchr.org/Documents/HRBodies /CRC/CRC.C.156_OPSC%20Guidelines.pdf

United Nations Office on Drugs and Crime. (2003). *Convention against transnational organized crime.* https://www.unodc.org/unodc/en/organized-crime/intro/UNTOC .html

United Nations Office on Drugs and Crime. (2013). *Comprehensive study on cybercrime.* https://www.unodc.org/documents/organized-crime/cybercrime/ CYBERCRIME_STUDY_210213.pdf

United Nations Office on Drugs and Crime. (2015). *Study on the effects of new infor-mation technologies on the abuse and exploitation of children.* https://www.unodc .org/documents/Cybercrime/Study_on_the_Effects.pdf

United States Department of Justice. (2007). *Department of justice announces inter-net crimes against children task forces in all 50 states.* http://www.usdoj.gov/opa/ pr/2007/October/07_ojp_061.html

United States Department of Justice. (2016). *National strategy for child exploitation prevention and interdiction: A report to congress.* https://www.justice.gov/psc/file /842411/download

United States Department of Justice. (2018, June 12). *More than 2,300 suspected online child sex offenders arrested during operation "Broken Heart"* [Press release]. https://www.justice.gov/opa/pr/more-2300-suspected-online-child-sex -offenders-arrested-during-operation-broken-heart

United States Department of Justice. (2019, June 11). *Nearly 1,700 suspected child sex predators arrested during operation "Broken Heart"* [Press release]. https:// www.justice.gov/opa/pr/nearly-1700-suspected-child-sex-predators-arrested-dur- ing-operation-broken-heart

von Weiler, J., Haardt-Becker, A., & Schulte, S. (2010). Care and treatment of child victims of child pornographic exploitation (CPE) in Germany. *Journal of Sexual Aggression, 16*(2), 211–222. https://doi.org/10.1080/13552601003759990

Webster, S., Davison, J., Bifulco, A., Gottschalk, P., Caretti, V., Pham, T., Grove- Hills, J., Turley, C., Tompkins, C., Ciulla, S., Milazzo, V., Schimmenti, A., & Craparo, G. (2012). *Final report: European online grooming project.* http://natcen .ac.uk/media/22514/european-online-grooming-projectfinalreport.pdf

Winters, G. M., Kaylor, L. E., & Jeglic, E. L. (2017). Sexual offenders contacting children online: An examination of transcripts of sexual grooming. *Journal of Sexual Aggression, 23*(1), 62–76. https://doi.org/10.1080/13552600.2016.1271146

Wolak, J., & Finkelhor, D. (2013). Are crimes by online predators different from crimes by sex offenders who know youth in-person? *Journal of Adolescent Health, 53*(6), 736–741. https://doi.org/10.1016/j.jadohealth.2013.06.010

Wolak, J., Finkelhor, D., & Mitchell, K. J. (2012a). Trends in law enforcement responses to technology-facilitated child sexual exploitation crimes: The third National Juvenile Online Victimization study (NJOV-3). http://unh.edu/ccrc/pdf/ CV268_Trends%20in%20LE%20Response%20Bulletin_4-13-12.pdf

Wolak, J., Finkelhor, D., & Mitchell, K. (2012b). Trends in arrests for child pornogra- phy production: The third National Juvenile Online Victimization study (NJOV-3). https://scholars.unh.edu/cgi/viewcontent.cgi?article=1046&context=ccrc

Wolak, J., Finkelhor, D., Mitchell, K. J., & Jones, L. (2011). Arrests for child por- nography production: Data at two time points from a national sample of U.S. law enforcement agencies. *Child Maltreatment, 16*(3), 184–195. https://doi.org/10 .1177/1077559511415837

Wolak, J., Finkelhor, D., Mitchell, K., & Ybarra, M. (2008). Online "predators" and their victims: Myths, realities, and implications for prevention and treatment. *American Psychologist, 63*(2), 111–128. https://doi.org/10.1037/0003-066x.63.2.111

Wolak, J., Liberatore, M., & Levine, B. N. (2014). Measuring a year of child por- nography trafficking by U.S. computers on a peer-to-peer network. *Child Abuse & Neglect, 38*(2), 347–356. https://doi.org/10.1016/j.chiabu.2013.10.018

Wolak, J., Mitchell, K., & Finkelhor, D. (2006). *Internet crimes against children: Five years later.* Washington, DC: Office of Juvenile Justice and Delinquency Prevention.

Wortley, R., & Smallbone, S. (2012). *Internet child pornography: Causes, investiga- tion, and prevention.* Santa Barbara, CA: ABC-CLIO.

Part III

SYSTEMATIC AND PRACTICAL CHALLENGES

Chapter 7

Controlling Minors

Extra-Legal Factors and the Decision to Use Force

Brian Lawton and Hyeyoung Lim

A defining characteristic of police work is the discretion that officers have available to them in making decisions about the proper course of action when interacting with the public. It has become increasingly common, through the implementation of new technologies, that a larger audience now has the opportunity to review these interactions after the fact. Of these actions, the ones that garner the greatest attention are those that involved the use of force by the officer. It is clear that the ability to use force allows the police to do their work, but questions arise when the citizens in these types of encounters are seen as particularly vulnerable.

Ava Ellis (age 4) 2015, Aiyana Jones (age 7) 2010, Tamir Rice (age 12) 2014, Andy Lopez Cruz (age 13) 2013, Michael Brown (age 18) 2014, Cameron Tillman (age 14) 2014, and Laquan McDonald (age 17) 2014 are just a few examples of incidents where juveniles were shot by the police during an encounter. Despite the relatively rare nature of these events, they do raise concerns about the police and whether these actions are the result of too much discretion, too little training, or some other factor. What cannot be overlooked is the assumption, by many, that extra-legal factors are playing a formal part of the decision-making process by the police during these encounters. In short, that particular characteristics of sex, race, and ethnicity result in greater force being used against citizens that are Hispanic/Latino, male, and Black/African-American.

This study seeks to address this issue by testing several hypotheses about the relationship between these extra-legal factors and whether the citizen in the encounter is a juvenile versus an adult. A series of logistic regression models are presented using six years of self-reported use-of-force data from a major metropolitan city in Texas. Due to the infrequency of incidents with a juvenile citizen (6.3%), propensity score matching was utilized to develop a one-to-one comparison of juvenile and adult incidents. This allows for a comparative analysis where concerns of a particular event being rare or over-shadowed by a large N can be addressed.

LITERATURE REVIEW

The body of research around the topic of police use of force and the discretion attributed to this decision-making process is extraordinarily diverse. Research studies in the field of sociology, criminology, criminal justice, public health, and geography have applied different approaches to understanding these rare events. Broadly speaking, many of the potential variables of interest, or potential explanators, can be broken down into three broad areas: individual, situational, and contextual. However, while this makes perfect sense when we are examining an adult population where research in this area has been well documented, the same cannot be said for studying a juvenile population. To that end, prior to the traditional breakdown of factors associated with police use of force, it is important to briefly touch on some of the relevant literature about the interaction between the police and juveniles.

Policing Juveniles

While the police are responsible for serving all members of society there has been evidence to suggest that the juveniles are overrepresented in regard to contact with the police and being subject to arrest (Leiber et al., 1998). The end result of this, particularly in regard to minority juveniles, is a body of research indicating that juveniles report a more negative perspective of the police than adults (Brunson & Miller, 2006; Brunson, 2007; Hurst & Frank, 2000; Taylor et al., 2001; to name only a few). The overwhelming cause seems focused on the juveniles' perspective that the police were targeting them for harassment both as juveniles and as racial minorities (Browning et al., 1994; Hurst et al., 2000).

Our earlier understanding of the interactions between the police and juveniles were reframed through the introduction of Tom Tyler's focus on procedural justice. Research comparing juveniles to adults found that adults are much more likely to comply with demands during an encounter with the police (Sunshine & Tyler, 2003). That finding could be partially explained by the frequency and opportunities which result in an interaction between the police and juveniles. Juveniles are more susceptible to police control and oversight as their behavior as a juvenile could be seen as an act of authority dispute, such as being active in public or congregating in large groups (Flood-Page et al., 2000; Aye-Maung, 1995).

Tyler's (1990) work suggests that when the legitimacy of the police increases, or seems evident, then citizens are more likely to be responsive to the police or police demands. Several authors have specifically looked at whether this same process is evident in the interactions between the police and juveniles. Fagan & Tyler (2005) found that juveniles indicated a higher legitimacy of the police when they felt that their interactions between them had been procedurally just; this finding was also present in the work of Piquero et al. (2005) and Reisig & Lloyd (2008).

While these findings demonstrated a link between perceptions of the police and procedural justice, most research in this area has not examined how this perception impacts cooperation between the juveniles and the police during interactions. Hinds (2009) found a link between juveniles' perception of the legitimacy of the police and the juveniles' willingness to assist the police, measured on a five-point scale. The results of these studies may suggest that while the interactions may be different between the police and juveniles, as compared to the police and adults, many of the same key factors are playing similar roles.

Explanations of Force

The topic of police use of force has garnered attention across numerous disciplines. One commonality across a body of this work is the breakdown of factors associated with incidents of police use of force being broken down into individual, situational, and contextual characteristics. Individual characteristics often refer to extra-legal factors of the encounter including information about the officer and the citizen. Similarly, contextual factors are generally extra-legal factors at various levels of aggregation such as the neighborhood and the Census Tract. Finally, the situational factors are the characteristics of the encounter such as the type of crime, the actions of the citizen, or their resistance to the authority of the police. Provided below is a brief literature of variables used in the presented analyses.

Individual

The discussion of race has dominated much of the literature around the topic of police use of force. This perspective has raised questions on whether officers are acting in a biased manner, or whether racial minorities are more at risk for having force used against them based on their actions, or their presence, in high-crime areas. While race, both officers' and citizens', has garnered this attention, the findings around it are mixed. There is ample evidence that racial minorities are over-represented in arrests (National Research Council, 2013), particularly among juveniles, the findings around force are less clear. While these findings are significant at the aggregate, they are not often sustained when a multivariate examination of the data is undertaken.

Lee et al. (2014) failed to find an impact of either officer or citizen race, while Shane et al. (2016) found that White citizens had a higher base rate for shootings than Black citizens. Klahm & Tillyer's (2010) content analysis of data on police use of force reported that neither officer nor citizen race impacted the use-of-force incident. Garner et al. (2002) found that the prevalence of force was associated with Black citizens, Hispanic officers, and both male citizens and officers. However, once resistance was controlled for, the impact of the citizen being Black was no longer significant. Bolger's (2015) meta-analysis of use-of-force decisions found evidence that citizen's race (effect size [ES]=.31), sex (ES=.37), and officer's sex (ES=.24) impacted whether the citizen had force used against them. This meta-analysis found no support that age of the citizen impacted the use of force.

Situational

Perhaps the most relevant situational variable to a discussion of police use of force is the measure of resistance on the part of the citizen. While there has been some debate on the operationalization of this measure, like the measure of force this is limited to the availability of information on the incident. Klinger (1994) makes a compelling argument for the separation of the concepts of resistance and demeanor, emphasizing the distinction between demeanor (legally permissible) and resistance (criminal behavior). While Klinger's works were emphasizing the impact on the decision to make an arrest, it's clear that this is equally relevant in regards to the use of force.

It's no surprise that citizen's resistance is consistently a predictor of the level of force used by the police because it is one of the legal factors that the police use force—responding to resistance. Bolger (2015) found that citizen resistance was not only significant in his meta-analysis of police use-of-force research, but that it had the highest ES of 1.46. One challenge of this type of research is that the reliance on secondary data often precludes understanding the escalation of the encounter, and we are limited to only the final summary of events.

Contextual

Unsurprising, there is mixed support for the impact that contextual factors have on police use of force. Bolger's (2015) meta-analysis failed to find support for the relationship between crime rate and associated force. (2014)

found that neighborhood violent crime was positively correlated with higher levels of force. Terrill & Reisig (2003) found officers using higher levels of force in more disadvantaged neighborhoods with high homicide rates. Lawton (2007) found only marginal support for measures of violent crime and racial heterogeneity. In their recent study, Fridell & Lim (2016) found selective moderation effects of neighborhood crime on the relationship between citizen race and police use of force. For example, the impact of race on the decision to use electronic control devices (stungun) was significant in neighborhoods with high rates of violent crime

This literature review was not intended to be exhaustive but was only meant to highlight the findings and emphasize those where our results are somewhat mixed. One additional piece that is necessary to highlight here is the work by Morrow et al. (2018) which at the time of this writing is the only article to focus on reported use of force against juveniles from a sample of juvenile arrestee population. Their results found that male juveniles and those arrested for misdemeanors were the only significant factors associated with the use of force against them. However, even these differences were found to be non-significant when situational-level characteristics such as resistance, demeanor and being disrespectful were taken into account.

Due to the limited amount of research in this area, the following hypotheses were defined assuming that the police would respond to adults and juveniles in a similar way. In short, the following hypotheses apply findings from adult populations to test against a juvenile population.

H_1: *Male juveniles are more likely to have a higher level of force used against them.*

H_2: *Black/African-American juveniles are more likely to have a higher level of force used against them.*

H_3: *Hispanic/Latino juveniles are more likely to have a higher level of force used against them.*

METHODOLOGY

Data for these analyses were obtained from a police department serving a major metropolitan city in the state of Texas. The city's primary police force was responsible for most day-to-day interactions between the police and the public and required that all use-of-force incidents were documented by submitting an official use-of-force report. The agency requires individual submission per incident. For example, if there were two officers and one citizen in an encounter and both officers used police force against the citizen, then there would be two reports submitted for one encounter. The data presented here include all reported incidents from January 1, 2009, through December 31, 2014. Over this six-year period, a total of 16,676 use-of-force reports were filed, for an average of 2,779 a year. All data reported here are secondary in nature.

As with any agency, the data suffers from issues of missing data across a number of key variables included in this study. To that end, 1,502 cases were removed from the analyses (9%), resulting in a database of 15,174 reports. Summary statistics (results not shown here) were run to test for some potential bias to the missing data, and results found no indication that this was the case. Variables most frequently missing were associated with officer characteristics such as race and sex.

Dependent Variable

The agency defines the term, *force*, as

- An officer pointing a firearm at a citizen.
- Any physical contact between an officer and citizen where the officer uses a weapon, or device, against the citizen.
- Any encounter where the citizen complains of having been injured, or when the citizen is in any pain, with the exception of minor pain.
- This excludes situations where the officer uses handcuffs on a citizen, or escorts them.[1]

The agency's use-of-force report form includes eight types of force: firearm, canine, impact weapon, taser, OC spray, weaponless, other, and none. The *none* category means that subject complained of pain but no force was used during the incident, and the *other* category represents the action that isn't categorized in any specific use-of-force category. Incidents where "none" was indicated were not included in the analyses, and other incidents were included.

The dependent variable was a measure of the level of force that the office reported using during their encounter with a citizen. Of those interactions where a police officer reported using force against a citizen, approximately three-quarters of them resulted in an arrest (75.8%). Due to the relatively rare nature of more extreme levels of force, the level of force was dichotomized as any impact weapon, firearm, canine, or action resulting in serious bodily harm or death (1) and OC spray, conducted energy devices, or weaponless technique (0). Despite the collapsing of these categories, the dichotomous distribution was still heavily weighted toward the low-end level of force with less than a fifth (16.5%) of the reports designating the more serious category of force. In other words, most reports (83.5%) indicated the use of OC spray or less-severe techniques being used against the citizen.

Independent Variables

As mentioned previously, there are three categories of potential correlates of the level of force used by the police during a police-citizen encounter. These are individual, situational, and contextual. The independent variables used in the models include officer characteristics such as race, sex, and ethnicity, as well as citizen's race, sex, and ethnicity. The situational variable included in the models is suspect resistance, measured with three categories: (1) passive or verbal resistance as well as other, (2) empty hand resistance or aggression, and (3) the use of a weapon or firearm. While no further information was provided on the citizen's actions which were labeled as "other," it was decided to treat them as a minimal display of force. It should also be clear that in situations where a citizen was reported as using multiple levels of resistance, only the highest is reported here.

Matching Variables

While the independent variables included measures at the individual and situational levels, the analyses here required the use of propensity score matching. To that end, a series of contextual measures were included, not in the model, but as matching variables for the propensity score matching analysis. The five-year average of the American Community Survey (2012–2016) at the Census Tract level where the incident occurred was used to match between adult and juvenile cases. This included measures of percent below the poverty line, percent Hispanic, percent Black, percent with less than a high school diploma, percent female-headed households with children, the five-year averaged violent crime rate, the five-year averaged property crime rate, and at the individual level, whether the police officer's rank was that of an officer, and whether the suspect was arrested.

Propensity scores were calculated using Stata 15.0's *psmatch2* command. This command allows for the calculation of the average treatment effect on the treated (ATT) which is used to pair a "treated" subject with a comparable "non-treated" subject. In this case, pairing juvenile and adult cases to allow for an analysis of the force employed, despite the majority of cases involving officer's using force against adults. To this end, the matching was limited to a one-to-one match for the simple comparison of police encounters with juveniles and adults. While propensity score matching has some limitations, it allows for the matching of treated and untreated cases to be reduced to a single measure.

ANALYSIS AND FINDINGS

Table 7.1 reports the simple descriptive statistics of the full data file. In short, the citizens were primarily adults (93.7%) and male (83.3%); approximately

Table 7.1 Descriptive Statistics of the Full Sample (N=15,174)

Variable	N	Mean	SD	Min	Max
Juvenile	15,174	.063	.244	0	1
Officer gender (M)	15,174	.956	.206	0	1
Citizen gender (M)	15,174	.833	.373	0	1
Officer race (Black)	15,174	.062	.242	0	1
Citizen race (Black)	15,174	.291	.454	0	1
Officer ethnicity (Hispanic)	15,174	.202	.402	0	1
Citizen ethnicity (Hispanic)	15,174	.342	.474	0	1
Citizen resistance	15,168	1.808	.440	1	3
C. resistance (verbal)	3,209	21.16			
C. resistance (aggressive)	11,665	76.91			
C. resistance (weapon)	294	1.94			
Officer force	15,174	.165	.371	0	1

Source: Data created by author study.

a third of the cases were Hispanic (34.2%) or Black (29.1%) and were most likely to use some form of empty hand resistance or aggression (76.9%). Officers were male (95.6%), less frequently Hispanic (20.2%) or Black (6.2%) than the population they interacted with, and reported using some form of weapon less frequently (16.5%).

In order to examine the association between the key variables of interest and whether the higher level of force was used, a series of logistic regression models were conducted with the dependent variable of officer's reported level of force. Several models were conducted to parse out the difference between force reported when the citizen was a juvenile (17 or younger) and as an adult. Table 7.2 reported the results of the initial full model. Here the variable of juvenile was included in the model as a dichotomous measure of whether the citizen was a juvenile. This key variable was significant ($p < .001$) with an odds ratio below 1, suggesting that juveniles are less likely to have a higher level of force used against them.

Most other individual variables are also statistically significant, with male officers less likely to use the higher level of force (OR= .729, $p < .01$), while male citizens were much more likely to have the higher level of force used against them (OR = 4.464, $p < .001$). In terms of race, Black officers were likely to use the higher level of force (OR = .768, $p < .05$), while Black citizens were more likely to have force used against them (OR = 1.336, $p < .001$). Ethnicity was only significant in regards to the citizen, with Hispanic citizens almost twice as likely to have the higher level of force used against them (OR=1.910, $p < .01$). The variable of resistance on the part of the citizen had mixed findings with the highest resistance on

Table 7.2 Logistic Regression

Variable	Full (N=15,168)		Juvenile (n=936)		Adult (n=14,205)	
	OR	SE	OR	SE	OR	SE
Juvenile	.638***	.070				
Officer gender (M)	.729**	.078	1.186	.599	.711**	.078
Citizen gender (M)	4.464***	.430	8.416***	3.935	4.317***	.426
Officer race (Black)	.768**	.078	.424	.265	.785*	.081
Citizen race (Black)	1.336***	.075	1.109	.453	1.349***	.077
Officer ethnicity (Hispanic)	1.097	.610	.928	.257	1.103	.063
Citizen ethnicity (Hispanic)	1.91**	.065	1.313	.483	1.184**	.066
Citizen resistance						
C. resistance (aggressive)	.423***	.021	.265***	.059	.433***	.022
C. resistance (weapon)	3.787***	.486	.995	.613	4.068***	.539
Pseudo R²	.0699		.1193		.0667	
BIC	−133271.922		−5948.563		−123676.442	

* = $p < .05$, ** = $p < .01$, *** = $p < .001$.
Source: Data created by author study.

the part of the citizen being almost four times as likely to be associated with the higher level of force (3.787, $p < .001$) as compared to the passive baseline measure, while the middle level of resistance was associated with less probability of the higher level of force being used against them (OR=.423, $p < .001$).

While this initial model has some surprising findings from prior studies on factors associated with the level of force employed, the primary question of whether the level of force used against juveniles was significantly different from that used against adults was confirmed. For that reason, two additional models (tables 7.3 and 7.4) report on logistic regression models that intended to parse out the difference between interactions between the police and adults versus juveniles.

Table 7.2 also reports the findings from an examination of the full juvenile sample. Here only two variables are statistically significant with the measure of the citizen's sex indicating that male juveniles were over eight times more likely to have a higher level of force used against them than female citizens (OR=8.416, $p < .001$); the only other variable of statistical significance was the measure of citizen's resistance where the second level was associated with a decreased likelihood of officer's using higher levels of force.

The same analysis was conducted for the adult population shown in table 7.2. Here the variable of citizen's sex is still significant (OR = 4.317, $p < .001$), although not to the extent that was present in the juvenile population. Measures of officer's sex (OR =.711, $p < .01$) and race (OR =.785, $p < .05$) follow a similar pattern to the full model. The citizen's measures of race follow the same pattern (OR=1.349, p < .001), however, in regards to citizen ethnicity we now see that this is statistically significant as well (OR=1.184, p < .01). Citizen resistance follows the same pattern as we saw in the full model with the highest level of resistance being more positively associated with a higher level of force (OR=4.068, p < .001) as compared to the baseline, while the medium level of resistance is negatively associated with the baseline (OR=.433, p < .001).

While the results are mixed in regards to prior research in this area, further analyses were conducted to try to control for possible factors that might be affecting the results of the comparative analyses. One concern was that the larger number of adults in the sample was resulting in more factors being found to be statistically significant. To that end a propensity score matching approach was used to identify a one-to-one match of juveniles to adults using primarily contextual measures gathered from the American Community Survey (2012–2016). Table 7.3 reports the average treatment effect on the treated (ATT) estimates provided by the *psmatch2* command calculated using Stata 15.0.

The command attempts to define a paired sample match of juveniles to adults using the key variables listed. Initial analyses suggested that almost all variables' means were statistically different (p < .05) between the juvenile and adult samples. Using the *psmatch2* command, the one-to-one selection was used to select adults that more closely resembled the juvenile population. Table 7.3A reports the means of the treated group (juveniles) and the means of the one-to-one ATT Control match (adults). While there is no perfect match, nor should one be expected, the means are relatively similar with the only statistically significant difference occurring with the variable of property crime, where the control group (adults) is approximately twice that of the juvenile's sample. It is worth noting while this difference is significant, the initial difference between the means was fourfold.

With this process completed a subset of the full data was identified with 961 juveniles and 961 adults. Descriptive statistics of this subset of the full data is reported in table 7.3B. The comparison between table 1 and table 3B demonstrates two important differences. First, there is a drop of approximately 11% in the presence of male officers in these incidents, and an increase of about 13% in citizen's ethnicity being Hispanic.

This new subset of data suggests that several of the relationships found with the full dataset are no longer present. Table 7.4 reports the logistic regression results for the combined matched sample (N=1,921).[2] The variable of juvenile continues to be significant here (OR=.736, p < .05) in the full model, however, referring back to table 7.2, it's clear that this impact has decreased both in terms of significance, as well as odds ratio. The variable of officer race continues to be significant (OR=.316, p < .05), however,

Table 7.3 Matching Statistics and Matched Sample

A. Matching Statistics Using PSMATCH2 in Stata

Variable	Treated	ATT Control	Difference	SE	T
Percent Hispanic	52.062	52.002	.060	.973	0.06
Percent Black	10.664	10.735	-.071	.398	-0.18
Percent less HS	24.070	24.073	-.003	.636	-0.00
Percent FHH with children	20.535	20.504	.032	.452	0.07
Percent below poverty	25.859	26.111	-.254	.570	-0.45
Violent crime rate	.002	.003	-.001	.002	-0.45
Property crime rate	.012	.025	-.012	.006	-2.02
Citizen arrested	.117	.117	.000	.015	0.00
Rank: officer	.792	.820	-.028	.018	-1.56

B. Descriptive Statistics of the Matched Sample (N=1922)

Variable	N	Mean	SD	Min	Max
Juvenile	1,922	.500	.500	0	1
Officer gender (M)	1,922	.944	.230	0	1
Citizen gender (M)	1,922	.723	.448	0	1
Officer race (Black)	1,922	.050	.219	0	1
Officer ethnicity (Hispanic)	1,922	.195	.396	0	1
Citizen race (Black)	1,922	.277	.448	0	1
Citizen ethnicity (Hispanic)	1,922	.476	.499	0	1
Citizen resistance	1,921	1.798	.471	1	3
C. resistance (verbal)	447	23.27			
C. resistance (aggressive)	1,416	73.71			
C. resistance (weapon)	58	3.02			
Officer force	1,922	.134	.340	0	1

Source: Data created by author study.

Table 7.4 Logistic Regression of the Matched Samples

Variable	Matched Full (N=1,921)		Matched Juvenile (n=961)		Matched Adult (n=960)	
	OR	SE	OR	SE	OR	SE
Juvenile	.736*	.112				
Officer gender (M)	1.101	.385	1.194	.603	1.115	.550
Citizen gender (M)	5.257***	1.301	8.480***	3.966	4.439***	1.376
Officer race (Black)	.316*	.154	.420	.262	.240	.186
Officer ethnicity (Hispanic)	1.062	.186	.918	.255	1.074	.252
Citizen race (Black)	1.051	.212	1.107	.452	1.096	.265
Citizen ethnicity (Hispanic)	1.116	.208	1.325	.488	1.014	.236
Citizen resistance						
C. resistance (aggressive)	.414***	.063	.260***	.058	.619*	.132
C. resistance (weapon)	6.029***	1.885	.975	.601	14.762***	6.163
Pseudo R²	.1225		.1209		.1416	
BIC	−13117.387		−5941.253		−5812.185	

* = $p < .05$, ** = $p < .01$, *** = $p < .001$.
Source: Data created by author study.

officer sex is no longer significant, and ethnicity continues to be non-significant. Citizen sex continues to be significant (OR=5.257, p < .001), while both citizen race and ethnicity are no longer significant. Of course, citizen resistance does continue to be significant both for the more extreme level of resistance (OR=6.029, p < .001) and the middle level of resistance (OR=.414, p < .001).

In terms of the matched juvenile model (n=961), it should come as no surprise that the results here mimic the results from table 7.2, which reported on the full juvenile sample (n=963). In short, citizen sex (OR = 8.480, p < .001) and middle level of resistance (OR=.260, p < .001) are the only variables that obtain statistical significance.

The final analysis produced examines the relationship between these same variables and the matched adult sample. As shown in the last column of table 7.4, we see that the only variables that obtain statistical significance are citizen sex (OR 4.439, p < .001) and citizen resistance both at the middle level (OR=.619, p < .05) and the high level (OR=14.762, p < .001).

DISCUSSION AND CONCLUSION

The idea that drove this research was a simple one. We recognize that the police have an enormous amount of discretion in their day-to-day interactions with the public. We would anticipate that certain types of encounters, particularly those that might require a more extreme response by the police, might limit the discretion that the officers can reasonably employ. In short, there is an expectation that juveniles are not going to be treated in the same way as adults. However, in police use-of-force encounters, particularly when the citizen resists, the officer may have limited latitude in treating juveniles differently from adults. To that end, these analyses were conducted to try and identify whether or not these differences occurred.

Initial results indicated that juveniles, overall, were less likely to have more serious levels of force used against them than adults. However, results demonstrated mixed support of other prior conclusions about the relationship between individual and situational factors related to the level of force employed by the police. One concern here was that the sample size, or overwhelming presence of adults, might be masking some variation unique to encounters between the police and the public. To that end, propensity score matching was employed to identify a one-to-one matched sample primarily using contextual indicators.

These results found two points of interest when comparing the juvenile and adult samples. First, extreme resistance on the part of the citizen was only a significant indicator of higher levels of force when conducted by adults. For juveniles, this higher level of resistance was not a significant indicator of police use of force. Second, while citizens' sex was significant for both juveniles and adults the odds ratio for juveniles was almost twice that of adults (4.4 vs. 8.4). Of course, this finding could also be interpreted not as an increased willingness to use force against male juveniles, but instead as resistance to using force against female juveniles.

The finding concerning the level of resistance could be explained by juveniles not using that more extreme level of resistance or police choosing not to report them using that level. A review of the data finds, however, that while within the matched sample there are more instances of adults using this most extreme level of resistance (n=41), there are instances of juveniles using this as well (n=17). This finding then might lend support to the idea that even in situations where citizens are employing higher levels of resistance, the fact that the citizen is a juvenile results in a less-severe response by the police.

The second finding that juvenile males are almost twice as likely to have higher levels of force used against them than the matched sample of adults might easily be explained by a greater contact between the police and juvenile males, as compared to the police and the adult population. In fact, looking at the data, there is no evidence to support that conclusion. In the matched sample, the police interact with the same proportion of juvenile females (.39) as they do adult females (.38) suggesting that when the police do use force against juvenile males, they are much more likely to employ higher levels of force than when interacting with juvenile females.

In regard to our initial proposed hypotheses, we failed to find support for either concerning race or ethnicity of the citizen or, for that matter, the officers'. As mentioned previously, only H_1 pertaining to the sex of the juvenile garnered any support.

There are some limitations in the current study. The primary limitation of the preceding analysis is a self-imposed one. Despite there being a database of almost 16,000 police use-of-force incidents, this research focuses on only a subset of approximately 2,000 to better separate out the key differences between adults and juveniles. Ideally, these analyses could be done with a larger sample, allowing for greater variation of the dependent variable as well as the measure of citizen resistance.

Further, the current study examines only the data from a single agency in Texas. For a variety of reasons, this results in some key differences in results from studies in cities due to large differences in the race and ethnicity of the location. A second site was not included in these analyses for two reasons: (1) it can be difficult to compare agencies with dissimilar training and rules around police use of force, as well as the data being measured differently, and (2) it is extremely difficult to find agencies that report this level of detail for interactions between the police and their juvenile population.

An additional limitation of the data is the inability to separate out the concepts of demeanor and resistance. This is a key point made by Klinger (1994) as a potential pitfall of using resistance as a correlate of the force used by the officer. It could be argued that the second level of resistance, which was continuously significant, but in the opposite predicted direction, might have been an indicator of demeanor as it touched only on passive resistance, but we are not comfortable making such an assumption.

The final limitation here is one common to much research that relies on self-report forms. These forms are completed following the event and provide no way of examining the interaction and potential escalation between the police and the citizen. It's not clear, for example, that the police didn't make a greater effort to interact with either age group, and further without a baseline of interactions we cannot be confident that in this jurisdiction the officers' discretion has not already excluded less serious events that the police may overlook from juveniles.

It needs to be emphasized that these analyses are looking at the actions of officers in a single municipality, so these findings should not be considered generalizable. Additional research should be conducted in this area, in particular, allowing for the perspective of police officers to discuss their own decision-making process to better illustrate and interpret these findings. A greater distinction of age, as compared to the current dichotomous measure of adult versus juvenile presented here, should also be addressed.

NOTES

1. The citation is not added to keep the agency anonymous.
2. In the matched adult sample, one of the adults was missing data on subject resistance. This resulted in a decrease in sample size formed 961 to 960 for this sample.

REFERENCES

Aye-Maung, N. (1995). *Young people, victimization and the police: British Crime Survey Findings on Experiences and Attitudes of 12 to 15-year olds*. London: HMSO.

Bolger, P. (2015). Just following orders: A meta-analysis of the correlates of American police officer use of force decisions. *American Journal of Criminal Justice, 40*, 466–492.

Bonnie, R., Johnson, R., Chemers, B., & Schuck, J. (2013). *Reforming juvenile justice: A developmental approach*. Washington, DC: The National Academies Press.

Browning, S., Cullen, F., Cao, L., Kopache, R., & Stevenson, T. (1994). Race and getting hassled by the police: A research note. *Police Studies, 17*(1), 1–11.

Brunson, R. (2007). "Police don't like Black People:" African-American young men's accumulated police experiences. *Criminology & Public Policy, 6*(1), 71–102.

Brunson, R., & Miller, J. (2006). Young black men and urban policing in the United States. *British Journal of Criminology, 46*, 613–640.

Flood-Page, C., Campbell, S., Harrington, V., & Miller, J. (2000). *Youth crime: Findings from the 1998/1999 youth lifestyles survey*. London: Home Office Research, Development and Statistics Directorate.

Fridell, L., & Lim, H. (2016). Assessing the racial aspects of police force using the implicit- and counter-bias perspectives. *Journal of Criminal Justice, 44*, 36–48.

Gaerner, J. Maxwell, C., & Heraux, C. (2002). Characteristics associated with the prevalence and severity of force used by the police. *Justice Quarterly, 19*(4), 705–747.

Hinds, L. (2009). Youth, police legitimacy and informal contact. *Journal of Police and Criminal Psychology, 24*(1), 10–21.

Hurst, Y., & Frank, J. (2000). How kids view cops: The nature of juvenile attitudes toward police. *Journal of Criminal Justice, 28*, 189–202.

Hurst, Y., Frank, J., & Browning, S. (2000). The attitudes of juveniles toward the police: A comparison of black and white youth. *Policing, 23*, 37–53.

Klahm, C., & Tillyer, R. (2010). Understanding police use of force: A review of the evidence. *Southwest Journal of Criminal Justice, 7*, 214–239.

Klinger, D. (1994). Demeanor or Crime? Why "Hostile" Citizens are more likely to Arrested. *Criminology, 32*(3), 475–493.

Lawton, B. (2007). Levels of nonlethal force. *Journal of Research in Crime and Delinquency, 44*, 163–184.

Lee, H., Vaughn, M., & Lim, H. (2014). The impact of neighborhood crime levels on police use of force: An examination at micro and meso levels. *Journal of Criminal Justice, 42*, 491–499.

Leiber, M., Nalla, M., & Farnworth, M. (1998). Explaining juveniles' attitudes toward the police. *Justice Quarterly, 15*, 151–174.

Morrow, W., Nuno, L., & Mulvey, P. (2018). Examining the situational- and suspect-level predictors of police use of force among a juvenile arrestee population. *Justice Policy Journal, 15*(1), 1–22.

Piquero, A., Fagan, J., Mulvey, E., Steinberg, L., & Odgers, C. (2005). Developmental trajectories of legal socialization among serious adolescent offenders. *The Journal of Criminal Law and Criminology, 96*, 267–298.

Reisig, M., & Lloyd, C. (2008). Procedural justice, police legitimacy, and helping the police fight crime: results from a survey of Jamaican adolescents. *Police Quarterly, 12*(1), 42–62.

Shane, J., Lawton, B., & Swenson, Zoe. (2017). The prevalence of fatal police shootings by U.S. police, 2015–2016: Patterns and answers from a new data set. *Journal of Criminal Justice, 52*, 101–111.

Skolnick, J., & Fyfe, J. (1993). *Above the law: Police and the excessive use of force.* New York: The Free Press.

Sunshine, J., & Tyler, T. (2003). The role of procedural justice and legitimacy in shaping public support for policing. *Law and Society Review, 37*(3), 513–547.

Taylor, T., Turner, K., Finn-Aage, E., & Winfree, L. (2001). Coppin' an attitude: Attitudinal differences among juveniles toward the police. *Journal of Criminal Justice, 29*, 295–305.

Terrill, W., & Resig, M. (2003). Neighborhood Context and Police Use of Force. *Journal of Research in Crime and Delinquency, 43*(3), 291–321.

Chapter 8

Medicolegal Death Investigation Systems and the Challenges in Child Death Investigation in the United States

Brandi C. McCleskey and Lily Mahler

As a guarantee of life, death can come at any time and from a range of causes. The individuals who are tasked with investigating deaths include a variety of professions ranging from law enforcement to medicine. A medicolegal death investigation serves to collect and preserve evidence while determining the cause of unexpected deaths, whether explained or unexplained. Offices specializing in death investigation are associated with a myriad of governmental hierarchy within state and local jurisdictions. This type of system began centuries ago and for many across the globe looks similar as it did in its inception. In the United States, the majority of investigative responsibility belongs to the coroner and/or medical examiner. Many states observe laws set forth decades ago outlining the electoral guidelines for coroners either within state governments or county governments. Other states have updated laws to recognize a medical examiner as the authoritative body of death investigation.

Death investigations are critical for many aspects of public health, criminal justice, and estate settlement. Investigation of unexpected deaths can have important legal implications, especially when tasked with providing evidence for use in a court of law prosecuting murder, child neglect or maltreatment, or other forms of interpersonal violence. The medicolegal death investigation is also paramount to the progression of public health practices including epidemiologic research, population health statistics, institution of injury, and death prevention programs, as well as impacting the overall quality of healthcare. The process of medicolegal death investigation involves collaboration among many groups with sometimes overlapping roles. This intermix comes with many challenges and can present a complex and confusing process to individuals unfamiliar with the medicolegal death investigation.

With the variety of death investigation systems in place within the United States and the lack of a unified database, research, and policies based on mortality data is dependent upon a death certificate. These are typically completed by a variety of individuals ranging from a county coroner to a palliative care physician. They not only outline the cause of death, which may fall within any range of ambiguity, but also the manner of death. The cause of death is the specific insult or injury that directly results in a person's death which usually falls into one of five categories: homicide, suicide, natural, accident, or undetermined. Certifiers are tasked with evaluating the history and circumstances of death to help assign a manner. The data from a death certificate are used for vital statistics at a national (and international) level. Information from the cause of death is coded using the International Classification of Disease (ICD) coding system to assist individuals in accessing mortality data and establishing causes of death statistics.

Many medical examiners and/or coroner offices around the country face a number of challenges related to staffing, resources, and ever-increasing case volumes related to epidemics of drugs, violence, and poor overall health. Many are understaffed and underresourced providing a host of issues including adherence to quality standards and investigative guidelines. The American Board of Medicolegal Death Investigation sets forth standards for death investigators, but not all have to obtain certification. The National Association of Medical Examiners awards accreditation based on forensic standards, but not all offices seek accreditation. Standardization of guidelines at a national level is lacking in consistency and, therefore, many jurisdictions function in isolation making the acquisition of accurate mortality data difficult.

THE HISTORY OF DEATH INVESTIGATION

Origination of the Coroner System

The Western culture's responsibility for investigating death is deeply rooted in history and has been documented as far back as the medieval period. Coroner-based systems put in place by Great Britain, and subsequently brought by colonists to the New World, are still widely in practice today in the United States. The tradition of the coroner system began in England during the eighth and ninth centuries and was eventually legitimized by King Richard I after the official election of "coroners" to office in 1194 (Spitz et al., 2006). The term "coroner" is derived from the Latin phrase *Custom*

Plactorium Coronae, which translates to Supervisor of the Crown's Pleas (Spitz et al., 2006).

Coroners, usually men of noble blood, were elected to enforce the Crown's rule of law as well as collect dues (Houston, 2014; Spitz et al., 2006). In the time of Medieval England, the King was privy to all property and possessions of his subjects. Coroners were sent to enforce the King's rule by collecting money and belongings from deceased individuals or individuals who had been accused of committing crimes (Spitz et al., 2006). With the primary responsibility of a coroner being to maintain the Crown's best interests, they were typically tasked with overseeing all aspects of death investigation. When the coroner was alerted of accidental or suspicious death, he would then interview all witnesses and potential suspects until ultimately making sole judgment on the manner and motive of the death (Spitz et al., 2006). Those individuals charged with homicide were taken into custody by the sheriff and the coroner confiscated their belongings for presentation to the king. The coroner also had the power to seize the property of individuals who committed suicide in addition to those who were simply accused of committing crimes, irrespective of sufficient evidence (Thorwald, 1965).

Death Investigation in the New World

English colonists brought the coroner system as they settled in North America and the first official death investigations were conducted as early as 1635 in the colony of New Plymouth (Hanzlick, 2007; Tilstone et al., 2006). In the early days of the British colonies, coroners had a relatively low reputation (Spitz et al., 2006). A death investigation was overseen by the coroner and the final verdict was given by a jury—the contribution of expertise from a physician was rare. The role of the coroner eventually merged with that of the sheriff, and only cases of severe and overt bodily injury were investigated typically without an autopsy (Spitz et al., 2006). Internal examination by autopsy was not permitted due to religious objection, and therefore, the cause of death was determined by examining the external surfaces of the body and compiling witness statements (Spitz et al., 2006).

The first official constitutional mention of coroners was documented in the state of Georgia's 1777 state constitution although very little detail is mentioned regarding the scope of the coroner's duties (Hanzlick, 2007; Thorpe, 1906). Other colonies followed suit and began to describe the official duties of a coroner, which mainly consisted of providing investigation over deaths deemed suspicious or unnatural in the case that a physician was not present (Choo & Choi, 2012). Coroners were most often lay-people elected by the popular vote and the training to become a coroner varied from intensive programs lasting weeks to none at all. If individuals did receive training, it primarily focused on determining whether a death was accidental or resulted from criminal means (Choo & Choi, 2012).

In 1811, Dr. Benjamin Rush, a well-known original member of Congress and a signer of the Declaration of Independence, published a work titled *On the Study of Medical Jurisprudence*, which served as one of the first texts addressing issues of medicolegal death investigation (Spitz et al., 2006). His watershed work began the movement to involve medically trained professionals in the process of death investigation. It was becoming more accepted for students of medicine to be taught the study of anatomy; however, the internal examination of the human body was still considered taboo by many in the early nineteenth century often resulting in protests outside of medical schools (Spitz et al., 2006).

Death Investigation since the Nineteenth Century

The transition from elected lay-person coroner death investigation became official in Maryland in 1860 when the first legislation was enacted requiring a physician to be present during an investigation (Hanzlick, 2015; National Research Council, 2009). Eight years later, the city of Baltimore appointed a physician as the sole coroner rather than relying on a democratic process to elect one. Over the next decade, Massachusetts replaced all coroners with physicians, a specialized group that would later be known as medical examiners (National Research Council, 2009). By the early twentieth century, medical examiners, a group that would eventually be comprised mostly of subspecialized forensic pathologists, were initially composed of physicians who received additional focused training in death investigation.

Baltimore, again at the forefront during the nineteenth century, appointed two forensic pathologists to perform all autopsies required by the coroner and state's attorney (Hanzlick, 2007). As early as 1918, both New York City and the state of Massachusetts had completely adopted the medical examiner system. Early adoption fueled the 1928 National Research Council's Committee on Medical Legal Problems to denounce the office of the coroner and went on to describe coroners incapable of adequately performing their duties (National Research Council, 2009). They went on to recommend transferring those duties to a medical examiner's office—an office that should be provided with adequate staff, facilities, and resources (National Research Council, 2009).

Later in the twentieth century, the New York City Medical Examiner's Office focused on pioneering the future by advocating for the training of future forensic pathologists under the leadership of Drs. Norris, Gonzales, and Helpern (Spitz et al., 2006). Dr. Milton Helpern was the third chief medical examiner of New York City and was also the founder of the National

Association of Medical Examiners (NAME) in 1977, which is still in operation today (Spitz et al., 2006). The NAME functions as a national organization for medical examiners as well as an accrediting body focused on maintaining quality standards for death investigation.

THE ESTABLISHMENT OF DEATH INVESTIGATION SYSTEMS

Although more than a century has passed since state governments recognized the benefit of having a specialized physician at the helm of death investigation, a myriad of systems still exists in the United States. Most medicolegal death investigation operations are instituted at the state, regional or district, or county level and each organization may be led by a coroner, medical examiner, or appointed individual such as a sheriff or state official. Less than half of the states have a state-wide death investigation system (Hanzlick & Fudenberg, 2014). The majority of the country's deaths are investigated within the confines of counties or regions, which occurs when multiple counties are covered by the same office (Hanzlick, 2015). The scope of the investigative jurisdiction within death investigation offices is typically outlined by state code (National Research Council, 2009).

Further complicating the quality of death investigation at a national level is that the individual offices may be led by individuals with a wide array of backgrounds—ranging from an elected lay-coroner to an elected physician-coroner to a medical examiner or a combination of both coroner and medical examiner. It is of paramount importance that the death investigation office (whether coroner- or medical examiner-led) remains an independent entity that reports to a commission or governing body rather than a law enforcement agency (National Research Council, 2009).

Transitioning to Medical Examiner–based Systems

Since the origins of the American death investigation system began with the English tradition of coroners in the 1700s, the majority of the country's death investigative systems began with coroners at the helm, and the trend to replace coroners with medical examiners has been a slow process. The need for this transition was brought to the forefront on a national platform in 1954 when the National Conference of Commissions on Uniform State Law initiated the Model Post-Mortem Examinations Act, "The Model Act," that recommended "each state have an office headed by a trained pathologist" (National Research Council, 2009). Throughout the remainder of the twentieth century, 15 states complied and implemented state-wide medical examiner systems, removing all elected coroner positions (National Research Council, 2009). During that same timeframe, primarily during the 1960s–1980s, 98 county-based medical examiner systems were established (Hanzlick, 2007).

The development of medical examiner systems has stalled since that initial push that ended in the 1980s. Currently, coroner jurisdictions far outnumber those that are overseen by medical examiners, but generally speaking, a little over half of the U.S. population are served by medical examiner based offices. This is typically related to the fact that more populous areas (cities or counties) dictate that death investigation be carried out by a medical examiner rather than a coroner, leaving the more rural, less populous areas to be served by an elected coroner (Hanzlick & Fudenberg, 2014). Some coroner/medical examiner jurisdictions utilize a "referral" system wherein a death can be referred to as a forensic pathologist for an autopsy to assist in a complete death investigation (Centers for Disease Control and Prevention, 2015a). Most recent data from the Centers for Disease Control and Prevention (2015b) illustrate that nearly half of the United States have state-wide medical examiner systems while the remaining half is a mixture of coroners and medical examiners covering states, counties, districts, or parishes (see figure 8.1). A lack of standardization and slow conversion to medical examiner death investigation systems has led to a multitude of issues including difficulties in acquiring, training, credentialing, and retaining staff to ensure the quality of death investigation and certification (Hanzlick, 2007).

Challenges for Medical Examiner–based Systems

The transition to a medical examiner–led system overall has many implications and the slow progress can be considered a multifactorial issue. Legislative, political, financial, geographical, and availability of personnel represent a number of hurdles that must be overcome when establishing a medical examiner system.

Many constitutional documents governing states and/or counties often contain laws designating the duties of a coroner and to construct an amendment to these laws is a lengthy and complex process (National Research Council, 2009). The position of a coroner is often a political office, elected by the popular vote, and therefore, firmly seated in the governing office. This same governing office would be responsible for rewriting the law, removing the coroner, and overcoming a significant conflict of interest, albeit for the betterment of the constituents. On the other hand, jurisdictions with limited resources could find having a locally seated coroner to be of benefit. These individuals are typically readily available throughout the investigation, invested in the community, and more equipped to respond in rural or sparsely

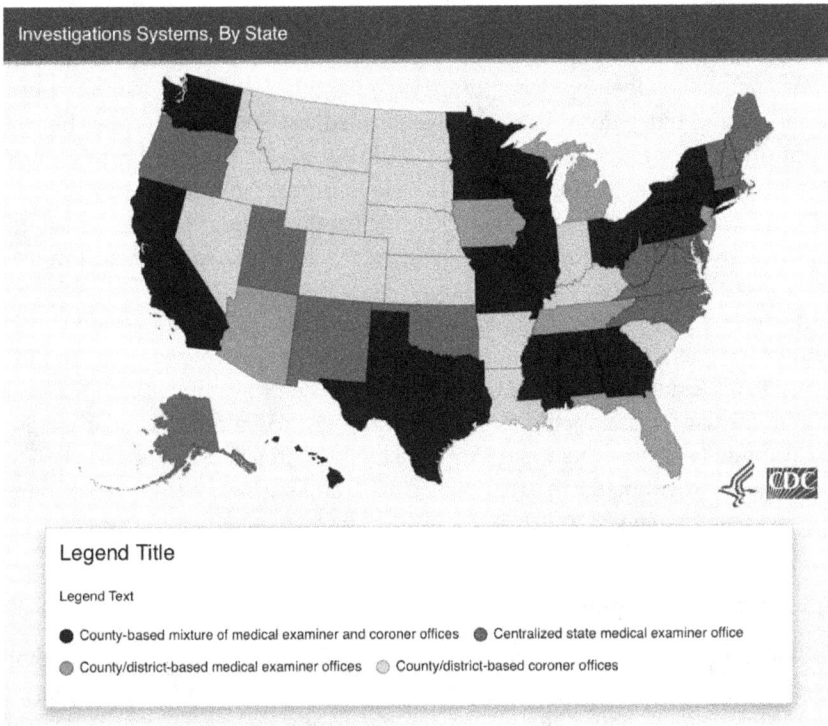

Figure 8.1　Map of Investigation Systems in the United States. *Source: Centers for Disease Control and Prevention (2015b).*

populated areas where reliance on a state or regional medical examiner may present delays throughout the process.

The typical requirements to become a coroner vary greatly among all jurisdictions throughout the United States. The majority are considered local government–elected officials with terms of varying lengths. No distinction for prior medical training or sole dedication to death investigation is required, although a few states designate a physician-coroner rather than lay-coroner. The training guidelines are highly variable ranging from no specifications to an initial week-long course to requiring annual continuing education (Frontline, 2011). For example, to be eligible to become a coroner in the state of Georgia one must (1) be at least 25 years of age, (2) have earned a high school diploma or GED, (3) be a registered voter, (4) lack any felony conviction, and (5) attend a week-long training session annually (Frontline, 2011; Hanzlick, 2007).

Perhaps the two largest factors limiting the transition to medical examiner systems are financial and availability of personnel (National Commission on Forensic Science, 2013). Medical examiners are almost always physicians who are appointed to the position rather than elected (Centers for Disease Control and Prevention, 2015a). Physician salaries can cause significant stress on the budgetary demands of a governmental office. Some states, counties, and cities do utilize a physician-medical examiner system, but the recruitment of interested physicians to fulfill this role in addition to clinical responsibilities may prove difficult. Like lay-coroners, physician-based medical examiners have the capacity to certify deaths based on scene investigation and external examination but must refer cases to a specialized forensic pathologist if an autopsy is necessary.

If the budgetary constraints are a nonissue, identifying a qualified candidate to serve as a medical examiner for a jurisdiction can often prove difficult. There is a shortage of well-trained and experienced forensic pathologists due to a number of factors such as limited training programs, low salaries, and underfunded systems (National Commission on Forensic Science, 2013). The shortage is exacerbated in areas with small populations, deficient tax base, and inadequate physician distribution.

Forensic Pathologists

Although general physicians may serve medical examiners, a forensic pathologist is a specialized physician in the field of death investigation. Becoming a physician, including a forensic pathologist, requires a lifelong dedication to learning and service to the community. Forensic pathology has its basis in Latin as *"forensis"* and *"pathos,"* but has evolved to encompass the study of deaths related to injury or disease that may be of interest to the legal "forum" or public (National Research Council, 2009). The forensic pathologist's career journey begins after graduating high school, earning at least a four-year bachelor's degree, matriculation from medical school (typically after another four years), and being accepted into a pathology residency training program. The typical pathology residency is four years followed by a one-year fellowship in forensic pathology. Each step beyond college requires successful completion of board examinations culminating in certification by the American Board of Pathology along with maintenance of that certification throughout the duration of their professional career. After this tenuous 13-year, at a minimum, journey, individuals are commonly well into their fourth decade of life when they begin practicing as a full-time medical examiner.

THE TEAM APPROACH TO DEATH INVESTIGATION

Regardless of the individual at the helm of death investigation, it is important to understand the interplay among investigating agencies during these often tense and emotional events. It is expected that sudden, unexpected, suspicious, or violent deaths be investigated thoroughly; this expectation also extends to deaths related to an injury, occurring during certain activities (such as at a workplace or during incarceration), occurring with a certain timeframe (such as after recent presentation to a hospital), or when there is a lack of physician presence (National Research Council, 2009).

The investigation at the scene of a deceased individual is of paramount importance and requires expertise from all involved. This typically includes law enforcement agencies as well as representatives from the coroner/medical examiner office. Competent medicolegal death investigators, often certified by the American Board of Medicolegal Death Investigators, are tasked with responding to the scene as a representative of the coroner/medical examiner's office (U.S. National Medicolegal Review Panel, 1999).

Both law enforcement officers and medicolegal death investigators approach the scene with integrity and caution, but the goal of a law enforcement officer is often to determine if a crime has been committed (Institute of Medicine, 2003). Once a lack of criminality is established, the law enforcement officer's involvement is usually limited. Conversely, the coroner/medical examiner's office is primarily focused on the patient-care aspect, mainly of the decedent, and determining how and why they died. This may include interviewing individuals at the scene, speaking with family, preserving evidence at the scene, and preparing the body for transport. The coroner/medical examiner's office works in parallel but independent of the law enforcement agency, and each has different tasks to accomplish (Holder et al., 2011). The coroner/medical examiner's office ultimately bears the responsibility for releasing a scene at which a deceased individual is found/removed (Holder et al., 2011).

Death Investigation's Role in the Legal System

A death investigation is often performed in a team-based atmosphere with qualified medicolegal death investigators, morgue personnel, transportation services, and the coroner/medical examiner. The goal of the team is unified— to collect, preserve, and process all physical information from the decedent. This physical evidence is collected in a manner that enables it to be used in a court of law, and the coroner/medical examiner serves as an agent of the criminal justice system if, in fact, the death is suspicious in nature (National Research Council, 2009). This simple fact further illustrates the importance of having a standardized approach to death investigation.

The American legal system is often reliant on the evidence presented and expert testimony educating the jury so that they may render the appropriate verdict. Expert witnesses are granted permission to testify based on their knowledge or expertise in a specific area relevant to the case being tried (Cornell Law School). Specific to forensic pathologists, they are asked to present their opinions in addition to facts established by an autopsy. This helps clarify how and why the individual is deceased, which is often too complex and technical for a nonexpert jury to determine on their own (Institute of Medicine, 2003).

The legal system in America is similar to that in Australia, Canada, and England in that the focus of achieving justice is based on revealing the truth which is accomplished in an adversarial manner (Iacobucci & Hamilton, 2010). This adversarial system relies on evidence being presented to an impartial decision-maker and helps ensure that all parties are treated fairly (Iacobucci & Hamilton, 2010). Expert witnesses often serve a vital role in this type of system as a provider of information so that the truth may be revealed and a decision reached.

The Family Physician after Death

The intricacies of determining if an autopsy is necessary to collect evidence or to help determine the cause of death is yet another benefit of having specialized training in forensic pathology (Institute of Medicine, 2003). This decision-making expertise allows for appropriate utilization of resources, death certification with accuracy and specificity, as well as complete end-of-life care by a physician. This patient-care aspect of death investigation cannot be overlooked and is often of immeasurable service to the families of decedents.

Family members are often left confused and emotional during times of unexpected death, and being informed of the process as well as knowing their loved one was being cared for by a physician even in their death provides a level of comfort. The medical examiner may very well be the only medical care provider the individual has encountered, and information derived from the autopsy could have a significant impact on living relatives. At the conclusion of the medicolegal death investigation, family members may be provided a report describing findings from the examination, but universally, they are provided a death certificate.

DEATH CERTIFICATION AND MORTALITY DATA

A death certificate is an official document that specifically states the cause of death for a deceased individual. The death certificate is completed by persons who are given the legal authority to do so. Generally, this is a licensed physician, medical examiner, forensic pathologist, or coroner and the responsible party varies by state. The United States has a Standard Certificate of Death, put forth by the Centers for Disease Control and Prevention (CDC) (National Center for Health Statistics, 2003). Each state has adopted this form although adjustments are made according to state laws.

Causes and Manners of Death

Information about the decedent, the decedent's family, and the cause of death are necessary details found on every death certificate. The immediate and any underlying causes of death should be recorded with specificity and accuracy. A separate section for significant contributing illnesses or factors is also available. The immediate cause of death is the final injury or insult that directly lead to death. The underlying cause(s) of death refers to any insult or disease that began the chain of events leading to the immediate cause of death. Other significant conditions (i.e., contributing factors) may include chronic diseases, risk factors, or other insults that may be associated with the death, but not directly related to the immediate cause of death.

The death certificate also serves as an official record of the manner of death. A determination often made by utilizing information from the scene and history, referred to as the circumstances surrounding the death, as well as information obtained from the autopsy (National Center for Health Statistics, 2003). The Standard Certificate of Death includes five main categories for the manner of death designation: natural, accident, suicide, homicide, and undetermined. The majority of cases that are assumed (accepted) by coroner/ medical examiner offices are typically found to be due to a natural disease process or illness, that is, a "natural death." Natural deaths also compose nearly the entirety of cases that are declined (not accepted) for further death investigation by a coroner/medical examiner office. An accidental manner of death is indicated in cases of non-intentional injury (such as motor vehicle collision, fall, and most cases of drug overdose). Although it is dependent on the jurisdiction, accidents make up the second-largest category of deaths at a coroner/medical examiner office (National Research Council, 2009). Suicide and homicide typically refer to deaths related to some sort of violence either initiated by the decedent themselves or another person. If a death remains undetermined at the conclusion of a thorough death investigation that often indicates the certifier has conflicting or missing information that renders them unable to conclusively determine the manner of death.

The Utility of Death Certificates

Death certificates serve a variety of functions within society. Personal legal matters including insurance allocation, distribution of assets, and closing of financial accounts are some of the tasks for which family members will need to show an official certificate of death. On a more public health platform, death certificates are the primary source of population-based mortality data statistics. Therefore, completion of death certificates often fulfills yet another role that coroner/medical examiners have which is that of a public health officer (Hanzlick, 2006; National Research Council, 2009).

Information derived from death certificates helps educate public officials and organizations on the overall health of the country and also aids in epidemiological investigations. Although access to death certification databases varies by state, some allow anyone to view the information and some restrict access to particular relatives. Completion of death certificates is often regulated by the state and is processed by central registration administrations. These state agencies send information to the Center for Disease Control and Prevention's National Center for Health Statistics (NCHS). The NCHS compiles population-based statistics from death certificates gathered by each state to both publish and provide ideas for future ways to improve the population's overall health. One of the systems it uses to monitor health statistics is the National Vital Statistics System (NVSS). In addition to monitoring health statistics, NCHS also serves to assist in the regulation of death reporting (Connolly et al., 2016).

Establishing Mortality Data

The NVSS is a decentralized, collaborative system of 57 regions (the 50 U.S. states, the District of Columbia, New York City, and 5 territories: Puerto Rico, the Virgin Islands, Guam, American Samoa, and the Northern Marianas). The system was first instituted in 1946 under the jurisdiction of the Federal Security Administration and began working with federal and state health agencies to collect birth and death records (Ventura, 2018). Other statistics were included over time such as marriage, divorce, infant birth and death, terminated pregnancies, surveys of hospitalizations, diagnoses, health insurance, smoking habits, demographics, educational attainment, and religion. States submit their vital statistics data electronically through the STEVE (Ventura, 2018).

The data collected by the NVSS is integral to study various public health indicators at the local, state, and national levels as well as health disparities by age, sex, race, ethnicity, and geography. Infant mortality, prenatal care, maternal risk factors, teen birth rates, trends in causes of death and rankings of said causes, and patterns of life expectancy are other important indicators reported by the vital statistics system. This wealth of data can reveal populations at risk and be used in planning programs and initiatives aimed at reducing health disparities. The NVSS is also a useful tool in predicting current and future population growth estimates at the national, state, and local levels. The NVSS is an extremely important source of rich data for public health efforts that benefit the entirety of the United States (Ventura, 2018).

Maintaining the integrity of the data output of the NVSS is of utmost importance. However, mortality data derived from death certificates poses more of a challenge than the reporting of birth data primarily because multiple sources are inputting the data (i.e., certifying deaths). Individuals who are responsible for completing death certificates may be physicians, funeral directors, coroners, or medical examiners. Data collection and standardization can be difficult owing to the vast variability in training and experiences among certifiers and the degrees of complexity in the cause of death statements.

Research has shown that death certificates are wrought with errors and these errors can have a significant impact on the vital statistics of a nation (Connolly et al., 2016; McGivern et al., 2017; Pritt et al., 2005). General physicians are rarely taught how to actually complete a death certificate during medical school or postgraduate training (Lakkireddy et al., 2004). The lack of a postmortem examination to augment clinical data or provide specificity to the cause of death statement is often a source of many errors as well.

Electronic Reporting and ICD Coding

Since 2003, states have been using revised versions of the United States standard birth certificate and death certificate along with electronic reporting systems for both. One proposed benefit of electronic reporting is the standardization of mortality data collection (Ventura, 2018). The NVSS developed a software program named the Mortality, Medical Indexing, Classification, and Retrieval (MICAR) system to process and code death records based on the ICD code. ICD coding is a familiar system to physicians and healthcare providers who use ICD codes to classify diagnoses, symptoms, injuries, and procedures during clinical care. This practice is common in the United States and in many countries worldwide. ICD codes were initially developed centuries ago for mortality data, but over many reiterations now serve the overall healthcare system (World Health Organization, 2019).

In theory, translating cause of death statements from death certificates into ICD codes should serve to standardize mortality data and help make it comparable throughout the United States and internationally. In reality, however, approximately 20% of death records cannot be processed by the MICAR system due to incomplete or incomprehensible information requiring the electronic system to be bypassed and an ICD code to be entered manually (Ventura, 2018). Records may also be wrought with errors that are miscoded by the MICAR system.

Analysis of the ICD code groupings helps develop the CDC's Rankable Causes of Death, the Leading Causes of Death, and The Selected 113 Causes of Death among other vital statistics tabulations (National Center for Health Statistics, 2020). Clearly, thorough and accurate reporting of mortality data has important implications for public health and improving the health of the nation as a whole; however, use of death certificates as the sole data source for mortality data is less clear (Kircher et al., 1985; Ventura, 2018). Primary data acquired from coroner/medical examiner offices is of infinite value but is often kept in a variety of formats some of which are inaccessible by researchers. A centralized database for standardized coroner/medical examiner data is definitely a goal for the future.

Research with Mortality Data

Perhaps the less immediately obvious impact of inaccurate mortality data is a financial one. Multiple funding organizations, including the National Institutes of Health (NIH), utilize the NVSS system to assist in resource allocation for research (National Institutes of Health; Star Metrics, 2019). The field of forensic pathology and medicolegal death investigation generates an abundance of useful primary data regarding epidemiology and surveillance of violent deaths, substance abuse, unintentional injury, hazardous environmental exposures, and infectious disease. Population-based epidemiological data generated by medical examiners can play a key role in public health research and intervention programs, optimizing trauma care, pharmacogenomics, and disease pathogenesis. However, if the ultimate source of this data is the death certificate its value is drastically diminished.

Despite the ubiquity of data generated in medical examiner offices, research efforts in medicolegal death investigation are quite limited. Although the data is limited in recent years, in the early twenty-first century only 11% of the United States' 125 medical schools had full-time faculty members that were forensic pathologists and only 38% of forensic pathology training programs had research opportunities for resident trainees (Nolte, 2004). Since then, the number of U.S. medical schools has increased substantially, while the number of forensic pathologists has not. Academic-based forensic pathologists are even scarcer in the United States and those associated with resident training programs do not always participate in research efforts.

Funding opportunities for forensic pathologists and projects related to medicolegal death investigation are available through the NIH, Centers for Disease Control and Prevention, National Institute of Justice, and the Department of Defense, as well as the American Academy of Forensic Sciences. Regardless of funding availability, reported barriers to the forensic pathologist pursuing research include time constraints with increased caseloads, a lack of protected research time, a lack of institutional support, issues of patient (decedent and relatives) confidentiality, and data acquisition, utilization, and storage (Nolte, 2004).

ADDITIONAL CHALLENGES TO QUALITY MEDICOLEGAL DEATH INVESTIGATION

Forensic Pathology Training

A subject already touched on in an earlier section, the lack of availability of forensic pathologists is an immense threat to the medicolegal death investigation system both in the United States and worldwide. As of 2013, there were only 500 board-certified forensic pathologists practicing full time in the United States. In order to provide adequate coverage to the population, estimates extrapolate that approximately 1,100 to 1,200 forensic pathologists are needed (resulting in nearly 3.7 forensic pathologists per 1 million people). So, this section briefly explains the reasons why there is such a shortage of forensic pathologists.

To begin, there are only 43 ACGME-accredited forensic pathology fellowship training programs available in the United States (Accreditation Council for Graduate Medical Education, 2020). Most programs are allowed to train one fellow per year. Some programs are accredited for additional spots, but these positions are often left unfunded. Approximately 42 of the 78 available positions were filled in 2014, and this percentage was relatively unchanged from data published nearly a decade earlier (National Research Council, 2009). Using historical data, it is estimated that out of the total forensic pathologists completing fellowship, two-thirds will become board certified and less than that will practice forensic pathology full time.

To further illustrate the desperate need for forensic pathologists: If we assume that 21 forensic pathologists are entering the workforce annually in addition to the ~500 currently in practice, it would take twenty-five years to create a workforce that would adequately serve the U.S. population! However, this figure utilizes unrealistic assumptions such as an absence of population growth during this time and that no current forensic pathologists will die or retire. In order to cease perpetuating this dire situation, the field of forensic pathology must become innovative in regard to recruitment, retention, and regulation.

Forensic Pathology Compensation

Some potential reasons for this shortage of forensic pathologists include a lack of exposure to pathology during the first two years of medical school, low salaries compared to other medical specialties, and the ever-growing amount of student debt following undergraduate collegiate and medical education. On average new physicians have greater than $170,000 (USD) of debt after completing the training. According to a survey conducted by the College of American Pathologists, the average salary of a pathologist is around $335,000 per year. In contrast, subspecialized forensic pathologists that are medical examiners, typically based in civil servant offices, make closer to $185,000 on average. Chief medical examiners, a promotion usually requiring many years of experience, net slightly better with annual incomes ranging between $190,000–$220,000 (National Commission on Forensic Science, 2013).

Considering medical examiner salaries are often tied to the state, county commission, or municipality budgets, this funding is quite variable and depends on the region served as well as the workload of each jurisdiction. On average, county systems receive more funding with a mean of $2.16 USD per capita, while state systems receive less (a mean of $1.41 USD per capita) (Hanzlick, 2007). The National Associate of Medical Examiners conducted a survey in 2001 that revealed the annual funding ranged from $30,000 to $16 million USD per office. Most offices spent between $2,000 and $3,000 USD for each autopsy, and the overall average expenditures totaled between $1,000,000 and $2,000,000 per year.

The survey also found a wide variation in workload between offices (Institute of Medicine, 2003). The number of autopsies performed annually, on a per capita basis, differed by a factor of 40. Over half of the offices reported performing more than the recommended 250 autopsies per pathologist annually, a factor that threatens the maintenance of accreditation for offices (Institute of Medicine, 2003). In addition to heavy workloads, many offices had inadequate facilities and a lack of ancillary resources necessary to perform autopsies. The average medical examiner facility was at least 20 years old (some over 50 years old) and lacked adequate space and storage. Most offices had body transport and radiology, but only 37% had in-house toxicology laboratories (Institute of Medicine, 2003).

Inadequate Resources

Facilities and Toxicology

Lacking access to adequate facilities for autopsy and capabilities of toxicological analysis has a disastrous impact on the quality of death investigation performed. Antiquated processes and guidelines can be quickly overrun by the ever-changing epidemics that plague the United States and beyond. One example that illustrates this quite well is the "opioid epidemic."

The past two decades of the "opioid epidemic" have put significant strain on medical examiner productivity and wellness as well as resources for all coroner/medical examiner offices (and healthcare in general). The rate of death related to opioid intoxication has quadrupled in the United States during that time frame reaching far over 16,000 deaths per year (Schiller & Mechanic, 2018). The term "opioid" encompasses natural and synthetic substances that stimulate the body's opioid receptors, resulting in a blockade of the body's pain signals (Schiller & Mechanic, 2018).

The NAME recently issued a position paper strongly urging medical examiners to continue to autopsy individuals suspected to have died from apparent intoxication (Davis & National Association of Medical Examiners and American College of Medical Toxicology Expert Panel on Evaluating and Reporting Opioid, 2014). With the recent surge of drug-related deaths, many offices have lost accreditation, medical examiners, and an ability to maintain a quality work product within a reasonable time frame (Davis & NAME and American College of Medical Toxicology Expert Panel on Evaluating and Reporting Opioid, 2014). Without overarching policies and appropriate funding in place, this strain will continue to greatly hinder the death investigation system's ability to adequately respond to any death including those of violent means. The judicial system and public health agencies are of course within the zone of impact from these ever-increasing challenges.

Sophisticated Testing Platforms

Diagnostic medicine is becoming more reliant on sophisticated methodologies such as advanced imaging solutions and molecular diagnostics. Most medical examiner offices in the country are utilizing digital radiology in the form of x-rays (plain radiographs), while rare offices are afforded the opportunity to have computed topography (CT) images to aid the postmortem examination.

Although "virtopsy" or postmortem examination by imaging has been discussed for years and has been established in other countries, research has demonstrated that imaging alone is not equivalent or superior to autopsy (Leth, 2007). However, having access to both radiology and autopsy data is of great importance to the medical examiner when determining the cause of death.

Data acquired through molecular diagnostics can also assist the medical examiner with specificity on the death certificate. A number of sudden cardiac deaths may be driven by a genetic mutation that would otherwise not be detectable without additional genetic testing. Having access to both radiologic and molecular diagnostic tools may soon become a basic necessity of death investigation systems worldwide.

CONCLUSION

The investigation of deaths in the medicolegal setting will always serve a vital role within a nation as it has done for centuries. Data generated by death certificates and the examination of how and why individuals die help inform the overall health of a nation and the world. Establishing a system of death investigation that is based on adequate training with adequate resources and functions within a standardized set of guidelines and expectations will continue to be a goal of this modern era and the centuries to come.

This chapter has limitations based on the availability of current studies and publications in the area of medicolegal death investigation. Although vital statistics and death investigation are integral in understanding why people die, these topics do not often generate interest among the general public, funding agencies, or policymakers. In current times, the global pandemic of COVID-19 infection has brought these deficiencies to the forefront as many are looking at mortality data to help understand the scope of the infection. Future studies should aim to educate the public on the value of forensic pathology, accurate death reporting, and policies for standardization of practice among coroners and medical examiners to obtain mortality data that adequately reflects the health of a nation.

REFERENCES

Accreditation Council for Graduate Medical Education. (2020). *Forensic Pathology Programs.* Retrieved January 7, 2020 from https://apps.acgme.org/ads/Public /Programs/Search?stateId=&specialtyId=59&specialtyCategoryTypeId=&numCode=300&city=

Centers for Disease Control and Prevention. (2015a). *Coroner/Medical Examiner Laws by State.* Retrieved January 7, 2020 from https://www.cdc.gov/phlp/publications/topic/coroner.html

Centers for Disease Control and Prevention. (2015b). *Death Investigation Systems.* Retrieved January 7, 2020 from https://www.cdc.gov/phlp/publications/coroner/death.html

Choo, T. M., & Choi, Y.-S. (2012). Historical Development of Forensic Pathology in the United States. *Korean Journal of Legal Medicine, 36,* 15–21.

Connolly, A. J., Finkbeiner, W. E., Ursell, P. C., & Davis, R. L. (2016). Death Certification. In *Autopsy Pathology: A Manual and Atlas* (Vol. 3, pp. 168–177). Elsevier. https://doi.org/https://doi.org/10.1016/B978-0-323-28780-7.00014-7

Cornell Law School. *Expert Witness.* Wex. Retrieved January 7, 2020 from https://www.law.cornell.edu/wex/expert_witness

Davis, G. G., & National Association of Medical Examiners and American College of Medical Toxicology Expert Panel on Evaluating and Reporting Opioid. (2014). National Association of Medical Examiners position paper: Recommendations for the Investigation, Diagnosis, and Certification of Deaths Related to Opioid Drugs. *Journal of Medical Toxicology, 10*, 100–106.

Frontline. (2011). *How Qualified Is Your Coroner?* PBS. Retrieved January 7, 2020 from https://www.pbs.org/wgbh/pages/frontline/post-mortem/things-to-know/how -qualified-is-your-coroner.html

Hanzlick, R. (2006). Medical Examiners, Coroners, and Public Health: A Review and Update. *Archives of Pathology & Laboratory Medicine, 130*, 1274–1282.

Hanzlick, R. (2007). The Conversion of Coroner Systems to Medical Examiner Systems in the United States: A Lull in the Action. *The American Journal of Forensic Medicine and Pathology, 28*, 279–283.

Hanzlick, R. L. (2015). The Future of Forensic Pathology: Is Regionalization a Key? *Academic Forensic Pathology, 5*, 516–525.

Hanzlick, R. L., & Fudenberg, J. (2014). Coroner Versus Medical Examiner Systems: Can We End The Debate? *Academic Forensic Pathology, 4*(1), 10–17.

Holder, E. H., Robinson, L., & Laub, J. H. (2011). *Death Investigation: A Guide for the Scene Investigator*. National Institute of Justice.

Houston, R. (2014). *The Coroners of Northern Britain C. 1300–1700*. Springer.

Iacobucci, F., & Hamilton, G. (2010). The Goudge Inquiry and the Role of Medical Expert Witnesses. *Canadian Medical Association Journal, 182*(1), 53–56.

Institute of Medicine. (2003). *Medicolegal Death Investigation System: Workshop Summary*. The National Academies Press. https://doi.org/doi:10.17226/10792

Kircher, T., Nelson, J., & Burdo, H. (1985). The Autopsy as a Measure of Accuracy of the Death Certificate. *New England Journal of Medicine, 313*, 1263–1269.

Lakkireddy, D. R., Gowda, M. S., Murray, C. W., Basarakodu, K. R., & Vacek, J. L. (2004). Death Certificate Completion: How Well are Physicians Trained and are Cardiovascular Causes Overstated? *The American Journal of Medicine, 117*, 492–498.

Leth, P. M. (2007). The Use of CT Scanning in Forensic Autopsy. *Forensic Science, Medicine, and Pathology, 3*(1), 65–69.

McGivern, L., Shulman, L., Carney, J. K., Shapiro, S., & Bundock, E. (2017, Nov/Dec). Death Certification Errors and the Effect on Mortality Statistics. *Public Health Rep, 132*(6), 669–675.

National Center for Health Statistics. (2003). *Physicians' Handbook on Medical Certification of Death*.

National Center for Health Statistics. (2020). *Vital Statistics Data*. Retrieved May 11, 2020 from http://www.cdc.gov/nchs/data_access/Vitalstatsonline.html

National Commission on Forensic Science. (2013). *Increasing the Number, Retention, and Quality of Board-Certified Forensic Pathologists*. United States Department of Justice.

National Institutes of Health. *Estimates of Funding for Various Research, Condition, and Disease Categories*. Retrieved January 7, 2020 from https://report.nih.gov/categorical_spending.aspx

National Research Council. (2009). *Strengthening Forensic Science in the United States: A Path Forward*. The National Academies Press.

Nolte, K. B. (2004). Research Issues in Forensic Pathology: A Survey of Academic Institutions Employing Forensic Pathologists. *Human Pathology, 35*, 532–535.

Pritt, B. S., Hardin, N. J., Richmond, J. A., & Shapiro, S. L. (2005). Death Certification Errors at an Academic Institution. *Archives of Pathology & Laboratory Medicine, 129*, 1476–1479.

Schiller, E. Y., & Mechanic, O. J. (2018). *Opioid overdose.* StatPearls.

Spitz, W. U., Spitz, D. J., & Fisher, R. S. (2006). *Spitz and Fisher's Medicolegal Investigation of Death: Guidelines for the Application of Pathology to Crime Investigation* (4th ed.). Charles C Thomas Publisher.

Star Metrics. (2019). *Federal RePORTER.* Retrieved January 7, 2020 from https://federalreporter.nih.gov/

Thorpe, F. N. (1906). *Constitution of Georgia February 5, 1777* The Avalon Project by Lillian Godman Law Library. Retrieved January 8 from https://avalon.law.yale.edu/18th_century/ga02.asp

Thorwald, J. (1965). *The Century of the Detective.* Houghton Mifflin Harcourt P.

Tilstone, W. J., Savage, K. A., & Clark, L. A. (2006). *Forensic Science: An Encyclopedia of History, Methods, and Techniques.* ABC-CLIO.

U.S. National Medicolegal Review Panel. (1999). *Death Investigation: A Guide for the Scene Investigator.* US Department of Justice.

Ventura, S. J. (2018, Mar). The U.S. National Vital Statistics System: Transitioning Into the 21st Century, 1990–2017. *Vital Health Stat, 1*(62), 1–84.

World Health Organization. (2019). *International Classification of Diseases (ICD) Information Sheet.* Retrieved January 7, 2020 from https://www.who.int/classifications/icd/factsheet/en/

Chapter 9

International Approaches to Pediatric Medicolegal Death Investigation

Alfredo E. Walker and Brandi C. McCleskey

According to the World Health Organization, childhood is defined as an age younger than or equal to 19 years, but the upper limit of 19 years can be lowered by any applicable legal definition in a particular jurisdiction (WHO, 2019). Groups are further classified by age such that an adolescent refers to individuals between 10 and 19 years of age, an infant as those less than 1 year of age, and a neonate as less than or equal to an age of 1 month.

The American Academy of Pediatrics (AAP) defined pediatrics as the specialty of medicine that deals with the physical, mental, and social health of children from birth to young adulthood (AAP, 2015). Pediatrics consists of a broad spectrum of health services that range from preventive healthcare to the diagnosis and treatment of acute and chronic diseases (AAP, 2015). There is marked variation in the common causes of death in the various subcategories of the pediatric age range, and given this marked variation, mortality statistics are reported according to these subcategories rather than as a single category. Based on this, pediatric mortality is reported according to pediatric age subcategory as neonatal, infancy, death under age 5 years, and adolescence (AAP, 2015).

Remarkable progress in child survival has occurred in the past three decades with millions of children now having better chances of survival than in 1990 (United Nations Children Emergency Fund [UNICEF], 2020). One in 27 children died before age 5 years in 2019, compared to 1 in 11 in 1990 (UNICEF, 2020). Progress in reducing child mortality rates has been accelerated in the 2000–2019 period compared with the 1990s, with the annual rate of reduction in the global under-five mortality rate increasing from 1.9 per cent in 1990–1999 to 3.7% in 2000–2019. Despite the global progress in reducing child mortality rates over the past few decades, an estimated 5.2 million children under age five died in 2019 (UNICEF, 2020).

The global under age 5 years mortality rate declined by 59% between 1990 and 2019, having moved from 93 deaths per 1,000 live births in 1990 to 38 per 1,000 live births in 2019 (UNICEF, 2020). However, despite this considerable progress, improving child survival remains a matter of urgent concern; in 2019 alone, approximately 14,000 deaths under age 5 years occurred daily (UNICEF, 2020). This is considered an intolerably high number of deaths which are largely preventable. Additionally, the overall burden of child and youth deaths remains high; in 2019, 7.4 million children, adolescents, and youth (0–14 years) died from mostly preventable or treatable causes.

The period of adolescence is associated with increasing amounts of time in an ever-expanding social environment within and beyond their immediate networks with interaction with a wider array of people (UNICEF, 2017). As children enter the second decade of life, their mortality rates from violence double more than those of their first 10 years of life (UNICEF, 2017). In 2015 alone, violence was responsible for the deaths of 82,000 adolescents worldwide (UNICEF, 2017). Every 7 minutes an adolescent is killed by an act of violence somewhere in the world (UNICEF, 2017). Those aged 15 to 19 years are particularly vulnerable, being three times more likely to die violently than younger adolescents who are aged 10 to 14 years (UNICEF, 2017). More adolescent deaths result from interpersonal than collective violence (UNICEF, 2017). In 2015, nearly two out of three victims died of homicide, while the rest were killed by conflicts (UNICEF, 2017).

It is imperative that pediatric deaths are investigated thoroughly and categorized appropriately in a standardized fashion utilizing expert input and collaboration. However, there is no single standardized international protocol for the investigation of these challenging deaths. Most developed medicolegal jurisdictions share similarities in their investigative approach, which typically involves concepts of a multidisciplinary team approach, collaboration, and centralization of information. Because it is not possible to cover the investigative protocols that exist in every medicolegal jurisdiction across the globe, this chapter presents an overview of the pediatric medicolegal death investigation practices in the Province of Ontario, Canada, the United States of America, the United Kingdom of Great Britain, Australia, and the Caribbean region.

MULTIDISCIPLINARY TEAMS IN MEDICOLEGAL DEATH INVESTIGATION

A multidisciplinary team (MDT) is a group of professionals who work together in a coordinated and collaborative manner (USDOJ, 2000). These types of teams are utilized in many fields including healthcare. In medicolegal death investigation, the MDT works to ensure an effective response to reports of suspected child abuse and neglect (USDOJ, 2000). No single profession or state agency can independently respond to these challenging cases adequately, and it is now well accepted that the best investigative response is through an MDT approach (USDOJ, 2000). This includes (and often extends beyond) joint investigations and inter-agency coordination that inform decision making (USDOJ, 2000). An MDT investigation requires the full participation and collaboration of team members by sharing their knowledge, skills, and expertise (USDOJ, 2000). Each member fulfills his/her professional role whilst taking the roles and responsibilities of the other members into consideration (USDOJ, 2000). The members of the MDT represent the government agencies and private practitioners who are responsible for investigating crimes against children and protecting and treating children (USDOJ, 2000). An MDT may focus on any combination of investigations, policy issues, and treatment of victims, their relatives, and perpetrators (USDOJ, 2000).

The MDT Approach

The MDT approach promotes well-coordinated child abuse investigations that benefit from the input and contribution of many stakeholders, especially law enforcement, coroners/medical examiners, prosecution agencies, and child protection services to ensure the successful conclusion of an investigation (USDOJ, 2000). It encourages and facilitates the sharing of key investigative details that allows each agency to acquire all the information it needs to effectively perform its duties. Some of the primary goals of this team include arriving at valid conclusions as to the circumstances of death, medical cause of death, manner of death; assisting with the prevention of deaths in similar circumstances in the future; determining whether or not there is a criminal liability; and, identifying any public health implications that may arise (Collins, 2019). The MDT approach minimizes the risk of dissemination of inaccurate information, the duplication of efforts, and inadvertent interference in the investigation of one agency by another agency, although investigations by various agencies will occur simultaneously and may complement each other (Collins, 2019).

Components of a Pediatric MDT
Medicolegal Death Investigation

Broadly speaking, the shared similarities of the better pediatric medicolegal death investigation frameworks outline a defined protocol for multi-agency involvement that consists of the following:

- Pediatric death reporting guidelines,
- Investigative protocols for the police,
- Care of the family,
- Activation of child protection concerns,
- Investigation by medical examiner or coroner,
- Death scene examination (with or without doll re-enactments),
- Minimum standards for the performance of postmortem examinations (inclusive of the nature and extent of ancillary investigations),
- Templates for reporting on the results of the postmortem examination,
- Case review by a pediatric multidisciplinary death investigation committee.

Each of the above components generates a varying amount of data of different types. Therefore, a vital portion of this process must involve the centralization of case data (Collins, 2019). The centralization of case data can take any form, but typically there is a Pediatric Death Review Team (PDRT) that acts as the central repository for collating, reporting, and sharing of information (Collins, 2019). This team coordinates the periodic review and evaluation of the investigative process, and provides feedback and updates on the progress and resolution of individual cases with the various stakeholder agencies (Collins, 2019). The role of the PDRT is most important when the outcome of the investigation of pediatric deaths can result in legal proceedings, particularly those that can disrupt family units through the removal of surviving siblings from the home and their subsequent placement into the hands of children's services, other childcare agencies, or foster care (Collins, 2019).

The starting point of the multidisciplinary medicolegal death investigative approach must be the mandatory reporting of every child death to a central hub by all participants using defined criteria (Collins, 2019). The local laws of a particular jurisdiction will define (a) what types of death must be reported, (b) who has an obligation to report such deaths, and (c) to which agency or organization. Depending on the jurisdiction, the police services, medical examiner's office, and/or coroner's office are usually the first agencies to be notified about any death of medicolegal concern. Once the circumstances of the death are established, the coroner or medical examiner will assume jurisdiction of the case if it falls under their legally defined authority to do so. If the death does not fall under their legal authority, then the case will not be accepted for investigation.

The mandatory nature for reporting certain categories of death must be part of the policy in a pediatric medicolegal death investigation (USDOJ, 2000). The relevant legislation in individual jurisdictions will mandate what types of pediatric deaths are reportable and to which oversight organizations (USDOJ, 2000; Collins, 2019). This is dependent on the nature of the medicolegal death investigation system that exists in that jurisdiction, whether it is a coroner's system or U.S.-style medical examiner's system, and the definition of the pediatric age range. Universally, medical personnel, law enforcement officers, medical examiners, and coroners can all report deaths. This approach will guarantee that every reportable death is captured, a file opened, and all investigative information pertinent to the case can be collected and collated (Collins, 2019). In most instances in pediatric medicolegal death investigation, the central hub for the collection and collation of information related to the death of a child is a child protection agency or a department of family services (Collins, 2019).

The collaborative investigative approach must begin shortly after the death of a child to ensure that appropriate information is gathered and shared in a timely manner (Collins, 2019). The collaborative intervention of the various partners during the investigation of a pediatric death will address the legal, medical, and/or social determinants of the cause of death (Collins, 2019). The ultimate aims are to (a) accurately determine and document the cause and manner of death, (b) identify risk factors that will inform prevention strategies aimed at protecting the health and well-being of other siblings and family members, and (c) facilitate criminal proceedings and the judicial process if indicated (Collins, 2019). As such there must be intersection of the functions of the major stakeholder organizations that feed into the process of centralization of information (figure 9.1) (Collins, 2019).

Utilizing Standardized Investigative Tools

With every report of a pediatric death that falls under the umbrella of medicolegal death investigation, information on the circumstances of death can be obtained from a variety of sources. Sources may include the police and coroner's investigative reports with details of the decedent's medical, birth and gestational history, the agonal illness, and description of the final sleep (if applicable) for babies and infants (Walker, 2019). In some jurisdictions, a standardized infant death investigation questionnaire is completed by the investigating coroner, police investigator, or pediatrician and is provided to the pathologist (Walker, 2019). In 1996, the Center for Disease Control and Prevention (CDC) developed and issued a Sudden Unexpected Infant Death Investigation Reporting Form (SUIDIRF) as a voluntary tool and template for the United States (CDC, 2021). Revisions of this form were issued in 2006, 2017, and 2020 prior to the most up to date version (CDC, 2021). The SUIDIRF serves to

- standardize data collection to help improve classification of sleep-related infant deaths.

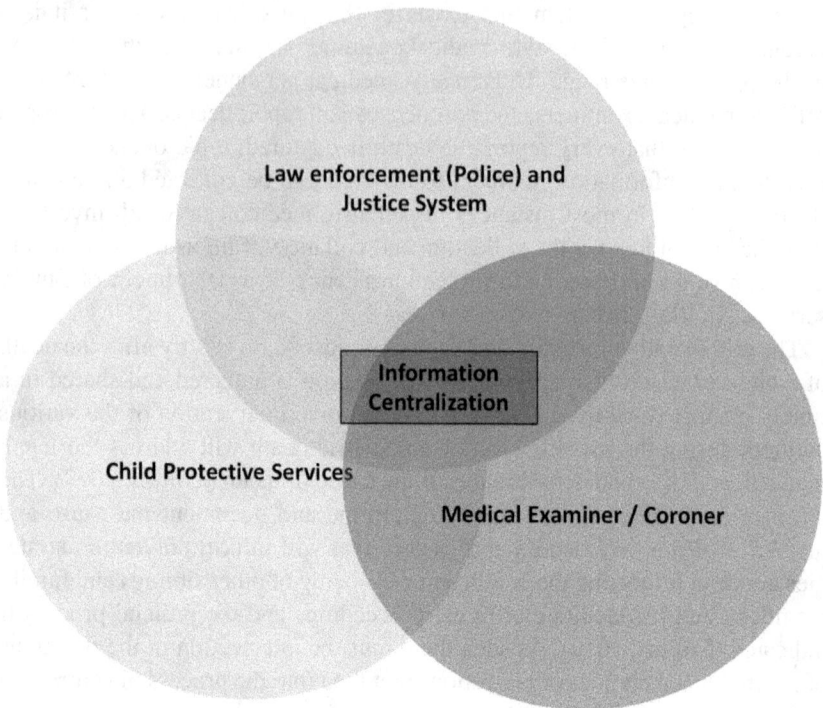

Figure 9.1   Diagrammatic Representation of the Centralization of Information. *Source*: Collins, 2019.

- assist in determining accurate cause of death by strengthening information about the circumstances of the death available before an autopsy.
- guide investigators through the steps involved in an investigation.
- allow investigators to document their findings easily and consistently.
- produce information that researchers can use to recognize new risk factors for sudden unexpected infant death and sudden infant death syndrome (SIDS).

In the United Kingdom, the equivalent form is called the Sudden Unexpected Death in Infancy (SUDI) questionnaire which was developed jointly in 2016 by the Royal College of Pathologists and the Royal College of Pediatrics and Child Health (Kennedy, 2016). In Ontario, Canada, the equivalent questionnaire was developed by the Office of the Chief Coroner for Ontario as the Investigation Questionnaire for Sudden Unexpected Deaths in Infants (DU1) (OCCO, 2013).

CHILD DEATH REVIEW TEAMS

The publication "A Program Manual for Child Death Review" produced by the National Center for Child Death Review (NCCDR) in 2005 states that the death of a child is a sentinel event and community responsibility that should urge communities to identify other children at risk for illness or injury. Death review requires multidisciplinary participation from the community and the review of case information should be comprehensive and broad (NCCDR, 2005). A review should lead to an understanding of risk factors and a focus on prevention by offering effective recommendations and actions to prevent deaths and keep children healthy, safe, and protected (NCCDR, 2005). Through comprehensive and multidisciplinary reviews of child deaths, a better understanding of how and why children die can be gleaned. The findings can be used to prevent other deaths and improve the health and safety of children (NCCDR, 2005). The objectives of the Child Death Review (CDR) are multifaceted as listed below:

- Ensure the accurate identification and uniform consistent reporting of the cause and manner of every child death.
- Improve communication and linkages among local and state agencies and enhance coordination of efforts.
- Improve agency responses in the investigation of child deaths.
- Improve agency responses to protect siblings and other children in the homes of deceased children.
- Improve criminal investigations and the prosecution of child homicides.
- Improve delivery of services to children, families, providers, and community members.
- Identify specific barriers and system issues involved in the deaths of children.
- Identify significant risk factors and trends in child deaths.
- Identify and advocate for needed changes in legislation, policy, and practices and expanded efforts in child health and safety to prevent child deaths.
- Increase public awareness and advocacy for the issues that affect the health and safety of children.

A CDR team should always have representatives from law enforcement, child protective services, prosecutor/district attorney, medical examiner/coroner, public health, pediatrician or other family health provider, and emergency medical services (NCCDR, 2005). Additional and ad hoc members from other agencies and professions should be considered for membership and provisions should be made for their inclusion on a case-appropriate basis (NCCDR, 2005). The purpose and objectives of CDR are consistent across the United States, but variations do exist on how the process is implemented by states and local communities (NCCDR, 2005). A CDR program can include a case review team, an advisory team, and/or program administration team and follow one of four different models (NCCDR, 2005).

The Case Review Team

A Case Review Team conducts comprehensive reviews of individual cases (NCCDR, 2005). These reviews should be performed in a timely manner and share comprehensive information compiled from multiple sources associated with the child's death (NCCDR, 2005). The process should identify and review system problems, work to improve communication and coordination among agencies involved, and examine any local trends and/or issues (NCCDR, 2005). Regular and repetitive iterations of this process help to improve investigative protocols and develop interagency agreements to improve reporting and procedures (NCCDR, 2005). Overall, the Case Review Team should enable systems to maintain integrity, accountability, and public health initiatives including community education, awareness, and prevention strategies (NCCDR, 2005).

The Advisory Team

The Advisory Team assesses the Case Review Team's findings and child mortality trends to inform recommendations and/or action plans (NCCDR, 2005). This team is responsible for identifying best practices, developing policies, and advocating for prevention programs (NCCDR, 2005). The Advisory Team would also serve to promote better communication among agencies both, local and larger (state, territory, country levels) (NCCDR, 2005). With this oversight, the Advisory Team can also advocate for the enhancement of the review process at the case level (NCCDR, 2005).

The Program Administration Team

The Program Administration Team will manage and/or support the Case Review Teams by promoting the development of local teams and providing training and technical assistance to the review teams (NCCDR, 2005). Collation of case review reports and child mortality data typically occurs at this level. The Program Administration Team prepares annual reports and links the review teams to prevention resources. As with the other teams, promoting multi-agency participation is a goal of the Program Administration Team (NCCDR, 2005).

Models of CDR Programs

Model 1: Local-only Reviews of Individual Cases, State Reviews of Local Findings, and State and Local Responses to Findings

In this model, a state agency provides oversight and coordination for a network of local review teams. Protocols or guidelines for local reviews are provided by the state with varying degrees of authority. Training and technical assistance are also provided to members of the local teams by the state who will also have a staffed state CDR coordinator position. Most reviews will be conducted at the local level with recommendations made for improvements to local policies and practices. Prevention initiatives will be implemented locally.

A local review team can serve a county, city, and/or regional jurisdiction. The agency coordinating the local teams can vary. The local review team will usually submit case review reports to a state agency or state CDR program office. Following this, a state advisory team will review the aggregate or individual findings of local teams and makes recommendations for improvements to state policies and practices. Most states that use this method will produce an annual report with child mortality data, CDR findings, and recommendations and may focus on child abuse deaths or all preventable deaths.

States vary as to whether local teams receive funding for reviews but except for a few states, they do not. States also vary in whether local reviews are mandated or are voluntary. Teams may also have sub-committees that review specific causes of deaths and report on these findings to their local or state CDR team. Most review meetings are held as retrospective reviews which usually take place after the investigation is mostly completed and all the gathered case information is readily available.

However, some teams have immediate response reviews that typically occur shortly after a death, usually for those deaths which are unexpected or unexplained. Applying this method allows the team to discuss case information immediately, thereby influencing the processes and procedures to be used during the active investigation of a child death. This type of review may also assist the child protective services in their efforts to protect other children involved. Immediate response review meetings are typically unscheduled, and the team coordinator usually contacts each team member to arrange these reviews as necessary. It is the responsibility of each team to establish criteria to identify deaths that require immediate response reviews and often only a select subgroup of the full death review team will participate in these types of reviews. If a team chooses an immediate response review but has standing meeting dates for retrospective reviews as well, then it is likely that the case will go through both types of review. In this way, the CDR process acts as a tool for coordinating death investigations and the delivery of services as well as a source of information for the identification of risk factors and prevention of other deaths in the future.

Model 2: State and Local Review of Individual Cases and State and Local Response to Findings

In this second model, a state-level committee reviews certain types of deaths or a representative sample of cases, while local teams review cases independently from the state team. There may be little or no coordination between the local and state reviews or the state may review the local findings. The local review teams may or may not operate under mandated or suggested state guidelines. Local teams rarely receive state funds for their reviews. As with the other approaches, the agency lead varies by jurisdiction.

Model 3: State-only Reviews of Individual Cases and State-level Responses to Findings

In this third model, no community reviews occur. Rather, a state-level CDR committee reviews child death cases and issues a state-level report of findings. These review panels usually involve state agency representatives. Most state-level reviews started as child abuse reviews, but some have expanded into other preventable causes of death. In several states, comprehensive case records are made available to an abstractor who prepares the case for the review team. In other states, agencies bring their own records to the review. The types and numbers of deaths reviewed usually represent only a proportion of all deaths in the state. A variation of this model is that a state agency may have an internal review team comprised of their own agency representatives. In this model, the deaths reviewed are usually of children who were in the care and custody of that agency (e.g., deaths of children in foster care). The state committee may also serve as the state-mandated review panel and conduct case reviews or review local case reviews of child abuse deaths.

Model 4: Local-only Review of Individual Cases and Local Response to Findings

In this fourth model, reviews are conducted in city or county jurisdictions only. These teams operate independently of the state although in some cases a state-level person may assist in bringing some of the teams together for training and/or technical assistance.

MEDICOLEGAL DEATH INVESTIGATION
IN SELECTED COUNTRIES

In order for a comprehensive review to occur after the death of a child, an examination is necessary by a physician, coroner, or medical examiner depending on the jurisdiction type. To understand how these deaths are investigated and examined in many mature systems, the process is outlined in the following sections. Much of the information is derived from personal knowledge and experiences of the author (AEW).

Canada

The geographical makeup of Canada is such that it consists of provinces and territories. Each province or territory possesses one of two medicolegal death investigation systems, either the traditional coroner's system or the U.S.-style medical examiner's system. The coroner's system is used in the majority of provinces and territories (like Ontario) and the medical examiner's system is used only in Alberta, Manitoba, Nova Scotia, and Newfoundland and Labrador.

Ontario

The Province of Ontario has the largest population (14.57 million) in Canada and operates the single largest medicolegal death investigation system in the world utilizing medical doctors as coroners. The coroner's system is overseen by the Office of the Chief Coroner for Ontario (OCCO), which supervises the death investigation process through Investigating and Regional Supervising coroners. Coroners investigate cases of sudden deaths and order postmortem examinations accordingly. Under the 2009 amendment of the Coroners Act of Ontario, only pathologists who are appropriately credentialed and registered by the Ontario Forensic Pathology Service (OFPS) may perform medicolegal postmortem examinations. The OFPS also includes the Chief Forensic Pathologist for the Province of Ontario who serves as one of three Deputy Chief Coroners. The OCCO and OFPS conduct medicolegal death investigations in a very collaborative manner.

The OFPS manages the pathologists that perform postmortem examinations therefore establishing a centralized protocol and repository for information related to the death. The pathologists are credentialed based on three categories:

Category A: Pathologists with recognized training and certification in forensic pathology which allows them to perform all types of medicolegal postmortem examinations, inclusive of homicides and criminally suspicious deaths, in both adults and the pediatric age groups.

Category B: Pathologists who are trained and certified in anatomical pathology which allows them to perform routine medicolegal postmortem examination on adults only in non-criminally suspicious cases.

Category C: Pathologists who are trained and certified in pediatric pathology and are only permitted to perform postmortem examinations in cases of non-criminally suspicious (i.e. natural) pediatric deaths that did not occur in a community-based setting.

The OFPS adheres to scientifically informed guidelines that its pathologists must follow when performing and reporting on medicolegal postmortem examinations. All postmortem examination findings are documented in a manner that will permit review by other pathologists (known as "peer review") as a quality assurance measure as necessary. All unnatural child deaths must be reviewed by a newly established committee known as the Child Injury Interpretation Committee (OFPS, 2017).

The OCCO is notified of all reportable pediatric deaths for medicolegal investigation. The investigating coroner will attend the scene of death or discovery of the body and gather all information pertinent to the decedent and the circumstances of the death. This activity is performed in conjunction with the police and will include an examination of the scene of death or discovery of the body. At his/her discretion, a Coroner's Warrant for Postmortem Examination is completed by the Investigating Coroner. The Coroner's Warrant for Postmortem Examination is the authoritative legal request for the performance of a medicolegal postmortem examination by a pathologist in Ontario. In a given geographical region of coverage, it is the Category A Pathologist who determines whether a postmortem examination can be performed by a Category C Pathologist or not; this decision being based on the known circumstances of death. This approach ensures that pediatric cases that require a forensic pathology eye at postmortem examination receive it, and minimizes the risk of a criminally suspicious death being missed.

As part of the completeness of the information gathering process, the investigating coroner will also complete a rather detailed Death Under of Age 5 years (DU5) Questionnaire as applicable. The DU5 Questionnaire consists of 28 pages that cover comprehensive questions about the demographics of the decedent, details of the person who discovered the body, specific details about the death, the circumstances of the final sleep and beddings, the sleep environment and ambient temperature, description of the body position when found, resuscitative attempts, mother's pregnancy (including obstetric history, the decedent's birth, postnatal history, immunization status, and other medical histories), death scene examination, and the medical and social histories of the birth parents. The child protection services, known as the Children

Aid Societies, will also be contacted, informed of the death, and asked if the child or family has a file with the agency and the nature of the matter.

Once the final postmortem examination report has been issued, the OCCO death investigation procedures may mandate a review of the case by the relevant expert death committee in certain circumstances. Seven expert death review committees were established for this purpose and these committees report to the Chief Coroner for Ontario. The Pediatric Death Review Committee (PDRC) and Child Injury Interpretation Committee (CIIC) are two of those committees. The CIIC serves to review only unnatural deaths.

United States

In the United States, the individual medicolegal death investigation system of each state can be a coroner's system, medical examiner's system, or a mixed coroner/medical examiner system. As such, the investigative approach adopted in a particular state can have slight variations depending on the law of the State. In most U.S. states, however, a multidisciplinary approach is utilized (Collins, 2019).

Again, the advantage of this approach is the creation of a centralized means for the collection of information and its sharing among the various investigating stakeholder agencies. The recipients of the information are responsible for disseminating relevant details to the other agencies while remaining objective and not directly involved in the activities of the other agencies. Periodic reviews are conducted, and they provide external quality assurance and ensure that the respective agencies are following best practice guidelines.

The standards for the performance of postmortem examinations are set by the National Association of Medical Examiners (NAME) (Peterson & Clark, 2006) with several additional position papers having been published over the years on the specialized assessments of injury (Case et al., 2001; Gill et al., 2013). The correct certification of both the cause and manner of death is dependent upon evaluation of all available data which includes information derived from the investigation, scene examination, postmortem examination, and ancillary studies. The 2013 NAME Position Paper provided recommendations on what constitutes the dataset to be produced during the postmortem examination of infants who died or are believed to have died of inflicted head trauma (Gill et al., 2013). In a similar manner to Ontario, it was stated that the evaluation and documentation of such infant deaths involve the production of a detail-oriented and thoroughly documented examination that is independently reviewable to support the multitude of inquiries that may follow from the public and the criminal justice system.

Dependent on the U.S. state laws, the nature of the medicolegal death investigation system and local and local quality assurance practices, CDR programs and CDR teams as outlined previously, may be employed accordingly (NCCDR, 2005).

United Kingdom

Individual professionals and agencies possess a statutory duty to investigate all sudden and unexpected deaths in infancy and childhood with due thoroughness, care, and compassion as stated in the 2015 interagency guidance document of the Department of Education on working together to safeguard and protect the welfare of children (Department of Education, 2015). This guidance is based around the regulatory structures in England, but the principles of the guidelines can also be applied in areas in which other systems are in place. Although it focuses primarily on SUDI, the principles broadly relate to all unexpected deaths in children from birth to age 18 years with the exclusion of stillbirths (Department of Education, 2015). Therefore, unexpected deaths in the early neonatal period, unexpected deaths for which a natural cause is not immediately apparent, and deaths from external causes, including accidents, suicides, and possible homicides are all included.

A report, typically referred to as the Kennedy Report, created by a collaborative committee, provides guidelines on the minimum expected standard of practice by specialist pediatric pathologists who are asked to perform investigations in both non-criminally and criminally suspicious deaths (Royal College of Pathologists [RCPath], 2016). Additional guidelines for the examination of suspicious infant deaths have also been established (RCPath, 2016). Unique to the United Kingdom, a "double-doctor" approach may be utilized in violent (i.e., homicide) deaths with joint efforts by a pediatric pathologist working alongside a forensic pathologist, whereas other countries would typically only use a forensic pathologist (RCPath, 2016). Requests for specialist pediatric pathology consultation opinions (cardiac pathology, neuropathology, ophthalmic pathology, and bone pathology) are made if needed.

On completion of the postmortem examination, the coroner should be immediately informed of the initial findings. These findings may also be discussed with the lead health professional and lead police investigator as required, with the coroner's permission (RCPath, 2016). If the initial findings of the postmortem examination suggest evidence of neglect or abuse, the police investigative team and children's social care should be informed immediately, and further investigations set in process (RCPath, 2016).

The UK government has established Child Death Overview Panels (CDOP), which have a statutory responsibility to systematically gather comprehensive data on children's deaths, to identify notable and potentially remediable factors, and to learn lessons and make recommendations to reduce the risk of future child deaths (Department of Education, 2015). The CDOP is a multi-agency panel that meets on a regular basis to review all child deaths. Each CDOP has the statutory duty to review the deaths of all children, irrespective of place of death (Department of Education, 2015). Cases of sudden unexpected deaths are scheduled for discussion at the CDOP after the conclusion of the full joint agency response, including the final case discussion and the coroner's inquiry (Department of Education, 2015).

The local CDOP manager should be notified whenever an infant dies and the responsibility to notify rests with the lead health professional following presentation (Department of Education, 2015). A copy of the report of the final case discussion should be sent to the CDOP manager for inclusion in the documentation compiled for the CDOP meeting. The CDOP manager should also be provided with other relevant documentation, including, where appropriate, completed forms and the initial report to the coroner and pathologist.

The CDOP should review all relevant information provided on the case from the different agencies involved and consider any relevant contributory factors in each domain (factors intrinsic to the infant, parenting capacity, family and environment, and service delivery) and form an opinion as to the relevance of such factors. The CDOP should form an opinion on the cause and category of the infant's death, and on whether they consider the death to have been preventable according to the definition of such (Department of Education, 2015). Learning points that arise from the review will be considered and used to inform appropriate recommendations.

Australia

South Australia

A Child Death and Serious Injury Review Committee has been responsible for reviewing the circumstances and causes of all child deaths in the state of South Australia since 2005 (Duncan & Byard, 2018). The committee consists of an MDT of experts who are drawn from pediatrics, education, disability, psychology, social work, child protection, public health, and justice. These experts come together to consider all information gathered about an infant's death. Their broad base of knowledge and experience facilitates a comprehensive overview of the circumstances of the death and identification of systemic issues that may have contributed to the quality-of-service provision to that infant and their family.

Apart from identifying events that actively contributed to the death, the review process can also identify the absence or omissions of services or regulatory/legislative mechanisms which could have created a different outcome. On conclusion of a death review, the committee can make recommendations to the government about changes to legislation, policy, or practice which could potentially lead to a reduction in the risk of deaths occurring under similar circumstances. Additionally, the committee also monitors the trends and patterns of all child deaths in its jurisdiction.

New South Wales

In New South Wales, the state government has produced guidelines on the roles and responsibilities of each agency (health, police, ambulance, forensic medicine, and the coroner), which is involved in the multidisciplinary approach to pediatric medicolegal death investigation, specifically in the relation of cases of SUDI (New South Wales Health Policy Directive, 2019). The roles and responsibilities of each of the participants and stakeholders in the death investigation process are detailed in the document. The process outlined in this document reflects that of the UK Kennedy Report.

Victoria

In Victoria, although a multidisciplinary approach does exist in practice, there is no single document that captures the roles and responsibilities that occur in New South Wales and elsewhere (Iles, 2020). A coroner's system of medicolegal death investigation exists with roles for the coroner, police, and forensic pathology services that include minimum standards for the performance of postmortem examinations and ancillary investigations. On the conclusion of the postmortem examination report, each death undergoes a multidisciplinary infant mortality case review by a board.

Caribbean

Despite the well-established protocols for interagency investigative collaboration that exist in many international jurisdictions, unfortunately, many of the island-state jurisdictions in the Caribbean region do not have similar structures in place and this situation exists for a variety of reasons that reflect limitations of both financial and appropriate human resource personnel to investigate pediatric medicolegal death investigation (Obenson, 2016). The medicolegal death investigation system in the English-speaking Caribbean (and indeed the wider Caribbean) cannot be neatly classified into either of the two traditional medicolegal death investigation systems (U.S. medical examiner system and the English coroner's system) (Obenson, 2016). They are probably more similar to the systems that exist in continental Europe, given the absence of an official equivalent to the medical examiner or coroner (Obenson, 2016).

Forensic pathologists exist to assist the police in their investigation and their services are only engaged when requested by police or magistrate acting as coroner (Obenson, 2016). Unlike the U.S. medical examiner's system, forensic pathologists in the Caribbean do not have any independent powers to initiate medicolegal death investigations and can only get involved in cases referred to them for postmortem examination (Obenson, 2016).

Typically, the process of medicolegal death investigation only starts when the police are notified of a sudden, unexpected, or suspicious death. A forensic postmortem examination will then be performed by either a qualified forensic pathologist or an anatomical pathologist without formal subspecialty training or qualifications in forensic pathology (Obenson, 2016). Most Caribbean jurisdictions do not possess a qualified forensic pathologist and most medicolegal postmortem examinations are performed by general anatomical pathologists (Obenson, 2016). The subspecialty services of pediatric, perinatal, cardiac, and neuropathologists generally do not exist (Walker & Breland, 2018, 2020). As such, there are no uniformly applied criteria for the medicolegal investigation and classification of both cause and manner of death in pediatric medicolegal death investigation which obviously affects data collection and analysis (Walker & Breland, 2018, 2020). Additionally, on a national level, there is no central repository for the standardized collection and analysis of such data (Walker & Breland, 2018, 2020)

In the Caribbean jurisdictions, the notification of death is usually straightforward in all cases when the death occurred and is certified outside of a medical facility, but death notification for medicolegal investigation can be problematic when the death is certified within a hospital, especially after a period of survival following inflicted injuries (Obenson, 2016). In most English-speaking jurisdictions in the Caribbean, deaths that occur outside of a hospital are reported to a government-employed, non-specialist medical doctor who is known as the District Medical Officer (DMO) (Obenson, 2016; Walker & Breland, 2018, 2020). DMOs are not required to possess any postgraduate training or qualifications in medicolegal death investigation or clinical forensic medicine to fulfill their role in medicolegal death investigation; however, they are the medical professionals who are tasked with viewing a body at the scene of death or discovery, the declaration of death, and ordering the removal of the body from the scene for postmortem examination at their request, most times without the involvement of forensic pathology at the scene (Obenson, 2016; Walker & Breland, 2018, 2020). It is not beyond the scope of imagination to predict the inherent medicolegal issues that have arisen in criminally suspicious deaths in this situation (Obenson, 2016; Walker & Breland, 2018, 2020).

Jamaica

In Jamaica, the Institute of Forensic Science and Legal Medicine (IFSLM) is the governmental agency that is charged with providing forensic pathology services for the island nation. It operates under the auspices of the Ministry of National Security and is headed by a non-medical director. Forensic pathologists are employed by the state and report to the director. These forensic pathologists play an important role in the pathological investigation of criminally suspicious/homicidal deaths to establish the medical cause of death and advise on the manner of death, but as already stated, they do not have the expansive executive powers to initiate medicolegal death investigations that a typical chief medical examiner or coroner would have in the respective alternative jurisdictions.

CONCLUSION

It has been established and accepted that the best investigative response to allegations of abuse and neglect is the MDT approach since no single profession or state agency possesses the ability to deal with these matters adequately. The stakeholder agencies can consist of the police or other law enforcement body child protection service, coroner/medical examiner's office, and the judicial system.

It has been demonstrated that the MDT approach promotes well-coordinated child abuse investigations that benefit from the input and contribution of many stakeholders, especially law enforcement, prosecution, and child protection services to ensure successful conclusion of an investigation with the correct determinations. It minimizes the risk of dissemination of inaccurate information, the duplication of efforts, and the inadvertent interference in the investigation of one agency by another agency, although investigations by various agencies will occur simultaneously. As such, the MDT approach encourages and facilitates the sharing of key investigative details which allows each stakeholder agency to acquire all the information needed to effectively perform its duties to arrive at valid conclusions on the circumstances of death, medical cause of death, manner of death, recommendations for the prevention of similar deaths in the future, the determination of criminal liability for a death, and the public health implications.

Despite this fact, no standardized international protocol exists for the medicolegal investigation of pediatric deaths but in most mature medicolegal jurisdictions, there is similarity in the individual investigative frameworks which have been developed and implemented. The main similarity of the investigative approaches involves the adoption of the concept of the MDT approach to pediatric medicolegal death investigation.

The pervasive common threads of pediatric medicolegal death investigation that run through the systems in the more mature medicolegal jurisdictions include centralization of the pediatric death investigation process, adoption of a multi-agency approach, review of the death investigation process, and review of the determinations and conclusions in each case, to ensure the accuracy and validity. This approach has provided the most consistent and best results thus far but can only be utilized if there are adequate resources and personnel to support it. Resource rich jurisdictions such as Ontario, Canada, the United States of America, the United Kingdom of Great Britain, and Australia can be said to all share these common threads of approach, whereas jurisdictions with limited resources and inadequate numbers of appropriately trained personnel (such as the Island States of the Caribbean region) tend to have suboptimal and inconsistent approaches to pediatric medicolegal death investigation.

Since no standardized international protocol exists for the medicolegal investigation of pediatric deaths, it is highly recommended that such a protocol be developed and implemented to ensure consistency across all jurisdictions. However, given the diverse nature of the medicolegal death investigation systems that exist worldwide, the legal systems in which they operate and the marked variability in available resources (both financial and personnel), it is recognized that the establishment and implementation of a standardized protocol will be extremely challenging, although it is the desirable ideal that should be strived for. The framework for a standardized protocol can be easily developed by utilizing the principles of the MDT approach as practiced in the more medicolegally mature jurisdictions. Therefore, it is recommended that scholars, researchers, and practitioners in the relevant fields be careful when comparing global children mortalities, especially the statistics of pediatric death investigation and death classification.

REFERENCES

American Academy of Pediatrics (2015). Definition of a Pediatrician, *135*(4), 780–781. https://doi.org/10.1542/peds.2015-0056 https://pediatrics.aappublications.org/content/pediatrics/135/4/780.full.pdf

Case, M., Graham, M., Handy, T., Jentzen, J., & Monteleone, J. (2001). Position Paper on Fatal Abusive Head Injuries in Infants and Young Children. *The American Journal of Forensic Medicine and Pathology*, 22(2), 112–122. https://doi.org/10.1097/00000433-200106000-00002

Centers for Disease Control and Prevention (2021) *SUIDI Reporting Form | CDC.* Cdc.gov. (2021). Retrieved from https://www.cdc.gov/sids/suidrf.html

Cohen, M., Scheimberg, I., Beckwith, J., & Hauck, F. (Eds.). (2019). *Investigation of Sudden Infant Death Syndrome (Diagnostic Pediatric Pathology)*. Cambridge: Cambridge University Press. doi:10.1017/9781108186001

Collins, G. (2019). Investigation of Deaths in Children: A Multidisciplinary Approach. *5th Annual Caribbean Medicolegal and Forensic Symposium*. Retrieved

from https://med.uottawa.ca/pathology/news/5th-annual-caribbean-medicolegal
-and-forensic-symposium-online-event.

Coroner's Act of Ontario (2009). https://www.ontario.ca/laws/statute/90c37/v11

Department of Education (2015). *Working Together to Safeguard Children: A Guide
to Inter-Agency Working to Safeguard and Promote the Welfare of Children.*

Duncan, J., & Byard, R. (2018). *SIDS Sudden Infant and Early Childhood
Death* (Chapter 6). Gill, J., Andrew, T., Gilliland, M., Love, J., Matshes, E., &
Reichard, R. (2013). National Association of Medical Examiners Position Paper:
Recommendations for the Postmortem Assessment of Suspected Head Trauma in
Infants and Young Children. *Academic Forensic Pathology, 4*(2), 206–213. https://
doi.org/10.23907/2014.032

Government of New South Wales (2019). *Procedures for Management of Sudden
Unexpected Death in Infancy. Policy Directive on SUDI.* Retrieved from https://
www1.health.nsw.gov.au/pds/ActivePDSDocuments/PD2019_035.pdf

Government of Trinidad and Tobago (2000). *The Children's Authority Act.*
Ttchildren.org. (2000). https://ttchildren.org/images/legislation/CHILDRENS
%20AUTHORITY%20ACT%2046.10.pdf.

HM Government Department of Education. (2018). *Working Together to Safeguard
Children.* GOV.UK. Retrieved July 31, 2021, from https://www.gov.uk/govern-
ment/publications/working-together-to-safeguard-children--2; https://data.unicef
.org/topic/child-protection/violence/violent-deaths/

Iles, L. (2020). *Head of Forensic Pathology Services*, Victorian Institute of Forensic
Medicine, Melbourne, Australia (Personal Communication).

Kennedy, H., et al. (November 2016). *Royal College of Pathologists (RCPath)
and the Royal College of Pediatrics and Child Health (RCPCH).* Sudden
Unexpected Death in Infancy and Childhood: Multiagency Guidelines for Care and
Investigation, 2nd Edition.
https://www.rcpath.org/uploads/assets/874ae50e-c754-4933-995a804e0ef728a4/
Sudden-unexpected-death-in-infancy-and-childhood-2e.pdf

National Center for Child Death Review (2005). *A Program Manual for Child
Death Review.* https://www.ncfrp.org/wp-content/uploads/NCRPCD-Docs/
ProgramManual.pdf.

Obenson, K. (2016). *Mechanics of Death Investigation in the English-speaking
Caribbean versus Canada*, Caribbean Association of Forensic Sciences, Inaugural
Conference.

Office of the Chief Coroner for Ontario (2011). *Investigation Questionnaire for
Sudden Unexpected Deaths in Children under the Age of Five (5).*

Office of the Chief Coroner for Ontario (2013). *Investigation Questionnaire for
Sudden Unexpected Deaths in Infants.*

Pathologists Registry alphabetical list | Ministry of the Solicitor General. Mcscs.jus
.gov.on.ca. (2010). Retrieved 31 July 2021, from https://www.mcscs.jus.gov.on.ca
/english/DeathInvestigations/Pathology/PathologistsRegistry/pathologists_registry
.html

Ontario Forensic Pathology Service (2012). *Guidelines for Autopsy Practice: Sudden
Unexpected Death in Infants and Children Under 5 Years*, 2nd Edition.

Ontario Forensic Pathology Service (2017). *Child Injury Interpretation Committee,* Memo Log 21–2172.

Peterson, G. F., Clark, S. C., National Association of Medical Examiners (2006). *Forensic Autopsy Performance Standards.* N.A.M.E. Annual Meeting, San Antonio, Texas.

The Children's Authority Act. Ttchildren.org. (2000). Retrieved July 31, 2021, from https://ttchildren.org/images/legislation/CHILDRENS%20AUTHORITY %20ACT%2046.10.pdf

UNICEF (2017). *UNICEF Data: Monitoring the Situation of Children and Women Violent Deaths.*

UNICEF (2020). *United Nations Inter-Agency Group for Child Mortality Estimation (UN IGME).* Retrieved July 30, 2021, from https://data.unicef.org/topic/child-survival/under-five-mortality/

US Department of Justice (2000). Forming a Multidisciplinary Team to Investigate Child Abuse. Office of Juvenile Justice and Delinquency Program. *OJJDP Portable Guides to Investigating Child Abuse.* Retrieved from

https://ojjdp.ojp.gov/library/publications/forming-multidisciplinary-team-investigate -child-abuse

Walker, A. E., & Breland, S. (2018). *Medicolegal Death Investigation Systems: The Coroner's System versus the US Medical Examiner System.* Second Annual Forensic Science Symposium, Belize National Forensic Science Services.

Walker, A. E., & Breland, S. (2020). *Medicolegal Death Investigation Systems: The Coroner's System versus the US Medical Examiner System.* 5th Annual Caribbean Medicolegal Symposium.

World Health Organization (2019). *Global Health Observatory Data.* Retrieved from https://www.who.int/gho/child_health/mortality/en/

Index

victimization indicators, 69, 70
Violent Crimes against Children
    International Task Force, 145
Virtopsy, 197. *See also* postmortem
    examination

YEH. *See* youth experiencing
    homelessness
youth, 3. *See also* children
youth experiencing homelessness, 4, 39

Contributors

Hyeyoung Lim is an associate professor at the Department of Criminal Justice, the University of Alabama at Birmingham. She holds a doctorate in criminal justice (PhD, Sam Houston State University, USA), ML in police administration (Dongguk University, Republic of Korea), MS in management information security (The University of Alabama at Birmingham, USA), and BS in computer Science (Sookmyung Women's University, Republic of Korea). She served as a special crime prevention committee member at the Seoul Probation Office in the Republic of Korea and trained as a professional counselor. Dr. Lim also worked at the Bill Blackwood Law Enforcement Management Institute of Texas (LEMIT) as a research director. Her primary research interests include crime analysis and prevention, police decision-making, policy and program evaluation, organizational behavior, police legitimacy, and police-community relations. A recently developed line of her research focuses on cybersecurity, cyber policing, and racial justice and equality. She is a founding member of the Center for Cyber Investigation and Cybercrime (CIC) in Boston, an associate editor of both the International Journal of Cybersecurity Intelligence and Cybercrime (IJCIC) and the Journal of Applied Security Research (JASR), and a guest editor for multiple journals.

Ana Beires is a researcher at Alternative and Response Women's Association, Portugal.

Ashley Boal is a senior research associate at WestEd's Justice & Prevention Research Center, USA.

Kyung-shick Choi is a professor of cybercrime and cybersecurity at Boston University, USA.

Asher Flynn is an associate professor of criminology at Monash University, Australia.

Li Sian Goh is a PhD candidate in criminology at the University of Pennsylvania, USA.

Ana Guerreiro is a lecturer of criminology at University Institute of Maia, Portugal.

Nicola Henry is an associate professor and a chief investigator on a Criminology Research Grant on anonymous and confidential reporting platforms for sexual assault survivors at RMIT, Australia.

Camila Iglesias is a PhD student in criminology at the Faculty of Law of the University of Porto, Portugal.

Lisa M. Jones is a research associate professor of psychology at the Crimes against Children Research Center (CCRC) at the University of New Hampshire, USA.

Brian Lawton is an associate professor in the Department of Criminal Justice at John Jay College of Criminal Justice, USA.

Hannarae Lee is an assistant professor of criminal justice at Bridgewater State University, USA.

Pamela MacDougall is a project coordinator with the Health and Justice Program at WestEd, USA.

Lily Mahler is a resident physician at the School of Medicine at the University of Alabama at Birmingham, USA.

Brandi C. McCleskey is an assistant professor of forensic pathology at the University of Alabama at Birmingham, USA.

Maria José Magalhães is an assistant professor of education sciences at the University of Porto, Portugal.

Chelsea Mainwaring is an associate lecturer in criminology at Monash University, Australia.

Anthony Petrosino is the director of the WestEd Justice & Prevention Research Center, USA.

Cátia Pontedeira is an assistant teacher in criminology at University Institute of Maia, Portugal.

Anastasia Powell is an associate professor in justice and legal studies and an associate member of the Centre for Applied Social Research (CASR) at RMIT, Australia.

Christina M. Rodriguez is an associate professor of psychology at University of Alabama at Birmingham, USA.

Rachel M. Schmitz is an associate professor of sociology at Oklahoma State University, USA.

Adrian J. Scott is a senior lecturer in psychology at Goldsmiths University of London, United Kingdom.

Margarida Teixeira is a researcher at Alternative and Response Women's Association, Portugal.

Kimberly A. Tyler is Willa Cather Professor of Sociology at the University of Nebraska-Lincoln, USA.

Alfredo E. Walker is an assistant professor of pathology at The Ottawa Hospital General Campus, Ontario, Canada.

www.ingramcontent.com/pod-product-compliance
Lightning Source LLC
Chambersburg PA
CBHW050643280326
41932CB00015B/2757